TATTERED KIMONOS in JAPAN

TATTERED KIMONOS in JAPAN

REMAKING LIVES FROM MEMORIES OF WORLD WAR II

ROBERT RAND

THE UNIVERSITY OF ALABAMA PRESS

Tuscaloosa

The University of Alabama Press
Tuscaloosa, Alabama 35487-0380
uapress.ua.edu

Typeface: Adobe Jenson Pro

Cover design: Lori Lynch

Cataloging-in-Publication data is available from the Library of Congress.
ISBN: 978-0-8173-2177-2
E-ISBN: 978-0-8173-9476-9

TO ERIKO, ARI, AND KAYA

Contents

Figures

Preface

I used to work in public radio, where I collaborated with a lot of really smart people who excelled at telling stories, which is what public radio does best. Along the way I received advice from colleagues, genuinely creative journalists more experienced than me, regarding how those stories could most effectively be told.

"Put your best tape first," one of them said. In other words, listen carefully to the interview voices and sounds collected on your recording device (the source material gathered while researching a story) and prioritize the most compelling stuff. Another colleague likened that process to "finding the poetry in news."

A third associate boiled it down to this: "Tell the big story in the smallest way possible through the experience of someone whose life is involved in the subject matter at hand."

All of that insight informs this book.

The big story here is World War II and its imprint on Japan, told in the smallest way possible through the experiences of Japan's war generation: the individuals who fought in the war or grew up during the war years; who remembered what it was like and grappled with the consequences of those recollections; and who managed, often against all odds, to carry those memories into the twenty-first century, where they crafted lives made from long-ago misfortune. Their stories constitute my best tape: interviews gathered over two decades of traveling to and through Japan and speaking with Japanese about their wartime pasts and postwar presents. Hopefully, readers will find poetry in some of what they told me.

This is a book about history, but caveat emptor: I do not write chronologically; and the book is not intended to be a comprehensive account of Japan, World War II, or the postwar years; nor is it intended to be a sociological or demographic analysis of Japan's war generation as a whole. It is a book about a select number of men and women whose postwar lives were profoundly shaped by wartime experiences.

Those experiences differ among individuals, of course, and individual postwar narratives also diverge. But the men and women you will meet here did have things in common; and the way they lived their postwar lives was influenced by a common, overarching set of ideas, beliefs, and themes. As you read through these pages, keep an eye out for them. They include:

Character. The war generation men and women I got to know were uniformly tenacious, resilient, thoughtful, and good-natured. Their stories illustrate these traits, and these traits helped them survive and thrive in the postwar years.

Bearing witness. The men and women I spoke with remembered the trauma of war, and went out of their way to talk about it. Doing so energized them and added purpose to their lives. They also shared a commitment to educate, so that future generations will never forget what Japan and its war generation went through.

Repentance. Japan was an aggressor state that started the Pacific war and carried out myriad war crimes. In the postwar years, public and private figures in Japan had to confront wartime behavior, and consider whether and how to repent and ask forgiveness.

Hiroshima, Nagasaki, and American air assaults on Japan. The effects of the atomic bombing of Hiroshima and Nagasaki, and of a monthslong firebombing campaign in 1945 against scores of Japanese cities, still resonate in Japan. Memories of those assaults by those who survived them sit in the inner sanctum of the war generation's psyche.

The endurance of tradition. Consoling dead souls. Practicing ancient religions. A culture of apology. The kimono. These Japanese traditions are supporting actors in this book, especially the kimono, which appears here and there, often tattered, as a powerful symbol of national identity and a metaphor for Japan's wartime experience.

While this book is the product of journalistic reporting and background research, there is a personal element that ought to be noted up front. World War II affected my life directly. I am American, and my father fought in the war and proudly spoke of his service until the day he died. I am also a Jew who grew up in a community of Holocaust survivors. All of this stoked my interest in the war years, and also made me mindful of the power of victimhood, memory, and shared suffering as I traveled around Japan. I see Japan through Jewish eyes, and that perspective is reflected in the chapters that follow.

A few style points: In Japan, first and last names can be written interchangeably; *Smith John* is as acceptable as *John Smith*. In this book, however, I follow the standard English-language preference of identifying characters by first names first and last names last. Second references may use first or last names, depending on the tone of the narrative. Subsequent references may also contain names (first or last) followed by *-san*, a genderless honorific suffix the Japanese regularly use when speaking respectfully with others, as in Komai-san or Saotome-san or Robert-san. Regarding the rendering of Japanese words into English: much as I standardize name practices for American and other English-language readers, I also avoid using diacritics to indicate long vowels in the text, though linguists might protest.

A point on methodology: My Japanese is not good enough to conduct serious interviews or read serious Japanese-language content. However, I worked on this book alongside a crew of extraordinarily proficient and completely bilingual Japanese-English language speakers (on occasion, including my wife). They were my interpreters and translators and fixers and research assistants from the beginning to the end of this project, covering every single interview, phone call, and written page of Japanese along the way. They know who they are. And their assistance made this book possible.

One final note. For some Americans, the Japanese experience in World War II remains a sensitive issue. As recently as 2015, seventy years after the war's end, a public opinion poll found that 29 percent of Americans thought Japan had not apologized sufficiently for its wartime actions; among older Americans, that figure was 50 percent.[1] I once produced a human-interest story from Tokyo for NPR about a Japanese soldier, a POW, who had suffered greatly in the war but who had, with intelligence and good humor, turned his life around in the postwar years. The piece aired on Pearl Harbor Day.[2] Some listeners responded with hostility, arguing that Japan had started the conflict and killed and tortured countless Americans, so who cares about a Japanese POW, especially on Pearl Harbor Day? Why don't you focus on our side, they said, on the men who died on December 7, 1941, and on the soldiers who fought with your father?

Reporting from the other side of my father's war does not, in my view, diminish American suffering; and telling stories about individual Japanese who built postwar lives on the back of wartime trauma does not downplay the wartime sacrifice or heroism of Americans. It simply informs, humanizes, and, hopefully, holds your interest and attention.

Acknowledgments

Special thanks to Taeko Hamamoto, Tiana Thompson, Maya Soma, and Yuko Mizuma for interpretation, translation, and research assistance; and to David Satterwhite in Japan for guidance and commiseration in the early stages of this project.

At the University of Alabama Press, gratitude to Dan Waterman for taking the cold call that pitched the project back in May 2020, and for graciously having shepherded it along the way. Credit, also, to his anonymous peer reviewer B, whose thoughtful and copious manuscript assessment really did make this a better book. And to copy editor Jessica Hinds-Bond, whose sharp eyes and meticulous mind caught some rogue errors and polished up the final manuscript.

Acknowledgment to the Fulbright Foundation and the Asian Cultural Council, whose fellowships generously supported research for this book inside Japan.

A version of the introduction and part 1 was published as "Mrs. Herskovitz's Kimono" in *Tablet*, August 2, 2017; and a version of chapter 13 was published as "The Diary of Anne" in *Tablet*, June 11, 2018.

And, finally, an endless and heartfelt expression of thanks to my wife, Eriko, and to our kids, Ari and Kaya, who journeyed with me throughout Japan and who inspire most everything I do. This book is dedicated to them.

TATTERED KIMONOS in JAPAN

Introduction

The Backstory

My father was a soldier in George S. Patton's army, European theater, World War II. Dad was a corporal, military policeman, born hard-edged and by disposition stubborn.

My father-in-law was also a soldier, an equally tough combatant, deployed to Asia by the Heavenly Sovereign, Emperor Hirohito of Japan. Father-in-law was polite and introspective, at least in the years I knew him. During the war he was a foot soldier, bivouacked in China, where most of the Imperial Army reposed.[1] He never revealed much about his wartime years, although I do recall him speaking once about the consistency and color of the dirt he slept on, and the fear that hung above, like a fog that wouldn't scatter.

My father was a Jew of east European stock, whose forbears worshipped God, spoke Yiddish, and endured as best they could the hard village life of the shtetl.

My father-in-law was samurai, with genuine warrior roots. Discipline and industriousness ran in his blood. He was not a religious man, unless you consider the golf ball to be a postwar deity. But he valued tradition, was faithful to his family, and revered Japan, prewar and post.

My father also was a reverent man, a patriot who honored his country. But he honored the diaspora of European Jewry too, whose ruin he saw

FIGURE 1. *Left*, the author's father-in-law (*middle row, center*), with his military unit in Japanese-occupied China, circa 1944. Courtesy of family. *Right*, the author's father standing beside his motorcycle at a military facility in Hampton Roads, Virginia, 1943, prior to European deployment. Courtesy of author.

sketched, in harrowing relief, when he and his US Army comrades freed a death camp called Buchenwald.[2]

Emancipating that place and tending to its survivors was a defining event in my father's life. The experience left a stomach-churning taste that lingered, a taste that affected the way he viewed the world. It elevated my father's sense of Jewishness, and it fed a preexisting arrogance that, in the postwar years, turned him into something of a xenophobe. He preferred the insular world of people who looked and thought like him; and, indeed, he raised his children in a suburban Jewish community where diversity was nonexistent, where intolerance of non-Jewishness flourished, where Israel stood like Mount Sinai above all else, with the possible exception of the American flag.

"I dislike foreigners," my father told me one day, out of the blue, when I was seventeen. It was a disturbing and profoundly disappointing thing to hear. It sent me reeling in the opposite direction, toward a life of foreign languages and cultures, and into the arms of my wife, who is from Japan, from the other side of my father's war.

My father's wartime name was Rudy. My father-in-law's was Kenichi.

They were born months apart, in 1925, on different halves of the planet. Each man died, eight decades later, without having met the other. I made sure of that. But for me the two were interlinked, by my marriage to be sure, but even more so by other more powerful things: the coincidence of contemporary births; the subsequent decades that shaped their lives and mindsets; and within those confines and above all else, the war in which they served. And because of those connections, I found meaning in their deaths, and inspiration in the manner each was laid to rest.

My father was interred in a Jewish cemetery named Shalom Memorial Park. A military honor guard showed up, ramrod in posture and dressed in finery. A young army corpsman played taps. Another saluted my mother. Both retrieved the American flag that draped my father's coffin and folded it gently, the better to exalt the spirit of the man who had died, and meticulously, the better to acknowledge the disciplined veteran and his military service.

We took the flag home and placed it near my father's safe, in which, upon inspection, I discovered an old envelope filled with a half-dozen photographs he had taken in Buchenwald. The photos depicted the usual Holocaust fare, horrific piles of corpses and bones, skeleton survivors with petrified faces. My father had kept the photos secret, under lock and key, so important were their memories and meaning to him. And now, to me.

My father-in-law was cremated, as Buddhism usually requires; and as it requires, his family surrounded his coffin as it slid into the crematory oven.[3] We were there afterward as well, when the deed had been done and Kenichi-san's remains, once cooled, were rolled out, all ashes and shards of bone, and presented before us: one last chance to honor his soul. And as Japanese tradition commands, the immediate family—the widow, the daughters and son—used giant chopsticks to pick up skeletal bits and pieces, depositing them into a cremation urn that, as it happened, was the clone of an oversized golf ball specially tailored for the occasion.

The ceremony is called *kotsuage*, and the idea, explained to me afterward, is noble: loved ones watch over the deceased until the very, very end, until the crematory ovens have settled and the soul of the fallen enters the enlightened eternal life.[4] I wasn't aware of the rationale as the event transpired, and except for the golf ball, all I could think of was Buchenwald and Auschwitz.

Those thoughts surprised and disturbed me. I knew, of course, where they came from, because I was my father's son and had been raised as a Jew in Skokie, Illinois, where synagogues and temples far outnumbered churches, and where thousands of Holocaust survivors lived among us interspersed. And I grew up next door to a Mrs. Herskovitz, who had experienced Auschwitz. My first glimpse at the numbers tattooed on her left forearm is a childhood snapshot memory.

My reaction to Kenichi's cremation troubled me mostly because it exposed ignorance of things Japanese, despite my marriage and multiple visits to Japan; and because I had conjured up, in the presence of Kenichi-san's remains, a memory of evil that falsely equated a righteous and praiseworthy Buddhist tradition with Hitler's Final Solution, a most profoundly malevolent proceeding.

Yet there was, in this unseemly juxtaposition, something else at play: a reminder of the simple truth that vision is shaped by experience, and that Judaism colored the focus through which I viewed Japan.

My father-in-law and my father. Soldiers from enemy armies in World War II. One spirit laid to rest as ashes in Japan. Another soul, of equal value, buried beneath the ground in a distant Jewish graveyard. They belonged, at least in my mind, to a common fraternity, and their stories, though written in different languages, shared a certain bond and narrative arc.

I knew my father's postwar record well, and that of his American generation. But the lives of the men of Japan who had fought and survived the Second World War, the postwar thoughts and feelings and experiences of soldiers like Kenichi-san who had returned, heads down, to a vanquished country: their histories—and the narratives of their fathers, mothers, brothers, wives, and sisters who had lived through the war at home—these I did not know.

So I set out across Japan in search of their stories, and in so doing encountered postwar tales of sorrow and joy, of resilience, recovery, anger, and regret; stories told to me by Japanese women and men of my father's generation who seemed genuinely pleased that an American was keen to ask them questions, and patient enough to stick around to hear what they had to say.

Part 1

HIROSHIMA

My father never fought in Asia, where father-in-law served; where Japan's war to expand empire took place; where, in the end, the course of conflict flowed back to the homeland, to Hiroshima and Nagasaki, like a death tide. My father was in Germany when the A-bombs hit those cities in August 1945. Three months earlier, in May, the German High Command had surrendered unconditionally. For soldiers like my dad, however, victory in Europe did not signal war's end. My father was given fresh battle gear and told to ship out to the Pacific. Hiroshima and Nagasaki cut short his embarkation. Dad thanked Harry Truman, the president who had ordered the atomic attacks, for saving his life. "I didn't think I would survive a frontline invasion in the Pacific," dad said.[1] Within months after Japan's surrender, my father, and thousands like him, boarded ships and sailed home.

1

The Tattered Kimono

On Thursday, August 8, 1946, one year and forty-eight hours after the United States dropped an atomic bomb on Hiroshima, the *New York Times* amusements section (pages 17 and 18) listed movies on Manhattan's screens that day. The war was not long over, and a victorious but weary America required mental repose. New York moviegoers had well-suited options.

The iconic Marx Brothers were at the midtown Globe Theatre in *A Night in Casablanca*, in which youngest sibling Groucho improbably encountered an escaped Nazi war criminal intent on ruining his day. "It's Your Night to Howl!" the Globe exclaimed.

Or, at the rival RKO cinemas, comics Bud Abbott and Lou Costello starred in *Little Giant*, about a clodhopping vacuum cleaner salesman and his unscrupulous boss. "IT'S LAFF TIME AT THE RKO!" the movie chain promised.

The Palace, on Broadway and Forty-Seventh, offered viewers more serious stuff. The theater presented *The Stranger*, a drama by Orson Welles, about a Nazi-hunting war crimes investigator. It was the first Hollywood film to show real footage of the Holocaust.[1]

The *Times* amusements section listed another novelty that day, a newsreel, screening at theaters across town, with other wartime images the public had not yet seen: images of a flattened Hiroshima, and of radiation-injured survivors. The screening was newsworthy, and the paper, in an above-the-fold article headlined "Reaction of Humans to Atom Bomb in Film," explained why.

"The frightful effects of atomic-bomb radioactivity on humans is revealed for the first time in newsreel footage made by Japanese camera men immediately after the bombing of Hiroshima and which the War Department has now released for public showing," the *Times* said. "It is the scenes of the burned-out city of Hiroshima and the pitiful sight of the maimed victims which stand out most harrowingly. . . . Most of the victims look as though they had been seared by an acetylene torch."[2]

The United States previously had suppressed images of the A-bomb's deadly indiscriminate bite and its prodigious capacity for destruction. Such explicit footage, it was thought, might unduly stoke emotions in occupied Japan, or raise uncomfortable questions at home about the decision to use the bomb in the first place. These newsreel pictures were an aberration, an early crack in censorship.[3]

The newsreel contained one particularly troubling segment, the *Times* noted, featuring a Hiroshima victim who had suffered an especially graphic injury: "The intensity of the radioactivity is demonstrated by the imprint of a dress design on a woman's body."

Her image and that injury, captured in a still photograph, lingered on the newsreel screen for four long seconds. The woman's face was hidden, but she appeared to be young. Her shoulders and back were exposed. Burned there into her skin, by the force of the explosion, was the checkerboard pattern of the kimono she was wearing when the A-bomb went off.[4]

The photo was subtle, lyrical, and horrifying. The woman, in a flash, was branded forever, the consequence of gamma rays and simple science: dark absorbs, but light reflects. Black stripes of kimono fabric took in thermal radiation and penetrated her flesh. White patches of kimono cloth reflected the heat, sparing the skin. What was left was a gruesome blueprint of the garment Japan holds most dear.

I first saw this photo in 2007, more than six decades after it had been shot. I had just arrived in Tokyo on a journalism fellowship and was searching the internet for story ideas. I googled "Japan Hiroshima Atomic Bomb," and the photo appeared in the image results.

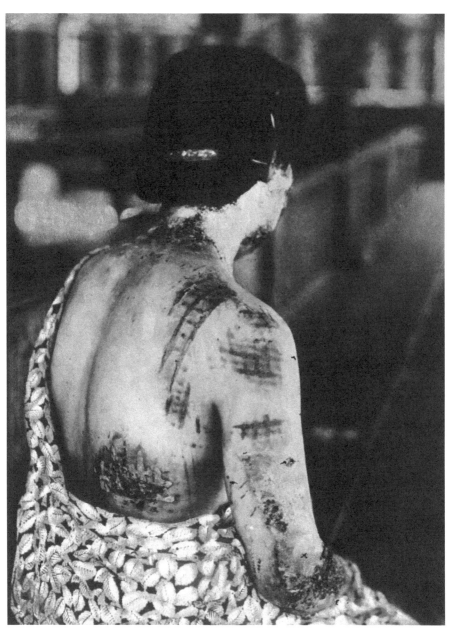

FIGURE 2. Hiroshima A-bomb survivor with kimono pattern burned into her skin by force of blast, at the Ujina Branch of the Hiroshima First Army Hospital. Photographed by Gonichi Kimura following the August 6, 1945, bombing. Courtesy of the Hiroshima Peace Memorial Museum.

For me, the markings on the woman's flesh recalled the concentration camp tattoos of Buchenwald or Auschwitz, and summoned up the memory of my childhood neighbor Mrs. Herskovitz, who, like the woman in the photo, bore the uncommon stain of war on her skin. It seemed to me that the photo of this unidentified woman from Hiroshima easily could rest beside snapshots of Jewish Holocaust victims in the gallery of twentieth-century suffering.

Mrs. Herskovitz and her survivor cohort had narratives I understood. But who was the woman in the Hiroshima photo? What was her name? What was her story? How long did she live after the war? Would knowledge of her life or death add value to my understanding of Japan, or of the Holocaust; or was my connection of this woman with Mrs. Herskovitz entirely subjective and without broader merit?

I traveled to Hiroshima in search of answers. First stop—the Hiroshima Peace Memorial Museum. It is a repository of memories, artifacts, pain, and suffering that illustrates, with archaeological precision, the human fallout of an atomic attack.[5]

A copy of the photograph was displayed there. The picture was in color. "Imprinted kimono pattern," a caption said. "The heat rays burned the dark parts of the kimono pattern into her skin." The photographer was identified as a man named Gonichi Kimura. He was said to have taken the picture at the "Ujina Branch of the Hiroshima First Army Hospital." Approximate date of the photo: August 15, 1945, nine days after the bombing.

It was a beginning, scraps of information that suggested pathways for further research. But the prize—details about the woman—was not there. She was not identified. The photo, in fact, appeared staged to maintain her anonymity. She was seated, looking away from the camera, precluding facial recognition, presumably because the snapshot was painfully intimate: the flowery blue dress she wore for the photo shoot was immodestly pulled down to the waist on her right side, fully exposing a scarred torso.

Later that day, I visited the peace museum's archive. There, hidden inside a weather-beaten volume of wartime photographs, I found the woman's name.

A curator, Shinobu Kikuraku, gently placed the book on a table in

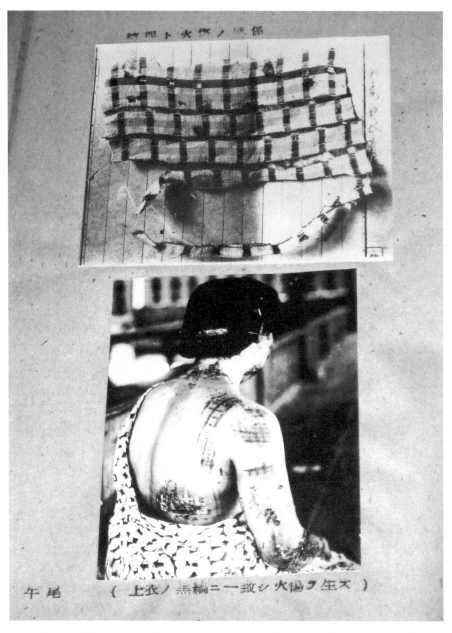

FIGURE 3. Original print of kimono-scarred survivor, with close-up of a tattered scrap of the kimono she was wearing when the A-bomb went off. Photographed by author in the Hiroshima Peace Memorial Museum archives, November 2007.

front of me. She handled it with white gloves. "It's very valuable," she said. The book was part of a medical report that a Japanese investigative team had prepared after the Hiroshima bombing. Its pages were yellowed and torn with age, conveying a fragility appropriate to the subject matter.[6]

A photo of the kimono-scarred woman was pasted onto an unnumbered page in the middle of the volume. The curator told me it was one of a handful of original prints. There was a second photo on the same page, equally stark, if not more so. It showed a single, charred, tattered scrap of cloth, taken from the kimono the woman had worn when the atomic bomb exploded.

Beneath the first photo, in handwritten text, was the woman's name, as well as a statement that the burns on her body were "in accordance with the black stripes of her clothing." Above the second photo, the one with the frayed piece of kimono cloth: a simple notation that the picture exhibited "the relationship between clothing and burns."

The curator told me that this volume was the only known source linking the woman's first and last names to the photo. At the curator's insistence, I agreed to protect the woman's privacy—posthumously if she were dead, contemporaneously if she were still alive—by using her first initial only in the narrative of this book. The woman's name was S. Ushio.[7]

≈

The search for S. Ushio's story required multiple visits to Hiroshima over the course of several years. Even then, only snippets of Ushio's life seemed clear and subject to confirmation.

On July 10, 1977, Hiroshima's main newspaper, the *Chugoku Shimbun*, published a list of *yukuefumeisha*—people who had gone missing after the atomic bombing. The list was based on information provided post-1945 by surviving family members who were looking for their loved ones. S. Ushio was on the list. She was reported to have been twenty-two years old on the day of the bombing, and she lived in the Kakomachi section of Hiroshima, a downtown area some eight-tenths of a mile south of ground zero, also known as the hypocenter. There was no information regarding her whereabouts at the time of the blast.

Two weeks earlier, on June 29, 1977, the *Chugoku Shimbun* had printed another list, of *muenbotoke*—bomb victims who had been identified but whose remains were never collected by family members. S. Ushio was not on this list. *Muenbotoke* means "a person (or their spirit) who died with no one to tend their grave."[8]

Taken together, the lists showed that somebody in S. Ushio's family had survived the bombing and had notified authorities that the woman was missing. There was no confirmation, however, whether she was dead or alive.

There are two large repositories of information in Hiroshima regarding A-bomb casualties: the National Peace Memorial Hall for the Atomic Bomb Victims, and Hiroshima City Hall. These buildings store all relevant, extant written records. I visited both places and asked staff researchers to look for any mention of an S. Ushio.[9] A young victim, "Sakuko Ushio—age 7," came up in each database. There were no references to an adult S. Ushio, however; and, therefore, still no proof of her whereabouts or whether she had died. Consequently, the *Chugoku Shimbun* article from 1977 was the only available public acknowledgment of S. Ushio that I could find.

Additional information about her life, however, could reasonably be inferred from other sources.

I showed the Ushio photos to Professor Yuko Tanaka, a Japanese culture and kimono expert at Tokyo's Hosei University.[10] Tanaka said the crosshatched garment that left its imprint on S. Ushio's back was a *yukata*, a commonly worn summertime kimono made of cotton. "It was very casual and inexpensive, the daily style of normal people during World War II," Tanaka said. At age twenty-two, Ushio would probably have been married. "I believe this lady was most likely a normal housewife."

Shinobu Kikuraku, the curator at the Hiroshima Memorial Peace Museum, provided information about Gonichi Kimura, the man who took S. Ushio's picture. Kimura had worked as a staff photographer for the Japanese army's Ship Training Division, based in Hiroshima (the city was an important port in southern Japan). The Ujina military hospital, where the photo was taken, was situated some two and a half miles from the A-bomb hypocenter. It was equally distant from Kakomachi, the district where S. Ushio lived.

The Ushio photo was one of dozens Kimura took in the days and months following the atomic bombing. Kimura wrote a brief accounting of his activities after the US attack, which the museum curator made available to me.[11] In it, Kimura made no mention of a kimono-scarred woman. He did, however, take photographs in Kakomachi, which revealed the neighborhood was flattened. "There were no buildings, only a solitary, strangely tall chimney standing in the midst of the burned-out area," Kimura wrote. "It was terribly eerie."

S. Ushio was probably elsewhere when the A-bomb fell. Had she been in Kakomachi, she most certainly would have died.

But she remained alive, at least in the weeks immediately after the bombing. The caption on the Ushio photo displayed in the peace museum said Kimura shot the picture approximately August 15. Masami Nishimoto, a *Chugoku Shimbun* reporter who has written about Kimura's photographs, told me that was wrong, that Kimura actually took the Ushio picture weeks later.[12]

Nishimoto explained that the photo was shot with color film, which was not available in Japan at the time. It was, however, used in the United States. Nishimoto said Kimura must have gotten the color film from a group of American military medical researchers (and accompanying photographers) who had arrived in Hiroshima on September 9, 1945, and had visited the Ujina hospital thereafter.[13] That is when Kimura would have snapped his photo, or perhaps even later, Nishimoto said. In either case, the provenance of S. Ushio's photo indicates she lived for at least a month after the Hiroshima attack.

But how long could she have stayed alive? For me, that was the most intriguing question. She had made it through the bombing and, despite her injuries, had somehow found her way to the Ujina military hospital. Could she have hung on for months or even years longer? Or did her injuries and exposure to radiation cut short her life?

≈

In Japanese, the word *genbaku* means "atomic bomb." It is as central to describing Japan's postwar experience as the word Holocaust is to the Jews, or Pearl Harbor, D-Day, and Stalingrad to the lexicon of World War II.

The Genbaku Retirement Home is nestled in the hills outside Hiroshima, a twenty-five-minute train ride plus a ten-minute taxi fare from the city's central rail station. The home is modern, the area quiet. There is no sign of the urban bustle that now thrives in contemporary Hiroshima, whose population exceeds one million. The Genbaku Retirement Home enjoys tranquility.

Some three hundred A-bomb survivors resided there when I visited in 2008. Survivors are known collectively as *hibakusha*, which means atomic bomb–affected people. Dr. Nanao Kamada was their chief medical officer.[14]

Dr. Kamada was a hematologist and radiation biologist. Since 1962, he had specialized in treating *hibakusha* who suffered from leukemia and other cancers. He was especially interested in helping people who had been within a one-third-mile radius of ground zero and, despite the odds, had managed to survive.

Nobody knows exactly how many people died in the immediate firestorm of the Hiroshima A-bomb. The Radiation Effects Research Foundation, a joint US-Japanese scientific group that monitors the health of *hibakusha*, estimates that between 90,000 and 166,000 people perished on August 6, 1945, or within the subsequent two to four months. The population of Hiroshima at the time of the bombing was between 340,000 and 350,000.[15]

When I visited the Genbaku Retirement Home, Dr. Kamada said approximately 240,000 Hiroshima and Nagasaki survivors were still alive in Japan. Their average age was seventy-six. Approximately 76,000 of them lived in Hiroshima.[16]

I showed Dr. Kamada S. Ushio's photograph and told him she was twenty-two years old on the day it was taken. "As a medical doctor specializing in treating survivors, can you diagnose how seriously this woman was injured and give me your opinion regarding how long she was likely to have lived?" I asked.

Dr. Kamada said the burns on S. Ushio's body were not uniformly serious. Her neck and elbow were "very severely injured." Her arm and upper back were not.

"So your question is how long she could have survived?" he asked.

"Yes."

He paused. "If she had been properly treated, she could have lived for more than twenty years. Do you know the distance she was from the hypocenter?"

"No," I said. "But she was in Hiroshima City. This picture was taken at the Ujina military hospital."

"The survival time depends on the dose of exposure," Dr. Kamada explained. "From this picture, I would speculate she was exposed around two kilometers [1.2 miles] from the hypocenter. So the radiation doses were not so hot, probably five to ten rads.[17] In those cases, someone can live ten or twenty or more years. So unless she had a malignant tumor, she could still be alive."

"Unless she had a malignant tumor, she could have survived?"

"Yes."

"Survived until when?" I asked. "Until today?"

"Today."

"Maybe this is not a fair question, but could you tell me what the odds are that she could still be alive?"

Dr. Kamada paused again to think.

"Eighty percent," he said.

"Eighty percent she could still be alive?"

"Yes. You said she was twenty-two years old?"

"Yes."

"She would be about eighty-five years old now."

I thanked Dr. Kamada for his time, and asked if I could take his photograph. He agreed.

A large bouquet of flowers sat on his desk. Dr. Kamada insisted that I include the flowers in the photo. "I love flowers," he told me.

We shook hands, and I returned to Hiroshima.[18]

≈

Japanese names that sound alike can be spelled in different ways. The variations depend on the choice of kanji, the Chinese characters that make up the bulk of Japan's writing system. Two completely different kanji characters can have identical pronunciations. That means the surname Ushio can be spelled in different ways.

The Hiroshima telephone directory listed nearly 150 Ushios with kanji that matched the spelling of S. Ushio's surname, as recorded in the old book of photos I saw in the peace museum archive. I called them all (with an interpreter's assistance), hoping to find S. Ushio herself, or a relative who might have known her.[19]

A woman named Motoko answered one of the calls. She said she knew an S. Ushio who was eighty-four years old, only one year shy of Dr. Kamada's estimation. This S. Ushio was the sister of Motoko's husband. She married at some point, and went by the name of S. Kiyokawa.

Motoko said S. Kiyokawa was a Hiroshima *hibakusha*.

I explained that I was looking for the woman in the kimono-burn photo, and asked if I could telephone S. Kiyokawa to inquire whether she had been treated at the Ujina military hospital in August or September 1945, and if so, whether she recalled posing for a photographer named Kimura.

"I don't know if it is a good idea to give you the number," Motoko said. "Even if you call, she is asleep most mornings and nights, so she probably wouldn't pick up the phone. She's old now and cannot hear well."

Motoko agreed to contact her sister-in-law on my behalf, nonetheless.

Meanwhile, I contacted a researcher at the National Peace Memorial Hall for the Atomic Bomb Victims, and asked whether they had any information about a survivor named S. Kiyokawa. They did not.[20]

Motoko called back later that day. She had spoken with S. Kiyokawa.

"She told me politely but firmly that she will not speak with you. She said she is very old and will not be calling you back. And she said 'it cannot be me in that picture.'"

Just as well, because I had forgotten to ask whether S. Kiyokawa spelled her maiden name with the same kanji used in my S. Ushio's surname. That oversight alone would have precluded my ability to confirm whether the two *hibakusha* might have been one and the same.

All the other Ushios I spoke with said they had never heard of an Ushio survivor whose first name was S. Based on the tone of some of those conversations—my calls occasionally triggered wariness and displeasure—information would not have been forthcoming, even if such knowledge existed.

≈

I do not know what became of S. Ushio. Inconspicuousness is a garment that history seems to have imposed on her, whether she wanted to wear it or not.

Masami Nishimoto, the *Chugoku Shimbun* expert on *genbaku* photography, has looked into the Ushio photo. He told me with certainty, based on records he claims to have seen, that S. Ushio died at age twenty-two, and that her body was probably transferred from Hiroshima to Ninoshima, a nearby island in the Seto Inland Sea that has been called the place of the sleeping dead. Ninoshima served as a quarantine station and emergency field hospital after the bombing. Tens of thousands of casualties were moved there, and many thousands died, their identities lost in the mayhem of emergency cremations and burials.[21]

Over the postwar years, remains of the Ninoshima dead were moved back to Hiroshima. Unidentified ashes, along with identified but unclaimed remains, were stored in the Atomic Bomb Memorial Mound, an underground repository of lost souls situated near the Hiroshima Peace Memorial Museum. Nishimoto surmised that S. Ushio's remains, identified or not, rest inside the Mound.[22]

Shinji Uemoto, a Hiroshima City Hall official responsible for the Memorial Mound, told me he had no record of S. Ushio's remains ever having been placed there.[23]

Nishimoto said it would not have been unusual, given the confusion of the times, for S. Ushio's name (which authorities had recorded when her photograph was taken) to have disappeared entirely from government registers. If that is what happened, and if S. Ushio's ashes are in the Mound, they probably sit unlabeled, resting with the many thousands of other unidentified remains that reside there.

There has never been a full accounting of everyone who died in Hiroshima. The A-bomb destroyed the public records of private lives many thousands of times over. The details of S. Ushio's life vanished in that whirlwind.

But S. Ushio's photograph is alive. It is eloquent and it is powerful. And it has the ability to rouse memories and to stir emotions, particularly among those Japanese of S. Ushio's generation who experienced the war themselves.

2

Watanabe-san and the Mound

I met Miyoko Watanabe one November morning outside a basement conference room in the Hiroshima Peace Memorial Museum.[1] I had just visited the museum's archive, where I had found the old book, yellowed with
time, that provided the name of S. Ushio.

Watanabe, a Hiroshima *hibakusha*, was in her late seventies. She had
just lectured to some high school students about the day the bomb went off.

"It is not easy for me to talk about my experience," she said. "For me
it is like airing my dirty linen in public." She speaks to children in order to
honor the victims and to promote peace, she said. She has told her story
more than one thousand times.[2]

Miyoko Watanabe was fifteen years old in 1945. She had been mobilized as a laborer in the Japan Steel Works, which made defense-related
supplies for the Japanese navy.[3] August 6 was a "no electricity day" at the
plant, so its workers had time off.[4] Watanabe was in her home, about one
and a half miles south of ground zero, when the bomb exploded. Her house
collapsed, exposing its bamboo frame. She was knocked unconscious. Her
injuries were not life threatening, although she suffered severe diarrhea.
Her father, who was closer to the hypocenter, was horribly burned.

"On the day of Japan's surrender," Watanabe recalled, "my father mum-
bled, 'Japan lost the war.' He died the next day, complaining of the cold."

The fire and heat, Miyoko Watanabe said, are what tormented most
other victims. She saw groups of people whose faces and clothes had been

burned black. "Almost naked and burned beyond recognition, they came tottering along, dangling their arms in front of them like ghosts," she recalled. "Some had their work pants burned away, save the elastic strings. Others had all their clothes burned except for the front part. They all kept chanting, 'Water! Give me water!'"

Their flesh was wet and "exposed juicily," Watanabe said. Peeled skin hung "from their fingertips like seaweed."

I told her I had come to Hiroshima to search for the story behind the kimono-scarred woman, S. Ushio, and that I had just made some progress. I pulled out my wallet and removed a small piece of paper, on which I had written S. Ushio's name.

"She is the woman in the photo?"

"Yes," I said.

"Ahh." Watanabe jumped back in her chair, and touched her shoulder, indicating, from memory, the spot where the pattern of S. Ushio's kimono was most pronounced.

"I always use the photo in my talks," Watanabe told me. "It is a picture that helps children understand the power of the bomb."

Miyoko Watanabe had a serious and scholarly way of engaging visitors. She spoke briskly, businesslike, and with confidence. Her pitch-black hair was shortly cropped, just so, and was thinning on top. She wore a navy blue blazer. A gold brooch in the shape of a flower was pinned to the lapel.

There was, to my eye, a patina of sadness about Watanabe-san, despite her self-assurance. The features of her face seemed to sag, drawn by all she had lived through. Even the flower on her lapel pointed downward. Hers was a life well exposed to the weather.

As we got to talking, I explained that the Ushio photo, in my opinion, was especially compelling because a kimono, the garment that symbolizes Japan, had scarred her skin. I asked Watanabe if she had any thoughts on the matter.

My question had the unexpected effect of transforming the nature of our conversation. Kimonos meant something to her. Her voice softened. Her staid bearing eased as she went back in time, to her childhood in prewar Japan.

Wearing a kimono was one of her earliest memories, she said. She recalled how her family, which was well to do, had collected a sizable number of kimonos, not everyday fare like S. Ushio's, but expensive, elegant garments; and how once, as a child, she had dressed in a beautiful kimono and marched in a parade.

"Watanabe-san," I said, "do you remember the first time you wore a nice kimono after the atomic bombing?"

"It was for a New Year's Day celebration, in 1948," she said. "I was very happy. I got to wear makeup for the first time ever, and even curled my hair."

The memory was powerful, and Miyoko Watanabe delighted in the pleasure of recounting it. She hugged herself at the recollection of how excited she was to have worn that garment. "It was a red kimono with long sleeves. It was so beautiful. I couldn't wait to put it on. It made feel me so proud."

"Do you know where the red kimono is today?" I asked.

"My mother gave it away to my niece. Without my permission! I was furious!"

Watanabe paused, then, unexpectedly, covered her face. She began to cry. Her mother had acted badly, and decades later, the pain and anger remained.

Watanabe explained that the kimono transfer occurred when she was childless. Since the niece was the only young girl in the extended family, the mother presented the garment to her.

Watanabe later adopted a daughter but lacked a kimono to give her. So she bought a brand-new one, equally beautiful. The purchase was her only option. It would have been inappropriate, she said, to ask her niece to return the original item.

When Miyoko Watanabe and I parted, I thanked her for sharing the red kimono tale with me. I pulled out a copy of the S. Ushio photograph, and pointed to it.

"I don't want this to be the only kimono story I tell."

⁓

During my conversation with Watanabe, I mentioned that a reporter for the *Chugoku Shimbun*, the local newspaper, had told me that S. Ushio's remains might be resting in the Atomic Bomb Memorial Mound.

"I went inside the burial mound once," Watanabe declared.

It was an unanticipated revelation. The Mound is a revered spot, one of the most solemn in Hiroshima. The remains of seventy thousand unidentified souls lay inside its vault, along with several thousand others whose identity is known but whose ashes are unclaimed.[5]

The vault inside the Mound is closed to the public. "No one can go in," a city hall spokesman told me. "Not even government officials. Only family members claiming remains are allowed inside."[6]

Japan is a rigidly bureaucratic country where rules are hardly ever broken. Watanabe's visit to the Mound was extraordinary.

"There is an old woman who takes care of the Mound," Watanabe explained. "She cleans it outside and inside. Even though it is prohibited, she let me inside the vault just one time because I knew her well. Her name is Toshiko Saeki."

I visited the Mound at lunchtime one autumn day.[7] It is smaller than I had imagined. A stone pagoda sits on its highest point, and trees hover on the periphery.

I was hoping to see Toshiko Saeki, but she wasn't there. However, a man on a motorcycle drove up. He wore a helmet, black suit, and tie. He parked the vehicle off to the side, dismounted, and approached the Mound, where he bent over and lit a candle. Straightening himself up, he put his hands together, closed his eyes, bowed, and prayed. When he was finished, he hopped back onto the motorcycle, fixed his helmet, and drove off, back to the business of the day.

All the while, directly behind the Mound, a large memorial bell tolled. Its resonant, metallic tones drifted through the trees and settled above the man, anointing his prayers in sound.

I asked Watanabe to describe what is inside the Mound. She told me its underground vault is lined with shelves. The shelves hold rows of containers filled with remains: the unidentified in wooden vessels, the identified in white china, with names written in black ink. The containers stand shoulder to shoulder, like soldiers at attention.

"I was so scared to go in," Watanabe said, "because ashes were really there."

"My mother once told me a story," she continued, "how one of her friends found a container inside the vault with the ashes of her son. She refused to take the remains. She felt it would be nice to keep them in the Mound, a place where so many people would come to pray for him. That would be good for his spirit."

Toshiko Saeki, Watanabe-san's friend, was a *hibakusha*. People called her the "guardian of the Mound" because of her constant presence there. She lost more than a dozen family members in the A-bomb attack, including her mother and younger sister. I never got to meet her, but I did read something she once said.

"The dead still cling to me," she declared. "So I decided to live with the victims."[8]

3

Scars and the Impersonal Nature of War

When I first visited Hiroshima, I didn't expect to meet somebody who had grown up in my hometown, let alone somebody who had made a career thinking, writing, and teaching about Japan. Robert Jacobs, who goes by the nickname Bo, is a professor at the Hiroshima Peace Institute of Hiroshima City University. He is interested in how exposure to radiation has affected people, families, and communities. He describes himself as "a historian of nuclear technologies and radiation technopolitics." And he has thought a lot about S. Ushio's photograph, and the symbolism of her kimono-scarred back.[1]

Bo and I were both raised in Skokie, Illinois, a village north of Chicago. When we were kids, Skokie had a sizable Jewish population that included roughly seven thousand Holocaust survivors. It was one of the largest clusters in the United States of eyewitnesses to the atrocities of Hitler's Final Solution.[2]

We also had similar connections to World War II, albeit on different fronts. My father fought in Europe. Bo's dad served in the Pacific theater. At a gathering in Germany after the Nazi capitulation, my father stood near General Dwight D. Eisenhower, leader of the Allied forces. Bo's father stood on a ship in Tokyo harbor when Japanese representatives, on board the USS *Missouri*, signed the Instrument of Surrender.

Bo is exceedingly thoughtful and articulate. I was curious to get his opinion about the Ushio photograph. We met one morning in downtown Hiroshima, less than a mile from ground zero.

He told me that in the years immediately following Japan's surrender, the United States suppressed images from Hiroshima and Nagasaki. General Douglas MacArthur, head of the Allied occupation forces in Japan, had imposed a strict censorship code in September 1945. It covered all forms of media, including newspapers, magazines, textbooks, radio, film, plays, and photographs, and applied to foreign as well as Japanese content. It banned criticism of the Allied Powers and prohibited the release of information regarding the radiation effects of the Hiroshima and Nagasaki bombings. The censorship regime continued until the occupation ended in 1952.[3]

"There was an extremely concerted effort to keep any photograph of actual victims or survivors out of the public domain," Bo said. The purpose was to skirt the issue of civilian casualties, and to bolster President Truman's assertion that the Japanese cities were military targets.[4]

The brief newsreel glimpse of S. Ushio, seen in 1946 by moviegoers in New York and elsewhere, appears to have been a departure from that practice.

The Allied occupation officially ended on April 28, 1952.[5] *Life* magazine, in its September 29 issue that year, published the first graphic Hiroshima photos, calling them "Atom Blasts through Eyes of Victims." S. Ushio was not among them. With time, however, her picture was published widely. "It's one of the photographs you encounter when you begin to read anything about Hiroshima," Bo said.

If that was so, I asked, why had S. Ushio remained an anonymous victim, her name hidden in the archives, the story of her life, and of her death, unknown?

If, in fact, she had died, Bo said, surviving family members would not have publicized her case. "Perhaps she was buried in a mass grave and wasn't honored properly. It might be easier just not to talk." Silence would avoid any embarrassment or shame at the impropriety, albeit forced by circumstances, of having failed to say a proper goodbye, of having failed to properly console and pay homage to her soul.

There was also the issue of humility. "I think there could be elements of not wanting to stand out and claim anything special about having her as a family member, compared to the other tens of thousands, hundreds of thousands who died. And," he added parenthetically, "there is a great stig-matization of *hibakusha*."

I halted the conversation at that point. How, I wondered, could any-body view A-bomb survivors disapprovingly? They were, it seemed to me, a hallowed class of noncombatants who had lived through the unimaginable, much like the Holocaust survivors Bo and I grew up with in Skokie. Our neighbors from Auschwitz may, on occasion, have kept to themselves, but not because they were shunned.

"Many *hibakusha*," Bo explained, "have tried to hide their exposure to radiation because along with radiation comes fear. People feared that *hiba-kusha* were still in some unknown way contaminated, that *hibakusha* were likely to have children with genetic problems who would make undesirable marriage partners. A-bomb survivors had reasons to downplay their iden-tification. That may have kept the Ushio family from publicly embracing her victimhood."[6]

Most Hiroshima and Nagasaki survivors could cloak their victim-hood, if they so chose, simply by keeping silent. There was nothing about the way they looked that gave them away. But the image of S. Ushio could not hide. Her kimono scars, publicly and forever displayed in her photo-graph, guaranteed that. It was similar for my childhood neighbor, Mrs. Herskovitz. The numbers tattooed on her left forearm identified her as a survivor whenever her shirtsleeve slipped up.

"That's what drew me to the Ushio photo," I told Bo. "When I first saw the kimono pattern burned onto her skin, I immediately thought of Ger-man concentration camp tattoos, and of the numbers on my neighbor's arm. Both imprints were a sort of wartime branding."

"What happened to Ushio took place in entirely different circum-stances from what happened to Mrs. Herskovitz," I added. Mrs. Hersko-vitz was a victim of genocide unleashed by a vile regime. S. Ushio was vic-timized by having been born in Japan, the aggressor nation responsible for unleashing war in the Pacific.

"But still," I said, "the Holocaust and the bombing of Hiroshima were equally horrifying for the victims, and the branding of S. Ushio and of Mrs. Herskovitz were equally appalling."

"It's the impersonal nature of the horror of war," Bo said. "The Jews were given those numbers to replace their individual identity, which was wiped from the slate as part of a mechanized process of killing. And the same is true for the woman with the kimono pattern burned on her. She was merely part of a city of hundreds of thousands of people who were, in a single instance, scorched and killed and irradiated. Her victimhood in war was completely impersonal."

At the same time, Bo noted, the kimono scars on S. Ushio's flesh were personal, in a most distinctive, invasive, and intimate way.

"There were so many people killed," he said, "so many scorched bodies. But she is marked specifically. She was burned in a specific way, and what that restores to her is her individuality. That's one of the only reasons that we even think of her. And that's one of the reasons this picture is important to us."

Part 2

NAGASAKI

My maternal grandfather, Abe Yellin, bore no concentration camp tattoo. He did not experience Auschwitz. But World War II broke his family nonetheless.

Abe was a devout man, and proudly so. He had come from a village called Lyubeshov, in the Russian Empire's Pale of Settlement, a western region designated for Jews.[1] Abe was a scholar, trained, he would boast, in Jewish theology by a disciple of Hayim Nahman Bialik, posthumously known as Israel's national poet.[2] Whatever sense I have of being Jewish is largely attributable to Abe.

World War I cut short my grandfather's studies. The German army took him prisoner and put him into forced labor. He managed to survive the conflict and emigrated to the United States along with other family members. They settled in Chicago.

One of Abe's younger sisters, whom he called Mary, stayed behind. "She very much wanted to come to America," Abe later recalled, "but her husband was doing well in business and wouldn't think of emigrating."[3]

Mary would have been my great-aunt.

Abe died in 1987. He left behind an unpublished autobiography in which he revealed that Mary had perished in the Holocaust. Sometime in 1942, Abe wrote, the Nazi army marched into Lyubeshov and "herded all Jewish families to the outskirts of town, had them dig one long grave, stripped all adults and children naked and shot them dead with machine guns. My sister's 3 children, aged 10-8-6, her in-law's family and possibly 200 other Jewish families perished." Abe said one of his cousins, named Moshe, "somehow crawled out of the mass grave alive and escaped into the forest." "I received a letter from him in 1950," Abe wrote, "describing the horror he had lived through."

I never doubted the veracity of Abe's story regarding his sister's death. Other witnesses to massacres in and around Lyubeshov told remarkably similar tales.[4] What puzzled me, however, was why Abe's sibling, the daughter of a devoutly religious family, was called Mary. It is not typically a Jewish name.[5]

Prior to his death, Abe submitted written testimony about his sister to Yad Vashem, the World Holocaust Remembrance Center in Israel. The document is stored in the center's central database of Holocaust victims. It officially lists her name, with a hyphen, as "Mary-Miriam."[6] That is how I learned that my great-aunt's Jewish name was Miriam. Abe never told me why he called her Mary.[7]

4

Apocalypse

On the eastern slope of Mount Iwaya overlooking the Urakami Valley, where Nagasaki lies, there is a burial ground called the Cemetery of Consolation of the Holy Mother Virgin Mary. A statue of Mary, sculpted in beaming white stone, stands atop a pedestal at the far end of the graveyard, bright and conspicuous against its surroundings. Mary's arms, draped in a mantle, are outstretched, palms up, beckoning the faithful in the valley below. Her face is serene. But her eyes, strikingly well chiseled, rivet forward, revealing a confluence of emotions—compassion, wisdom, anger, sorrow—all etched by the history of what took place there.

At the other end of the cemetery, towering over a congregation of headstones, is a tall, simple white cross. It points to the sky and to the heavens beyond. You can see it at a distance today from the Nagasaki Atomic Bomb Museum, near ground zero, where the *genbaku*, as the Japanese call it, exploded more than seventy-five years ago, turning the Urakami into a valley of death.

Catholic survivors say the Virgin Mary led the souls of those who died to heaven.[1]

Nagasaki has been the center of Catholicism in Japan since the last half of the sixteenth century, when missionaries from Spain and Portugal introduced the religion. Catholics have always been a small minority in Japan, where the main faiths are Shinto and Buddhism. Today, even among all Japanese Christians (who constitute about 1 percent of the country's

FIGURE 4. Cemetery of Consolation of the Holy Mother Virgin Mary,
Nagasaki, March 2008. Photograph by author.

population), Catholics make up the smaller part: an estimated 40 percent, with Protestants accounting for the rest.[2]

But within that Christian minority, the Catholic community of Nagasaki, with some sixty thousand believers, is the hub of the Church of Rome in Japan.[3] In 2020, Catholics made up 4.4 percent of all city inhabitants, more than four times the national norm.[4] Before the atomic bombing, the proportion was even larger: 6 to 8 percent of Nagasaki's wartime population was Catholic.[5] Despite their minority status, and indeed because of it, Nagasaki Catholics own a compelling and often heartrending story, a narrative that reveals the short- and long-term impacts of the atomic bombing on a single community of victims.

Nagasaki's official account of what transpired on August 9, 1945, begins laconically. "It was a hot summer day," say the *Nagasaki Atomic Bomb Damage Records*, the city's comprehensive history of the bombing and assessment of the devastation it caused.[6] At 11:00 a.m., when an American B-29 bomber named *Bockscar* approached overhead, the temperature had already reached nearly eighty-four degrees Fahrenheit.[7] By nighttime, it would hit ninety-one. The air was muggy, the relative humidity at 71 percent.[8] The Japanese have a word for this unpleasant mix of atmospheric moisture and heat: *mushiatsui*. It was a stifling setting for the events that would soon play out.

Mrs. Yamada was twenty-nine years old back then, the mother of four children, including a three-year-old son named Shinichi. She worked at a kimono fabric store in Nagasaki. By 11:00 a.m. she had taken her ten-month-old daughter to the hospital for a doctor's visit and was heading home. She lived in the southern part of the Urakami Valley, in an area called Zenzamachi. Her home was about a mile from what would soon be called the hypocenter, or heart of the explosion.

On the other side of town that morning, Kio Tanaka was working in the fields. Tanaka was from a farming family. She had three children, including an infant boy named Yoshihiro. Her home was in the northern part of the Urakami Valley, a little more than a mile from ground zero.[9]

As the two women went about their business, a morning ground fog that had covered Nagasaki was dissipating. From the sky, the B-29 initially encountered a fluffy cloud cover, obscuring its target (the Mitsubishi Steel and Arms Works) and causing the crew to consider bombing by radar.[10] Just after 11:00, however, the clouds split. The bombardier eyed the city below, and at 11:02 let loose a five-ton plutonium bomb named Fat Man.

Some forty seconds later, the device detonated, discharging the pent-up power of a US military bent on ending the war. The force was twenty-one kilotons of TNT. The Hiroshima bomb dropped three days earlier, named Little Boy, had released twelve and a half kilotons.[11]

The burst point was a third of a mile above the ground. Fat Man missed the Mitsubishi complex by a mile or so, although the blast did destroy it.[12] The bomb instead went off over a tennis court. The explosion spit out a nuclear fireball that raised the ground temperature to between five thousand and seven thousand degrees Fahrenheit.[13] Most of Nagasaki, at least the prewar version of it, ceased to exist.

The instantaneous consequence of the blast was the pulverization of three square miles of the city.[14] The Urakami Church stood within that zone, a third of a mile northeast of ground zero. The church was the spiritual heart of Nagasaki's sizable Catholic community, and the largest Catholic church in the Far East. Two priests and twenty-four parishioners were in the building when the bomb went off. They died preparing for the Feast of the Assumption of Mary six days later, which marks the Virgin Mary's ascent to heaven at the end of her life.[15]

The exact number of people who died in Nagasaki is unknown. According to the Nagasaki Atomic Bomb Museum, the estimated death toll would rise within months to 73,884. The number injured was 74,909. Nagasaki's population at the time of the bombing was approximately 240,000, among them an estimated 15,000 to 20,000 Catholics, some 10,000 of whom were killed.[16]

Not everyone died instantly within that three-square-mile footprint of destruction. Short-term survival depended on location and luck. Long-term survival hinged on severity of injury, gravity of radiation exposure, and immediacy of access to medical and other care.

The Nagasaki Medical College was located between a third and a half mile from the hypocenter, directly south of the Urakami Church.[17] The

A-bomb flattened most of the college's buildings. Nearly nine hundred staff members and students died immediately or shortly thereafter from injuries or radiation exposure, while thick concrete walls shielded some occupants. Later on, a group of surviving medical researchers wondered how far away from ground zero you had to be in order to survive. They looked at death rates according to hypocenter proximity and found that 100 percent of Nagasaki residents who were within a third of a mile of the blast point died immediately. Ninety percent within six-tenths of a mile perished sooner or later. Fifty percent within nine-tenths of a mile were likely to die, as would 10 percent within one and a quarter miles.[18] This was the topographic calculus of death, and the terrain a young man with a camera would soon traverse, barely one day after the blast.

5

Sacred Images, Two Mothers

Yosuke Yamahata, a twenty-eight-year-old army photographer, arrived in Nagasaki at 2:00 a.m. on August 10, fifteen hours after the US attack. He exited a train at Michino-o station, two and a half miles north of ground zero. The depot had survived the explosion and became an aid station and transit point in and out of the city, ferrying the injured away from the disaster.[1]

The Japanese government had dispatched Yamahata to Nagasaki to capture the explosion's terrible aftermath. The photographs might be useful for military propaganda against the United States, the thinking went.[2]

Yamahata traveled with two companions, including Jun Higashi, a writer. Overnight, the men walked south from the train station toward the military police headquarters at the opposite end of the city. The journey took nearly two hours. The mushroom cloud had moved off. The night was clear. Moonlight illuminated the route, as did the light of many small fires—"elf-fires," Yamahata called them—smoldering in the detritus.[3]

They made their way through the hypocenter. "Near the center of the explosion the blast was so strong that all living beings and objects had been turned to powder," Higashi wrote. "There were no corpses to be seen."[4]

The men reached the military police outpost in southern Nagasaki before dawn. When the sun came up, Yamahata began taking photos. "Not a single cloud blocked the direct rays of the August sunlight, which shone down mercilessly on Nagasaki, on that second day after the blast," Yamahata later recalled.[5]

By day's end, the men had retraced their steps and returned to Michino-o station. Yamahata had taken 119 photos. They remain the primary visual chronicle of the Nagasaki attack, taken in its immediate aftermath, when death and suffering were still fresh on the canvas.[6]

That same morning, after dawn, Mrs. Yamada and her young son, Shinichi, had descended a hill near the southern military police headquarters. Despite the stifling August heat and humidity—the *mushiatsui*—the Yamadas wore thick, padded winter kimonos, which replaced the soiled garments they had been wearing at the time of the explosion. A hood covered Shinichi's head. The winter gear was the only attire close at hand in the postbombing chaos.

They approached an aid station, where they were given *onigiri*—rice balls. Yosuke Yamahata saw them and took their photograph.[7] The snapshot would become one of the most iconic images of the Nagasaki tragedy.

Bandages swaddled Mrs. Yamada's head, framing her dazed eyes and tightly drawn lips. Splotches of blood lined the son's face. He gazed forward, with a mix of curiosity, bewilderment, and fear. He held a white rice ball in his right hand. The mother held one in her left. Chalk-colored dust covered the ground around them, like a coating of frozen ice crystals. Behind, a chilling, ghostlike haze hung over debris and hills. It was nuclear winter in August.

"That is one miserable picture," Mrs. Yamada said years later. "I do not like looking at it."[8]

Three and a half miles north of where the Yamadas stood, Kio Tanaka appeared some hours later in the midafternoon at a temporary relief center in front of Michino-o station.[9] She wore a loose-fitting striped kimono, and had walked to the station barefoot.[10] A large bruise blemished the right side of her face. She sat down next to a wagon, the ground around her covered by what appeared to be straw. She cradled her infant son, Yoshihiro, in her arms. His head was bloodied and his body frail. His eyes barely opened.

Tanaka's kimono was slightly unfastened, exposing her left breast. She tried to feed the infant. A man who appeared to be a relief worker offered assistance, holding Yoshihiro's head to the mother's nipple. The worker backed off. The baby had latched on.

FIGURE 5. Mrs. Yamada and her son holding rice balls at an aid station in Nagasaki, August 10, 1945. Photograph by Yosuke Yamahata, courtesy of Shogo Yamahata, IDG films. Photo restoration by TX Unlimited, San Francisco.

This sequence of events was captured on film by Yosuke Yamahata, who had already made his way back to Michino-o station by the time Kio Tanaka had arrived. The photographs were among the last of his Nagasaki journey.[11]

Yamahata's final shot of Kio Tanaka is the most well known. It is a visual masterpiece with religious overtones. Tanaka's kimono, and the way she wears it, suggests the mantle of the Virgin Mary. Tanaka is cradling Yoshihiro, as Mary once cradled the Christ child. Yoshihiro is swaddled in white cloth, grasping the edge of his mother's kimono with two tiny fingers, holding on to life.

"The image bears a striking resemblance to conventional Madonna and child iconography," said Karen Fraser, an art historian specializing in Japanese photography.[12] Depictions of the Virgin Mary cradling baby Jesus, or of Jesus suckling her breast, are central to the Catholic faith.[13] The intimation of religion in the Tanaka picture "further underscores the poignancy of the photo given Nagasaki's long, complex Christian history," according to Fraser.

"Some would say there's not much to say here other than to acknowledge the visual coincidence, but given Nagasaki's connections to the Virgin Mary, I think this is one of those cases where a portrait arises to the level of a symbol," said Matthew Milliner, a specialist in Christian art history. "The Yamahata photograph speaks as a Marian image because of the compassion it elicits."[14]

Osamu Giovanni Micico is a Japanese Catholic painter based in Florence, Italy. His 2019 work *Holy Mother of Sorrow and Hope* was painted for the Urakami Church to commemorate Nagasaki's A-bomb victims. The painting now hangs on the wall of the Urakami sanctuary. I asked Micico for his thoughts about the Kio Tanaka picture.

"The image would beautifully turn into a painting; I would love to do that!" he told me via email.[15] "Look at the way the Nagasaki survivor holds the baby, look at her gaze and the tilt of her head. The image resembles Gothic paintings of the nursing Madonna and Child, in which Mary looks into her heart and contemplates the destiny of her Son and the Salvation of humanity. The mother in this photograph may be surrounded by sorrow and destruction, but she casts her gaze forward, beyond her child and beyond the moment. What is there beyond? I see Hope."

FIGURE 6. Kio Tanaka and her infant son at an aid station, Nagasaki, August 10, 1945.
Photograph by Yosuke Yamahata, courtesy of Shogo Yamahata, IDG films.
Photo restoration by TX Unlimited, San Francisco.

FIGURE 7. *The Virgin of Humility*, Lippo Memmi, circa 1340. Gemäldegalerie, Berlin.

Figure 8. *Madonna and Child*, Duccio di Buoninsegna, circa 1290–1300.
Metropolitan Museum of Art, New York.

6

Missionaries, Banishment, and Resurrection

On the day after the atomic bomb exploded, Dr. Tatsuichiro Akizuki, a physician at Nagasaki's First Urakami Hospital, checked on a severely wounded man he had earlier treated. The hospital, run by a group of Japanese Catholic Franciscans, was less than a mile from the hypocenter. The facility's interior had been destroyed by the blast and subsequent fires, but the building's concrete shell still stood. Akizuki had narrowly escaped injury from a collapsing ceiling, and he (along with other surviving staff, including priests, monks, and nurses) assisted many of the area's injured.

Akizuki did what he could to comfort his patient, who was near death, and then moved on to look after others. As he walked away, the sound of desperate voices followed him.

"Jesus! Mary! Joseph!" they cried.

These were wails of grief from the patient's loved ones. Akizuki later said the experience left him feeling lifeless. In the days ahead, Akizuki reported similar scenes across the blast zone. "They prayed to Mary with all their hearts," he said of the Catholic injured.[1]

Invocations of the Virgin Mary, along with those of Jesus, had been a religious ritual among Nagasaki Catholics since Christianity first came to Japan in 1549, when a Spanish Jesuit missionary named Francis Xavier landed in Kyushu, the southernmost of Japan's four main islands.[2] Nagasaki is situated in northern Kyushu on a large natural harbor that opens onto Pacific waters. The city would become Japan's primary port of entry for foreign trade, culture, and influence, including religion. It was Japan's "window to the West." Xavier was later canonized for spreading the faith.

By the late 1500s, Nagasaki drew other Catholic missionaries from Spain and Portugal. The countries were Japan's leading partners in foreign commerce, selling goods, guns, and God, as one historian put it.[3] At the time, Japan was disunified, fractured into warring states. The firearms appealed to local military rulers, *daimyo*, who were fighting to assert regional control against neighboring lords. In return, the *daimyo*, primarily Buddhist, tolerated, at least initially, the influx of European Catholic proselytizers.

It was a quid pro quo with religious and political consequences. In 1580, a provincial *daimyo*, Omura Sumitada, the first Japanese warlord to have been baptized, gave the Jesuits jurisdiction over Nagasaki. He was under siege from samurai rivals, and so his conversion to Catholicism and ceding of Nagasaki were calculated to earn Portuguese support, enhancing his base of power. He took the Christian name Don Bartolome. Portuguese ships took control of Nagasaki harbor. And Christianity took deeper root there.[4]

By the beginning of the seventeenth century, European missionaries had built some two hundred churches and converted from three to five hundred thousand Japanese to Catholicism.[5] Nagasaki had become a bright shining light of Christianity, a "Rome of Japan."[6]

Japan's leaders soon changed course. Worried that Catholicism would lead to political unrest and Western domination, Toyotomi Hideyoshi, one of the era's most powerful *daimyo*, outlawed Christianity in 1614. Persecution of believers followed. Some Catholics were burned at the stake. Suspected Christians were forced to trample on images of Mary and Jesus to prove they had renounced the faith. This practice, known as *fumi-e*, was central to writer Shusaku Endo's 1969 novel *Silence*, a powerful period tale later turned into a movie by director Martin Scorsese. To stamp—or not to stamp—on the holiest of Christian icons was an existential choice for Japanese Catholics. Endo called the decision "the most painful act of love that has ever been performed."[7]

By the 1630s, Tokugawa Iemitsu, one of Hideyoshi's successors, controlled a newly unified Japan. The era of warring *daimyo* had ended. Wielding power as shogun, or commander in chief of an entire nation, Iemitsu issued a series of edicts dramatically restricting any Japanese contact with the outside world.

Japanese ships were "strictly forbidden to leave for foreign countries." No Japanese could go abroad. "If there is anyone who attempts to do so secretly, he must be executed."[8] The shogunate expelled all foreigners except the Dutch, who were allowed to live on a small, man-made island in Nagasaki Bay. Merchants from Holland had first sailed into Japan in 1600.[9] They were Protestants and deemed less threatening than Catholic outsiders. And the Dutch promised not to promote Christianity in Japan. Violation of this assurance meant imprisonment. Holland would remain Japan's only link to the West until the mid-nineteenth century.

The assault on Catholicism forced believers underground. Survival required ingenuity and adaptation. The faithful carved likenesses of Mary into Buddhist figurines. In the Japanese tea ceremony, they rotated tea bowls three times, symbolizing the Trinity of Father, Son, and Holy Spirit. For funerals, crosses were hidden inside Buddhist statues.[10] These "Hidden Christians" sheltered in the Urakami Valley or on remote nearby islands. They were mostly poor farmers, and they lived in silence, in the shadows, without Bibles or priests or houses of prayer, for more than two hundred years.

Two centuries of seclusion passed. By the second half of the nineteenth century, "barbarians" (the Japanese epithet for Americans and Europeans) pressed for commercial and diplomatic links with Japan in what was becoming a shrinking and modernizing world. Japan's wall of isolation collapsed, and its political system adjusted. *Bunmei kaika*—civilization and enlightenment—became the guiding principles of governance. That meant westernization, industrialization, and, as the Japanese emperor declared, an end to "evil customs of the past."[11]

In 1873, Japan lifted its ban on Christianity. Hidden Christians, some twenty thousand of them, resurfaced.[12] In Nagasaki, a newly revived community of Catholics built a new house of worship on grounds where their ancestors had been forced to perform *fumi-e*.[13] Construction of the Urakami Church began in 1895. The building was completed in 1925. It was formally christened the Immaculate Conception Cathedral, also known as Saint Mary's.

The atomic bombing of Nagasaki ripped the Urakami Church apart. However, some of the building's brick exterior structure held ground against the blast. The remaining slabs of broken wall loomed above the surrounding flattened terrain, like hollowed-out towers of misery that could be seen for miles.

For Nagasaki's surviving Catholics, the Urakami ruins would become sacred territory, a magnet for worshippers amid all the destruction. Within months of the bombing, congregants built a small wooden interim church there. In 1959, Nagasaki erected a new Urakami Cathedral, designed to resemble the old house of worship.

Takashi Nagai, a Catholic theologian, writer, and medical doctor, was a leading proponent of rebuilding the church.[14] He likened the cathedral's rebirth to the Virgin Mary's ascent to heaven. He believed a newly resurrected church would demonstrate Christianity's capacity to overcome hardship. The cathedral, he said, would become "a hill of blossoming flowers to point the hearts of the children freely to heaven."[15]

The reconstructed cathedral became an architectural icon and is, as its predecessor was, the spiritual seat of Catholicism in Nagasaki, and in Japan. It represents nearly five difficult centuries of Christian continuity, and displays the postwar resolve of Nagasaki Catholics to reclaim their lives and to breathe again.

The twenty-first-century cathedral is an active place, offering Mass and prayer seven days a week, baptisms, musical choirs, rosary workshops, a church school, and a monthly online magazine.[16] It welcomes locals and tourists, dignitaries and pilgrims, young and old. For the Catholic *hibakusha* of the Urakami congregation (those who have died and the dwindling number remaining), the church was and is more than a place to gather or to pray: it is a repository of memories; an archive of recollections from the old days when the original sanctuary still stood, when parents and uncles and aunts and siblings who are no longer around took them there to pray.[17]

Yoshitoshi Fukahori and Masahito Hirose were Nagasaki Catholics who, in their later years, curated such memories. They were determined and compassionate men, members of Japan's war generation, who were devoted to collecting and preserving the visual and written record of what happened on August 9, 1945, and thereafter. They were also responsible, in part, for ensuring that images of their compatriots Kio Tanaka and the Yamada mother and son would not fade.

7

Searching for the Kimono-Draped Nursing Mother and Child

On the morning of August 9, 2017, Yoshitoshi Fukahori put on a black suit, white shirt, and black tie, and set out to bear witness. It was the seventy-second anniversary of the Nagasaki attack, and the Nagasaki city government had chosen Fukahori, then eighty-eight years old, to deliver the Pledge for Peace, an address presented annually by a representative of the *hibakusha* community at the city's ceremony of remembrance.

The Pledge for Peace took place at the Nagasaki Peace Park, a large, open, tree-lined swath of land near ground zero. A towering bronze Peace Statue presided over the space. Thirty-two feet tall, the sculpture depicted an austere, well-muscled man. His sinewy right arm pointed to the sky, where the A-bomb once held sway. His left arm reached out horizontally, palm down, in a gesture for peace. A lectern and microphone, intended for Fukahori, sat beneath the sculpture.

Fukahori was a photo archivist at the Nagasaki Foundation for the Promotion of Peace, a public-private educational organization affiliated with the Nagasaki Atomic Bomb Museum. He looked after a collection of thousands of images shot on August 9, 1945, and in the following days, months, and years. "Photographs don't lie," he said.[1]

Fukahori was far from the hypocenter when the A-bomb fell, but his sister Chizuko was near ground zero and perished. Afterward, on the ninth of every month, once in the morning and again in the evening, Fukahori, a religious Catholic, went to the Urakami Cathedral "to speak to Chizuko." On sunny mornings, a rainbow of light from the building's arching, stained glass windows illuminated the sanctuary, where Fukahori, with folded hands, would call up his sibling's spirit to engage in conversation.

"How is it there?" he would ask regarding Chizuko's life in heaven. "Do you feel at ease there? I'm doing fine, by some means or other."

"I never forget the ninth of the month," Fukahori mused. "If I forget, my sister will hit me."[2]

At the Peace Park, a young woman dressed in black led Fukahori onto the ceremonial plaza. He was a genial man, with an owlish face and prominent white eyebrows. Despite his age, he looked strong and determined this day. But his gait was tentative. The woman gripped his right arm, to steady him.

At center stage, she released her hold so Fukahori could execute an obligatory bow to the audience. As he bent at the waist, he stumbled forward, but managed to regain his footing on his own. He bowed a second time, effortlessly.

The woman grasped his arm, and the two approached the Peace Statue. When they reached the sculpture, Fukahori bowed again, this time longer and deeper. Then, having reached the microphone, he pulled some papers out of an inside suit pocket, unfolded them, and proceeded to speak in a calm, resolute voice.

"Pledge for Peace," he began.[3]

Fukahori said he was sixteen years old on the morning the atomic bomb fell. He was working in a student mobilization brigade more than two miles from the hypocenter. The distance from ground zero saved him. In the evening, he was ordered to return to Nagasaki City. He arrived there the next day.

"It was as if we had wandered into another world," he recalled. He reached a demolished home. "Inside, my eighteen-year-old sister lay dead, looking as if she was embracing the beam of the house in her right arm. I still regret that I did not force myself to go home earlier. If I had made it, I might have been able to speak with her one last time."

Fukahori also spoke of his archival work. "We have collected and examined more than four thousand photos taken by many people," he said. "Believing in the power of the photos, which convey the truth of what happened under the mushroom cloud, we pledge that we will continue to convey the reality of the atomic bombing, and continue to use all our abilities toward eternal world peace and the abolition of nuclear weapons."

I visited Fukahori in 2008 to see his photo archive and, in particular, to ask him about the Yamahata images shot immediately after the bombing.

"Following the war, after General MacArthur came to Japan, we were not allowed to see anything about August 9," he said. The Allied publishing ban on photographs of Hiroshima and Nagasaki (including those in Fukahori's collection) meant that A-bomb victims had to wait seven years—until the Allied occupation ended—to view images of what they had been through.[4]

Fukahori opened a book that had been sitting on his desk. "This is where the Yamahata photos first appeared," he said. "The book is called *Atomized Nagasaki*. It came out when the Americans left, in 1952."[5]

The image of a youngster's face, expressionless and blood spattered, filled the book's cover. It belonged to the rice ball boy, Shinichi Yamada. The photo of Kio Tanaka, breastfeeding her dying child, was inside the book.

Fukahori said the Tanaka photo, in particular, was hard to forget. Its impact, he said, is palpable. "When we saw this picture for the first time, we realized that this happened to a normal civilian peacefully living in a town. It made us feel the terrible tragedy that the atomic bomb brought to Japan."

Kio Tanaka was thirty years old when the photo was taken. She died sixty-one years later, in 2006, at age ninety-one. Obituaries told some of her story.[6] She was said to have been a kind, gentle woman. Two of her children were killed in the bombing, including the baby, Yoshihiro. The kimono Kio Tanaka wore in the photo, the Madonna-like mantle that Yoshihiro weakly clung to, wasn't hers. The blast had set fire to her clothing, as well as the skin on her back. For the trek to the Nagasaki medical aid station, she had borrowed a kimono from a neighbor, whose house had survived.

After the war, Tanaka bore four more children, the "reincarnation," she said, of those she had lost. "I love all of my little ones, whether they are dead or alive," she said. "But if I only think about my dead children, I will not be able to love the ones who are still with me."[7]

Fukahori said he never met Kio Tanaka. But he told me she used to sell vegetables at a local market in Sumiyoshi, in the northwestern corner of the city. "The market is still there," he said. "It's not far from Michino-o station, where Tanaka-san received medical aid, and where her photograph was taken. Are you going there?" he asked.

I went to the market the next day.

"Did you know this lady?" I asked a Sumiyoshi merchant, showing him the photo of Kio Tanaka.

"She used to sell vegetables around here," he said.

"She used to have her cart over there, down the street," a nearby woman added, pointing to the end of a road.

"There's a Miss Mitsura who used to work with her," the man said. "I'm not sure she's here today."

She was.

≈

Chiwa Mitsura, age seventy-five, quietly sat on a low squat chair on the fringes of Sumiyoshi market. She eschewed any hint of the boisterously singsong hawking of wares common among Japanese street merchants. Instead, she perched calmly on her marketplace seat, overseeing a modest spread of fruits and vegetables displayed on the pavement before her.

Her attire, however, was exuberant and splashy, disclosing a certain puckishness of character this day. Her apron, which dominated the ensemble, displayed bright orange, blue, and pink daffodils hovering over a background of black and white squares, like flapping butterflies above a checkerboard field. She wore a soft khaki hat, which also featured blossoms. Her shirt was stitched in red and black gingham. Her pants were brown tartan plaid. It all blended nicely with the produce at her feet: dark green onions, broccoli, and spinach, light green cabbage, red strawberries, white radishes, and orange carrots.

"Are you Mitsura-san?" I asked, wanting to confirm her identity.

FIGURE 9. Chiwa Mitsura, friend of Kio Tanaka, selling vegetables at Sumiyoshi market, Nagasaki, March 2008. Photograph by author.

"Yes, I am Mitsura."

I asked her about Kio Tanaka.

"I knew Tanaka-san for about twenty years," Mitsura said. "She was a very strong and kind woman. And she liked to wear clothing similar to what I have on today," she added.

The women were from the same neighborhood, and had met before Mitsura, who was fifteen years younger, had started selling vegetables. "I visited at her house sometimes. Her daughter-in-law kept the place very clean."

Chiwa Mitsura and Kio Tanaka both survived the A-bomb, but they never spoke of those days. "We would talk about this and that, how many vegetables did you sell today, that kind of thing. You know, she grew all the vegetables she sold. She would come here lugging a hand-pulled cart filled with them. Cabbage. Spinach. Cucumbers. Sweet potatoes. Her garden was quite far away from her house, and she had to hike a long way uphill to get there. She was very patient with her work. We used to laugh a lot," Mitsura said, enjoying the memory. "Sometimes she would bring me *manju*, little cakes, and we'd eat them together."

"Do you remember the first time you saw the famous photograph of Mrs. Tanaka?" I asked.

"Only recently," she said. "Tanaka-san was still alive, and I saw the picture in a newspaper. That's when I realized who she was, that she was *hibakusha*. I never asked her about the photo, however."

Mitsura said her friend suffered from osteoporosis and walked hunched over. The two women were Buddhists. "That's how I found out she died," Mitsura said. "We belonged to the same religious group."

Chiwa Mitsura and Kio Tanaka were uncomplicated women who had lived through the ghastliness of August 9. They lacked riches and spent their days as the smallest of entrepreneurs in a market where other grocers were far better stocked. Nonetheless, year after year, they persevered, selling produce from the fringes of Sumiyoshi.

"She worked very hard," Chiwa Mitsura said of her friend. "She worked until the last day of her life."

8

Searching for the Rice Ball Boy and His Mother

In his Pledge for Peace speech, Yoshitoshi Fukahori recalled one especially hard memory after the A-bomb attack on Nagasaki. "I saw the Urakami Church burning down," he recalled. "While tears overflowed, I felt anger and thought the world was going to end."

It did not. The new cathedral on a "hill of blossoming flowers," as Takashi Nagai put it, evidenced Nagasaki's reawakening. It was on that hill, sometime before the cathedral was completed, that Mrs. Yamada's child—the rice ball boy in Yosuke Yamahata's iconic photo—was baptized.[1]

"I always call them the rice ball family," Yoshitoshi Fukahori told me.

Pointing to the image of the Yamadas in *Atomized Nagasaki*, he said: "This picture is formally called 'A Mother and Child Holding Rice Balls.' Rice balls were the emergency food being distributed to civilians." Fukahori said the photo is probably Yosuke Yamahata's most famous. "It's very interesting that those two people are wearing winter clothes, lined with cotton for warmth, even though it was very, very hot. After the bomb, they wanted to go down to where the rice balls were being distributed, but the mother was covered in blood, and they didn't have anything to wear. So they went to an underground bomb shelter and were given the kimonos. This poor, little boy was wearing this thick kimono in that heat. And he had his mother's blood on his face. But that's how he was dressed when the picture was taken. The image of the boy is actually more famous than his mother's. The mother survived, although she recently died. The child is still alive, however."

"Would it be possible to speak with the surviving child, the rice ball boy?" I asked.

"I'm not sure," Fukahori said. "I hear he is very reluctant to be in public. Although, two or three years ago we held a photo exhibit here that included the rice ball family photo. The son showed up, looked at the photo, and said 'That's me.'"

"What is the son's name?" I asked.

"I can't remember," he said.

I asked Fukahori how I could gather more information about the son and his mother. "Hirose," he said.

≈

"Ahhh," said Masahito Hirose, grinning at the black-and-white image I had shown him of a baby-faced teenager in a soldier-style cap. He was looking at a photo of himself from the BBC's website, published several years earlier, after an interview with one of its journalists.[2]

"I'm a little famous in Japan," he said, chuckling.

The atomic bombings of Nagasaki and Hiroshima produced two types of *hibakusha*: those who spoke about their experiences, and those who did not. The latter remained quiet for various reasons: a desire for privacy; a fear of stigma; a reluctance to relive the pain. Hirose belonged to the former group, and he readily agreed to meet with me to talk about the rice ball family, whom he had met.

Masahito Hirose was fifteen on the day the atomic bomb fell. He had been pulled out of school to work at a Nagasaki ship engine plant near what would become the hypocenter. As a precaution against anticipated American air raids in the weeks before August 9, however, some factory operations and laborers, including Hirose, had moved outside the city. That put him three miles away when the nuclear device exploded. "I was very fortunate," he said. His arms suffered injuries from broken glass.

Hirose taught high school English after the war. He was mostly known, however, for his work preserving war memories and advocating government compensation to *hibakusha* for radiation illnesses. Hirose often spoke publicly about his war experiences, in Japanese and in English.[3] He helped direct the Nagasaki Atomic Bomb Testimonial Society, which assembled survivor stories, many of which he translated into English.[4] He died in 2016. One obituary said he had been giving interviews from his hospital bed.[5]

I met Hirose at the Nagasaki Atomic Bomb Museum, where he was a volunteer.[6] It was springtime, and we sat next to a window overlooking a garden filled with rows of yellow, pink, and blue flowers. Inside, many hundreds of multicolored origami paper cranes, fastened together in long garlands, flowed from elevated hanging rods like rainbow waterfalls. Muzak quietly streamed from the museum's sound system. A nearby poster shaped like a heart declared *Heiwa*, or peace. The ambiance was entirely at odds with what Hirose and other survivors witnessed here in 1945.

"I am Catholic, and so are the Yamadas," Hirose said. "We all lived in the same district and used to go to the same church. It was one Sunday after Mass. I was speaking with the priest, and suddenly he turned and called out to somebody, 'How are you? It has been a long time!' When I looked over to see whom the priest was speaking to, I saw a middle-aged father with his family. 'Mr. Hirose,' the priest said, 'do you not know that person? He is the boy from the rice ball photo.'"

The boy's real name was Shinichi, but Hirose said as an adult, when appearing in public, he used a pseudonym, Shigeru, to preserve his privacy. The two men became acquaintances.

"At the time I first met the son, his mother happened to be in the hospital," Hirose said. "And after she came back home, I immediately went to see her. She was actually doing very well. She told me, of course, that she went through some difficult times after the war, but now she was having the happiest moments of her life. She had grandchildren who were very nice to her. She was very content."

"When I approached her about the photograph," Hirose continued, "she became slightly cold. She did not want to talk about it. But I told her I felt great relief at meeting her. It was as if my soul had been saved. With that, she opened up a little and told me about her life."

Hirose said Mrs. Yamada had raised four children: her son, Shinichi, and three daughters. Her husband had been a factory worker. In the postwar years, Mrs. Yamada sold rice balls and sweets in a local market to help support the family. "Because I was working on Sundays," she told Hirose, "I was worried whether my children were going to church. As for me, I went to evening mass."

Mrs. Yamada said that in the 1950s, after the Yamahata picture was published, journalists learned that she and her son were in the photo. "Different newspaper and magazine people would come and ask about that photo and my story," she said. "I really did not like that. I continued to decline interviews, and eventually people stopped pestering me about that picture. I do not like remembering that time in my life."

Hirose had multiple conversations with Mrs. Yamada, and later recorded what she had to say in a book.[7] Shinichi, however, never spoke with Hirose about what happened on August 9. "He was very young, and didn't have any memory of the atomic bombing," Hirose said. Shinichi only found out about the rice ball photograph postwar, in middle school, when a teacher told him about it. "He had to confront the issue because people wanted to discuss it with him," Hirose said. "It was quite chaotic. He started to feel distant from the Nagasaki experience."

Mrs. Yamada had passed away by the time I met Masahito Hirose. I wanted to speak with Shinichi, but he refused multiple interview requests that Hirose conveyed on my behalf.

"It's like he puts some kind of invisible wall around himself," Hirose said. "That's how I see it."

As for Mrs. Yamada, whatever celebrity she had was unwelcome, and like her son, she had shunned publicity. Whether by chance or design, even her first name remained something of a secret. I couldn't find it in published sources. And Hirose, her biographer, never revealed it. In his book he called her Nobu-san, a pseudonym.

"Don't you know her real name?" I asked.

"I respected her anonymity," he said. "And I don't remember her first name."

I asked Hirose if he knew where Mrs. Yamada was buried. He said her remains might lie in the cemetery of their common house of worship, the Shiroyama Catholic Church. I told him I would visit the place to look for her grave, and to search for more information about the rice ball mother and her son.

≈

The Shiroyama church is a short drive from the A-bomb museum. After saying goodbye to Hirose, I left the building and approached some taxis that were idling on the street. Three drivers waited around, chatting.

"I would like to go to the Shiroyama Catholic Church," I said.[8]

One of the drivers pointed to another.

"Go with him. He's Catholic."

Inside the church, a Miss Kataoka worked reception.

"Do you have a Mrs. Yamada buried in your cemetery? She probably died sometime in the nineties. She was the woman in the famous photograph of the rice ball mother and child," I said.

"Yes. She's buried here."

"The same woman who was in the rice ball photo?"

"Yes."

"I would like to visit her to pay my respects."

Miss Kataoka produced a cemetery map and wrote down the exact location of Mrs. Yamada's grave.

"Did you know her?" I asked.

"I did."

"What was her first name?"

"Womi."

≈

The Shiroyama graveyard is officially called the Cemetery of Consolation of the Holy Mother Virgin Mary. It is situated some distance from the church, on the eastern slope of Mount Iwaya, looking onto the Urakami Valley. A taxi driver had trouble finding the place and asked a dispatcher for assistance. "It's near such-and-such an apartment complex." "Ah," the driver said. He quickly made a sharp left turn. "Now I know what you're talking about."

We stopped at the base of the mountain, where I exited the cab. The cemetery was a fifteen-minute walk away, uphill, at the end of a series of steep steps and paths that wound through clusters of traditional Japanese houses and gardens. It was springtime. The gardens displayed a mix of flowers, green onions, radishes, and more.

"I have a lot of spinach," said Kiwa Nishiyama, a local farmer. "It's all organic. No pesticides. Very healthy. Why don't you take some?"

Kiwa Nishiyama had just finished tilling her garden. She was bending over a metal basin washing dirt off her hands when I walked by. Seventy-five years old, she lived downhill from the cemetery, next to the graveyard access path. Wearing a flowery apron and denim cap, she had a playful disposition and was eager to engage the improbable foreigner who had appeared out of nowhere.

"My grandchildren can speak English!" she said, laughing at the serendipity of encountering an American.

Nishiyama was in elementary school when the A-bomb was dropped. She lived far from the hypocenter and emerged unscathed. Her garden, on this mountain slope, was far closer to ground zero. "Everything was burned around here," she said.

"This is a very religious area," she added, nodding up toward the cemetery. "Many believe in Jesus Christ. At dusk, and in the morning, lots of people go there to pray."

"Have you seen the photograph of the rice ball family," I asked, "the one taken here after the A-bomb fell, with the mother and son holding *onigiri?*"

"Yes, yes, I know it. I've seen the picture in the Atomic Bomb Museum."

"The mother is buried up there, in the cemetery."

"Oh, I see," she said. "You know, not long ago the woman in another famous photograph, Tanaka-san, the one breastfeeding her baby, she died. I saw it on television. Her oldest son is head of the residents' association around here, where I live. He organizes things around town. He used to work for the local government."

"What is his name?"

"Tanaka."

"Do you know Mr. Tanaka?"

"Yes. He said that it was him in the picture. The baby. 'The baby is me,' he said."

I told Kiwa that in fact, the breastfeeding infant died not long after the photograph was taken.

"The baby died? Hmm. He said that it was him."

She handed me a bunch of spinach. I offered my business card in return. "I will put it in my lucky charm bag," she said.

"I'm honored that you're putting it there."

"I pray for peace," she said.

≈

The cemetery was now just a short walk away. It occupied a flat piece of land carved from the forested mountainside. A few private gardens, like Kiwa Nishiyama's, lay nearby.

The graveyard had a pleasing, mathematical symmetry, characteristic of Japan's devotion to detail and orderliness. Dozens of rows of identically shaped tombstones, some eight hundred of them, stood in ranks, shoulder to shoulder, like Catholic soldiers. Colorful bouquets of flowers adorned nearly every marker. A tall white cross was at one end of the graveyard. The even whiter statue of the Holy Mother Virgin Mary stood atop a gray, marble pedestal at the other. Her arms reached out, palms up, in a gesture radiating tranquility, peace, and, above all, faith. Her face, calm yet knowing, watched over the entire space, consoling the souls interred before her.

Nagasaki was visible from the cemetery grounds, but distance muted the noise of city traffic. A black hawk, wings spread, flew overhead. Green and white *uguisu*, Japanese bush warblers, flitted above the surrounding woods, singing *ho ho ke kyo*. It is said that the warbler's song welcomes the spring.[9] The scene was utterly peaceful, contrary in the extreme to what took place here on August 9, 1945.

A gold-lettered inscription on one side of tombstone number 282 read: "Yamada Family Gravestone." Engraved on the opposite side, in red: "Yamada, Womi." The tombstone reported that Mrs. Yamada had died at age seventy-four on February 3, 1991, in "Year Three of the Heisei Era," according to the Japanese calendar. A certain Kiyoshi Yamada, presumably her husband, was interred alongside her. His death preceded hers by ten years.

Their baptismal names were also carved into the tombstone marble. His was Paolo. Womi Yamada's Christian name was Mary.

9

Hibaku no María

In October 1945, Kaemon Noguchi, who belonged to a cloistered Catholic religious order called the Trappists, returned to his native Nagasaki in search of a souvenir. He had just been discharged from the army and was about to travel to distant Hokkaido, the northernmost Japanese island, to live in a monastery. Before departing, he went to visit the ruins of the Urakami Church, where he had prayed before the war.

"I wished to find a keepsake of the cathedral to bring with me," he later recalled. "Yet I found nothing but a heap of rubble."[1]

Noguchi wandered over the Urakami debris, imploring the Virgin Mary "to let me encounter anything at all associated to the church."

"Some time passed," he said. "I was praying silently. And all of a sudden I saw the holy face of the Virgin, blackened by fire, looking at me with a sorrowful air. I cried with joy. 'Thank you, Our Lady. Thank you!'"

Noguchi had stumbled across a relic that would later be called *Hibaku no Maria*—Bombed Mary, also known as the Wounded Madonna. For Nagasaki's Christians, this wooden, slightly less than life-sized head of the Holy Mother would, more than any other artifact, embody the experience of a Catholic community that had endured an atomic cataclysm.

"The appearance of the war-ravaged religious icon is haunting," the Japanese newspaper *Asahi Shimbun* wrote. "The Madonna's eyes have become scorched, black hollows, the right cheek is charred, and a crack runs like a streaking tear down her face."[2]

"She has a disfigured, miserable face, but she appeared before us in that way," said Shigemi Fukahori, a Nagasaki *hibakusha* who, years later, oversaw the construction of a special shrine inside the Urakami Cathedral to display the statue. "Those who have seen the Mary who survived the atomic bombing, they admire her so much, you know, seeing her in such a state."[3]

Shigemi Fukahori grew up in Nagasaki's Catholic enclave not far from another Fukahori, Yoshitoshi, the A-bomb photo collector. "I know him very well. We're something like second cousins," Shigemi said.

Shigemi was fourteen when the atomic bomb fell, two years younger than Yoshitoshi. Distance from ground zero saved him, just as it had saved his cousin. Shigemi was working in a factory more than two miles away from the blast point. His mother, two brothers, and two sisters were only a half mile from the hypocenter. They all perished.

Shigemi pursued Catholic theological studies after the war and became a fixture at the rebuilt Urakami Cathedral, which was located near his home. Like his cousin, he played a public role in preserving memories of the Nagasaki experience. Three years after Yoshitoshi gave the Pledge

FIGURE 10. Bombed Mary (*Hibaku no Maria*), iconic wooden image of the Virgin Mary that survived the Nagasaki atomic bombing, preserved at Urakami Cathedral, Nagasaki.

for Peace, Shigemi received the same honor, and on a bigger occasion: the seventy-fifth anniversary of the Nagasaki attack. His message emphasized a central *hibakusha* concern: will recollections of what happened in Nagasaki and Hiroshima fade after Japan's war generation dies off?

Shigemi Fukahori was eighty-nine when he delivered the Pledge for Peace. He showed no signs of old-age frailty, however. The audience, which included Japanese prime minister Shinzo Abe, saw a straight-backed, wiry man, white haired, bespectacled, and sure footed. Dressed in black with a white carnation rosette attached to his breast pocket, he looked confident and dignified.

On the day he took the podium, the cohort of *hibakusha* was dwindling. Of the estimated 650,000 who had survived the Hiroshima and Nagasaki bombings, some 136,000 were still alive. Their average age exceeded eighty-three.[4] In the previous year, more than nine thousand *hibakusha* had died, one-third of them in Nagasaki.[5]

The passage of time and the passing of survivors had already affected the collective memory of Japan. A survey found that in 2015, fewer than 30 percent of all Japanese could name the dates of the atomic bombings (among Hiroshima and Nagasaki residents, the numbers were higher).[6] For Americans, that would be like forgetting that Pearl Harbor Day is December 7, or that the World Trade Center attack took place on 9/11. The governor of Hiroshima Prefecture worried that "fading memories, not only in Japan but around the world," would make people complacent about nuclear war.[7]

Holding the text of his speech with steady hands, Shigemi Fukahori got right to the point. "This year marks seventy-five years since the bombing, and the *hibakusha* are passing away one after another." He told his story, what he saw on August 9, and the terror he experienced. "I don't want anyone ever again to feel that kind of fear," he said. To prevent nuclear war means to preserve memories, and he exhorted his grandchildren's generation never to forget. "I am hoping that as many people as possible will bond with each other, particularly young people. I would like to ask them to firmly take the baton for peace from us, and keep running for the future."[8]

The Pledge for Peace was a secular proceeding. Nine months earlier, in

November 2019, Nagasaki hosted a religious event: the visit of Pope Francis. It was an occasion of singular importance for Urakami Catholics, and for Shigemi Fukahori in particular.

≈

"The Pope visited the Wounded Mary statue," Shigemi Fukahori said. "I led him there."

On November 24, 2019, Pope Francis spoke at the Atomic Bomb Hypocenter Park, a memorial field situated just south of the Nagasaki Peace Park, where the Pledge for Peace is delivered. As the pontiff entered the Hypocenter Park grounds, Fukahori, along with another survivor, gave Pope Francis a wreath of flowers. The pope took it and smiled. Fukahori held on to the wreath and, breaking ranks with protocol, continued to walk with Francis, clinging to the flowers and the opportunity to stroll with the bishop of Rome. He reluctantly let go when Japanese archbishop Mitsuaki Takami and a white-gloved official gently grabbed his arms and pulled him back. Fukahori then paused, looked around, clasped his hands, and grinned, having grabbed the experience of a lifetime.[9]

"Dear Brothers and Sisters," Pope Francis began, "This place makes us deeply aware of the pain and horror we human beings are capable of inflicting upon one another." Francis then spoke of the Bombed Mary statue, and of a cross that had also survived the nuclear attack. "The damaged cross and statue of Our Lady remind us once more of the unspeakable horror suffered in the flesh by the victims of the bombing and their families."[10]

Later that day, the pope celebrated Mass before thousands of worshippers at Nagasaki's baseball stadium.[11] *Hibaku no Maria* was there as well, prominently displayed on the stage within a small wooden shrine. At the beginning of the Mass, Francis approached the statue, gazed at its face, reverentially swung a thurible (a metal container of incense suspended from chains), and bowed.

Afterward, the wooden bust of Mary was returned to its home in the special chamber inside the Urakami Cathedral. "I go to that room where *Mary-sama* resides every day," Shigemi Fukahori said, using the Japanese honorific form of naming Mary. He said alongside Mary there is a list with the names of known Nagasaki A-bomb victims. "Whole families perished," he said, "but the bombing also wiped out families whose names we still don't know. So I go there every day to pray before *Mary-sama* for those people. And I never forget that *Mary-sama* sacrificed herself so that those who died in Nagasaki can be led to God in heaven."

Part 3

FIREBOMBED CITIES

Six months before the destruction of Nagasaki, American planes firebombed the Japanese port city of Kobe for the first time.[1] The raids—part of a nationwide air assault on Japan—would continue through the end of the war, killing more than seven thousand Kobe residents and leaving more than four hundred thousand locals homeless.[2] My wife's mother, Yoko, was in Kobe when the raids began. She was fourteen years old and lived there with her mother, Koh, a kimono tailor.

Yoko once told me that an American B-29 flew so low to the ground that she could see the pilot's face. The plane seemed to target her, she claimed. Yoko said she ran for her life and slipped away. She and Koh then fled to the countryside, where they lived out the duration of the war.

Yoko's memory runs contrary to the historical record: American bombers flew at high altitudes, with the pilots well out of sight.[3] But Yoko was young back then, and her recollections reshaped and personalized the trauma, which made them more impactful.

10

Tokyo

The human remains discovered in Tokyo on June 11, 1967, had not received a proper burial. There were no cemeteries or religious rites, no graves or headstones, no urns for ashes. There was instead an old, subterranean sarcophagus: a bomb shelter, dating back to World War II, that a work crew had found entirely by chance nearly fifty feet beneath the surface of a railroad construction site.

"Inside it were six human skeletons huddled close together," remembered Katsumoto Saotome, a Tokyo native. "Two of them were children and the other four adults. Their gender could not be determined."[1]

Saotome first learned of the underground shelter on June 13, two days after it had been unearthed, from a local newspaper report. He later recounted what he had read.

"The positions of the bones suggested they had been cowering in terror, and one of the adult skeletons was cradling two Buddhist memorial tablets in its arms. There were signs that the shelter had been engulfed in flames. Burn marks were visible on one set of bones, and a rusted steel helmet and decayed water bucket lay close by."

The grim discovery shook Katsumoto Saotome, who wanted to "pray for the souls of the victims." "There could be no salvation for the souls of the dead without an investigation of the facts," he said.[2]

Saotome spent the next fifty-plus years educating a largely forgetful world about the singular event that destroyed the shelter, entombed its occupants, and burned to the ground vast swaths of Tokyo.

On the night of March 9–10, 1945, more than three hundred American B-29 Superfortresses descended on Tokyo from South Pacific waters, releasing, over the course of three hours, a storm of wind and fire that razed sixteen square miles of the city. The weapons of choice were incendiary bombs filled with white phosphorus and a jellied gasoline, recently developed by Harvard scientists, called napalm.[3] Tokyo was "scorched, boiled, and baked to death," Air Force general Curtis LeMay, the author of the assault, said later.[4] The conflagration blackened the ground and illuminated the sky. The flames produced so much light that American pilots could "almost read a paper in the cockpit."[5] By the end of the raid, between eighty and one hundred thousand people were dead, and the stench of death touched the B-29s overhead. The "Great Tokyo Air Raid," as it has been called, destroyed one quarter of the city and rendered more than a million homeless.[6] Among them, a twelve-year-old boy, Katsumoto Saotome.

"I remember it was a very windy day," Saotome told me. "The fire invited the wind, and the wind invited the fires. There were flames everywhere. Everything was completely red, from north to south to west to east. There was nothing to do but run away."[7]

I met Saotome on a spring day in Tokyo sixty-three years later. The venue, his choice, was the retro lounge of the Hilltop Hotel, an art deco building that housed the US Women's Army Corps in the immediate postwar years. The facility, spared by American air raids, was situated in the city's Ochanomizu district, a hip tapestry of music shops, guitar stores, and university hangouts. The hotel had long been a magnet for famous Japanese authors seeking a comfortable, secluded room to hunker down and write.[8] Saotome, the author of novels and numerous journalistic works, felt comfortable there. I wondered whether he had selected the Hilltop for its literary appeal or for the irony of a Tokyo bombing survivor holding sway over tea with an American writer in a building once requisitioned by US occupation forces.

The March 1945 American firebombing of Tokyo was part of a nine-month-long blitz of US incendiary attacks on the Japanese mainland.

General LeMay had believed that air power was the only way to force Japan to surrender.[9] Its "paper cities" packed with wooden structures were highly combustible, and therefore especially vulnerable. In the days after the Tokyo assault, B-29s also targeted Osaka, Nagoya, and Kobe (Japan's second-, third-, and fifth-largest cities behind Tokyo), and Tokyo was severely hit again in the months leading up to Japan's capitulation in August.[10]

"My house was completely destroyed in the bombings," Saotome recalled. "We had no place to stay. For a long time I wandered around like a street dog picking up anything I could use. I was hungry every day. I believed I was going to die."

In all, the firebombings destroyed or partially damaged more than sixty Japanese cities, leaving a quarter of Japan's urban population homeless and causing approximately 806,000 civilian casualties, including an estimated 300,000 deaths.[11]

Saotome spoke of these things calmly, belying the grim nature of the story he told. He sat with one leg crossed over the other, hands gently folded on a knee. Yet he had seen much, and his drawn face and sunken cheeks revealed the cost.

"I'm a very old man," he said. He was seventy-six.

What bothered Katsumoto Saotome this day about the incendiary air campaign, and the firebombing of Tokyo in particular, was a troublesome case of memory loss, both in Japan and abroad. The Tokyo death toll equaled or exceeded that of Hiroshima and of Nagasaki. But the March 1945 attack on the Japanese capital, one of the deadliest air raids in history, is less well remembered. Hiroshima and Nagasaki have their atomic bomb museums and memorial peace parks. The Japanese government compensated A-bomb survivors for their suffering. But in Tokyo, there is not a single memorial exclusively dedicated to firebombing victims. And the government left those victims empty handed.

"Tokyo did not receive as much attention as Hiroshima or Nagasaki because it was attacked with conventional weapons," Saotome said. "It makes a huge difference. The world's attention is on nuclear weapons. And right after the war we were ruled by the United States. The Japanese government kept a low profile, and civilians—the Tokyo bombing victims—were overlooked and left behind. There was no acknowledgment of their suffering. I think this makes their suffering more severe as time passes."

How to compensate the pain and suffering of Japan's war casualties had always been tricky. The government had long embraced the concept of helping out a limited class of victims: legislation funding medical care for some *hibakusha*, for instance, dated back to 1957.[12] But in a painstakingly intricate and slow postwar dance between morality and budgetary constraints, the government continued to struggle to define and contain the list of other compensation-eligible recipients.

"Military families who lost loved ones were compensated after the war," Saotome told me. "Civilians, who died in higher numbers, were not. The government did not give them a penny. I would say there is no difference between these lives. Loss feels the same, whether it is military or civilian."

The families of dead soldiers received military pensions. Ordinary civilians, lacking "an employment relationship" with the government, did not. Firebombing victims fell into that category. *Hibakusha*, the A-bomb survivors, received some health and welfare benefits. But determining compensation eligibility for *hibakusha* was anything but straightforward. Is a survivor who lived beyond a certain distance from ground zero entitled to benefits? What about those exposed to "black rain," the post-blast precipitation laden with radioactive debris? Is a survivor who moved abroad benefit eligible? What about the potential hereditary impact of radiation on the children of A-bomb survivors? These and other permutations confounded a cost-conscious government, riled various survivor groups, and produced generations of survivor lawsuits that never seemed to end because of determined plaintiffs, a slow-moving court system, multiple appeals, and fact patterns that defied easy answers.[13]

Saotome was a plaintiffs' witness in one of those lawsuits, which ultimately failed.

In December 2020, more than a decade after our Hilltop Hotel interview, I contacted Saotome via email—the coronavirus pandemic upended a Japan reporting trip and in-person interview I had planned—and asked him to look back on his work on behalf of the Tokyo air raid victims.

He was eighty-seven years old at the time, and in weakened health. But the passage of time seemed to have hardened his resolve and doubled the frustration of not having accomplished more.

"Air raid victims are still fighting for postwar compensation at this moment," he said. "It was the Japanese government that started the war. It should take responsibility, compensate, and atone for the many victims involved. If the lives of the people continue to be neglected, it will not be possible to console the souls of those who died."

By tradition in Japan, the living must tend to the souls of the dead. Consoling fallen spirits is a moral imperative. Saotome's first instinct back in 1967, when he read about that underground bunker, was to pray for the spirits of the victims found within. Failure to do so, it is thought, would expose dead souls to an unsettled afterlife as wandering spirits, or souls gone astray.[14]

I asked Saotome whether this tenet of Japanese faith, a determination to console the souls of firebombing victims, was what kept him going all these years.

"It was not consolation," he said. "It was anger."

After the war, he said, General LeMay, commander of the Tokyo air raids, was tasked with training Japan's new Air Self-Defense Force. In 1964, the Japanese government awarded LeMay one of its highest honors, the Grand Cordon of the Order of the Rising Sun, for his "great contribution" to building Japan's national defense capabilities.[15] The gesture did not sit right with Saotome then, and his hard feelings festered for more than fifty years.

"I don't understand why the Japanese government would make such a decision," he told me. "As a person who was born in Japan and experienced the air raids, I will not give up pursuing accountability for this war, nor will I remain silent about its victims. As long as I am alive, I will continue to write about them, talk about them, and tell their stories, so that the people who were burned to death will not be dismissed as mere numbers, and so that we will not forget that they also had personalities and lives."

Katsumoto Saotome told me he had written more than one hundred books and articles about air raids, war, and civilian deaths.[16] He oversaw the collection of more than a thousand personal histories from Tokyo bombing survivors. In 2002, he founded a museum, the Center of the Tokyo Raids and War Damage, the only facility in the Japanese capital solely dedicated to the firebombings.[17] A memory gap regarding the Great Tokyo Air Raid may persist, but Katsumoto Saotome did his best to reduce it.

He passed away in May 2022. He was ninety. The cause of death was organ failure.[18]

Yoko Ono, like Saotome, was a twelve-year-old child living in Tokyo on the night of March 9–10, 1945. And like Saotome, she carried into adulthood consequential memories of what happened then and in subsequent days and weeks. Her wartime recollections nurtured what would become a well-branded commitment to peace activism. They also incited bursts of artistic creativity.

"I remember the severe bombing in Tokyo," she recalled afterward, "hiding in an air raid shelter listening to the sound of the bombs coming closer and then going away, and feeling that my mother and I lived another day. I remember being evacuated to the country; the food shortage, and starving; going to the next village to find rice for my brother and sister; being stoned by the village kids who hated people from the city."[19]

Yoko Ono came from a family of privilege. Her father was a banker. Her mother had aristocratic roots.[20] The Great Tokyo Air Raid leveled the family tree.

"I remember how I cried at the end of the war, how bombed out Tokyo looked when I returned from the country on the back of a truck."

Decades later, after her husband—musician and Beatles' cofounder John Lennon—had been assassinated, after Ono had become a performance artist in her own right, she was asked to compose music for a play about Hiroshima. "Songs flooded into my head," she said, "and I kept writing and recording. The memory of being a young child in Japan during the second World War came back to me."

In these songs, Ono translated her wartime memories into an idiosyncratic language, a cacophonous mix of words, wails, and grunts that somehow accomplished exactly what she had set out to accomplish: to convey the horror of war, to "purge my anger, pain and fear," and in so doing, to raise up the necessity of peace.

One song is a mournful, hard-edged track called "I'm Dying." The music is heavy metal. The lyrics are sparse, featuring grief-filled cries of "no, no, no, no" and "help me." The effect is a performance testimonial that seems to have risen from battlefield ruins. She called another song "Kurushi." It is a softer, soulful, piano-driven piece. The word *kurushi* "in Japanese means something like 'tormented,' 'pained' and 'suffocating,'" she said.[21]

I met Yoko Ono in Tokyo at the old Hotel Okura, a stately facility near the American Embassy that, in its heyday, numbered Ronald Reagan, Barack Obama, Mikhail Gorbachev, and Princess Diana as overnight guests.[22] Ono had performed the night before with her Plastic Ono Band at the Tokyo International Forum, a large, glass-paneled exhibition space downtown. At the Hotel Okura, she was dressed in her trademark outfit: black pants, low-cut black shirt, black hat, and sunglasses slipped down her nose. She looked tired. An assistant asked if she wanted something to drink. "Yes," she said, "strong green tea, please."

I had attended the concert, which opened with Ono in soliloquy, presenting an a cappella homage to her husband and to the circumstances of his death. "It happened at the time of my life when I least expected," she sang. "I don't even remember how it happened. But it happened. It happened. I know it happened. And I know there is no return, no way."

I asked her about "Kurushi," which she performed early on in the concert, with her son, Sean Lennon, at the piano. The piece, she said, was certainly rooted in her own wartime experience. But she also pointed to Sadako Sasaki, a young Hiroshima bombing victim who died in 1955, at age twelve, from leukemia due to radiation exposure. In the weeks before her death, from her bed in the Hiroshima Red Cross Hospital, Sadako had folded one thousand tiny paper cranes.[23] That cathartic act of imagination posthumously made Sadako famous, turning her into something of a Japanese Anne Frank: a young, innocent casualty of war who came to symbolize suffering and peace. A statue of Sadako, holding aloft a paper crane, stands prominently in the Hiroshima Peace Memorial Park.[24]

"'Kurushi' has a lot to do with the inspiration I had from Sadako's life," Ono said. "She was suffering and about to die, and everyone was very worried about it. And they all started to make paper cranes. And she did pass away, and maybe they're still making these paper cranes to console her spirit. Any opportunity I have to remind audiences of what happened to her is very good. I was here in Japan at that time, although not in Hiroshima. But it is part of our experience in the sense that it's in our blood. We are connected with blood. We're like the blood family."

Thanks to her marriage to John Lennon, Yoko Ono is one of the most well-known members of Japan's war generation. The world, however, for the most part did not see her as a wartime survivor. She instead was the Japanese woman at John Lennon's side: the Beatles' odd fifth wheel, an interesting, offbeat, rebellious, thoughtful, and devoted-to-her-husband adjunct to the main act.

But at her Tokyo concert, a good deal more was at play. She beguiled a completely packed auditorium, not so much with her artistic skills as with her very presence, her charisma, sincerity, and passion. She talked about the war, in Japanese, before a young, empathetic audience whose parents or grandparents may very well have survived the American incendiary attacks on Tokyo. She recalled the horrors of Hiroshima, and spoke of trauma and of shared sorrow.

At the end of her concert, Yoko Ono and Sean Lennon performed John Lennon's iconic "Give Peace a Chance." "All we are saying is give peace a chance," they sang. "All we are saying is give peace a chance."

"*Minasan*, everyone, once again," Sean implored. The audience joined in. "All we are saying is give peace a chance."

Sean's mother raised her left hand, formed a V-shaped peace sign, and waved it back and forth in time with the music. Most of the audience did the same.

"All we are saying is give peace a chance."

It was a powerful moment. Sean Lennon's singing voice sounded very much like his father's. The hand of John Lennon seemed to have reached down from the sky to touch his family there on that Tokyo stage.

When it had ended, Yoko Ono and her son thanked the audience.

"Arigato gozaimashita," they said. "Ono-san! Ono-san!" someone yelled. Sean put his hand on his mother's back and escorted her off stage left. The septuagenarian widow with roots in World War II had wrapped up another concert, leaving the crowd delighted. It was a splendid event to have grown out of long-ago misfortune.

11

Tokushima

On July 4, 1945, American Independence Day, US B-29s attacked Tokushima, the largest municipality on Shikoku, the smallest of Japan's main islands. Incendiary bombs destroyed 62 percent of the city, leaving more than a thousand dead.[1] The assault was part of the ongoing Allied air offensive targeting major population centers, which hastened Japan's defeat.

Tokushima's postwar economic recovery proceeded methodically. Crews reconstructed buildings and bridges and restored the central train station. Taxis and buses replaced pedal-powered rickshaws. A black market economy gave way to more regulated economic fare. By 1955, nursery school children were playing with Hula-Hoops: it was one indicator that things had settled, that trade in nonessential consumer goods was able to flourish.[2]

At that time, twenty-year-old Tadashi Okamoto was working as an apprentice in a Tokushima kimono shop. He came from a farming family that lived on a mountainside homestead far from the city. He was there during the July bombings, and his family survived unscathed.

Okamoto moved to Tokushima after the war. By 1960, he had opened up his own storefront clothing shop. His company expanded, renovated, and relocated, having tapped into a lucrative niche apparel market unique to the region. By 2010, the business had marked its fiftieth anniversary. It had become a Tokushima institution, a cultural hub filled with wildly colored kimonos, dancing shoes, hats, and other paraphernalia, all earmarked for the one social enterprise that mattered most to the city's residents: a four-hundred-year-old folk dance that gave life to Tokushima's postwar revival.

The dance is called Awa Odori: *Awa*, the feudal administrative name for Tokushima, and *Odori* meaning dance.[3] It is the Tokushima embodiment of a traditional art form performed by communities all over Japan during *obon*, the summertime celebration honoring ancestral spirits.

Awa Odori in Tokushima is a well-organized public enterprise. Dancers in groups of up to fifty parade, in sync, up and down city streets accompanied by a mesmerizing symphony of drums, flutes, and gongs. Men wear lightweight cotton coats over shorts or pants. Women wear summer kimonos and half-moon-shaped straw hats pulled down to partially cover the eyes, creating a rakish, mysterious look. Everyone chants *Erai yatcha erai yatcha yoi-yoi-yoi!*, roughly meaning "Some fools dance while other fools watch." Once unleashed, an Awa Odori performance resembles a flash mob.

"The men's dance involves bending over a bit with legs slightly bowed, raising the hands a little above the forehead, and lightly waving the wrists up and down," a Japanese children's website explains. "The women turn the palms inward and gracefully move the wrists. There's a saying that if you raise your hands and move your legs forward you're doing the Awa Odori."[4]

Awa Odori is more than a quaint bit of folklore. It was an important spiritual and economic force behind Tokushima's recovery after the war. Suppressed by necessity during the war years, Awa Odori returned in 1946.

"It gave those people hope," said Hisako Nakamura, a professor of dance studies at Tokushima University.[5] "Being able to dance freely and to be creative is nothing extraordinary to us now. But it was back then." Seijuro Shinomaya, an Awa Odori master and former soldier who survived the chaos of wartime Manchuria, even called it the dance of peace.[6]

Economically, the dance became a tourist magnet. Each year Awa Odori performances in Tokushima drew increasingly larger numbers of curious spectators from other regions of Japan. Tourists populated inns and poured money into the local economy. "People gathered," Nakamura said. "Things were sold. The shopping district revitalized. They expanded the performance hall. It enriched the area." By the twenty-first century, Tokushima's annual Awa Odori festival had become one of the largest dance events in Japan, drawing one hundred thousand dancers and more than a million visitors each August.[7]

"It's fun!" Tadashi Okamoto exclaimed.

Okamoto was something of a Tokushima icon. His age (midseventies when I visited his shop) commanded respect. So did his fifty years of experience as an Awa Odori dancer. But the key to Okamoto's stature was his role as Tokushima's main supplier of Awa Odori merchandise to the city's large and utterly devoted community of dancers. Emi Tanaka, a Tokushima businesswoman, was one such dance enthusiast. "Awa Odori is my reason to exist," she told me. "My whole identity is wrapped up in it. I found my purpose in life through the dance."[8] And she found her dance attire at Okamoto's place.

Okamoto called his store Okachu, an abbreviated rendering of his last and first names. The shop was shiny, with bright lighting and no whiff of disarray. Neatly packed cubby shelves lined the walls. Shoppers bustled about, purchasing Awa Odori clothing, shoes, fans, and musical instruments. There were even shock-absorbing insoles on sale (twelve dollars a pair) specially fashioned to fit *geta*, the traditional wooden sandals Awa Odori performers wear.

Okachu was a no-nonsense business enterprise. Okamoto was a meticulous and driven proprietor. He roamed the shop neatly dressed in a suit and tie. His gray hair was carefully slicked back to cover a baldpate. His conversation was direct and singular in purpose: the unadulterated promotion of Awa Odori. Okamoto's worldview, explained on Okachu.com (his store's website) was: "I put as much effort into my work as into my dancing."

I told Okamoto I was interested in the connection between Awa Odori and World War II.

"Hai, hai," he said. "Yes, yes."

He retrieved a small album of old black-and-white photographs and asked me to follow him into a back room, covered with tatamis, the straw mats ubiquitous in Japan. We removed our shoes before entering, and sat on cushions, knees tucked under the legs in the traditional Japanese style.

The album held rare snapshots of Awa Odori performances in the years immediately following Japan's defeat. Okamoto explained that Tokushima strove for some sense of normalcy after the war, and its citizens embraced dance as one of the sure things that gave them pleasure. It was as if peacetime really couldn't arrive until Awa Odori reappeared.

The photos, dating back to 1946, were mostly of children, six or eight or ten years old, dressed in their Awa Odori best, posing in groups or caught in full dance motion. I wondered whether the focus on children meant that the bulk of prewar adult dancers had lost their lives, or perhaps their willingness to dance. Okamoto wasn't sure. But the children were survivors, he said, and as such, had been tasked with preserving the dance form.

Okamoto pointed to one little girl in a photo. He said she was three years old at the time. "She's nearing her seventies now," he said, "and still dancing."

≈

Okamoto didn't take up Awa Odori until 1959, when, at his brother's urging, he joined a dance group, or *ren*. On occasion, the *ren* traveled internationally to promote Awa Odori and to foster Tokushima tourism. One of those trips was to Europe, where Okamoto, who had become group leader, found himself stepping around a repugnant World War II memory that, if handled improperly, could have tarnished Japan's reputation.

At issue was the *manji*, a religious symbol that had been part of Japanese Buddhism for more than a thousand years.[9] In Tokushima and elsewhere in Japan, the *manji* is benign, or even uplifting. It means "good fortune" and often appears on temples or religious materials. On maps it has designated the location of Buddhist shrines. It has even morphed into the twenty-first-century lexicon of teenage schoolgirls, for whom *manji* symbolizes strength, the upper class, or, in emoji form, "yay."[10] To Western eyes, however, the *manji* projects something nefarious: it resembles an inverted swastika, conjuring up memories of Hitler's Third Reich.

In 2006, Okamoto brought his *ren* to Germany. The group, called

Hachisuka after an ancient Tokushima clan, visited six cities in connection with that year's World Cup soccer finals. The women in the group normally wore brightly patterned performance kimonos featuring red and white decorative *manji*.[11] Okamoto recognized that the emblem—long ago a Hachisuka lord's family crest—might provoke unwelcome recollections of the Axis alliance and all that it stood for, even six decades postwar. In advance of the trip, Okamoto tactfully ordered his dancers to shelve the costume. "The Buddhist swastika has a longer history than the Nazi swastika," Okamoto told a Japanese reporter. "But we should give due consideration, because we perform a happy dance."[12]

Ten years later, in 2016, Okamoto's *ren* traveled to Taiwan, where Nazis were irrelevant and Awa Odori shone unabashedly. The *ren* women put on their traditional *manji* kimono and danced all smiles and worry free.[13] That same year, Japan stopped putting *manji* on maps for foreign tourists, a nod to the sensibilities of travelers to Tokyo for two top-tier international sporting events: the 2019 Rugby World Cup and the 2020 Olympics.[14]

≈

The Tokushima Awa Odori festival hall is a short walk from Okachu, Tadashi Okamoto's store. The facility, known as the Awa Odori Kaikan, is a city landmark, the artistic and educational hub for everything about the dance form. The building's design accentuates its importance. It is an eye-catching mix of geometry and architecture, an inverted trapezoid with a glass facade that stands tall, like an exclamation point. Its collection showcases costumes, props, instruments, and history. One exhibit features an Awa Odori dancing robot manufactured by a consortium of the town's engineers.

A 250-seat auditorium is the museum's focal point. In the evenings, Tokushima's *ren* appear onstage. The city has more than thirty dance associations, so they rotate performances, one each night. When I visited, a group named Uzuki-ren was on deck.[15] One man, Kazuyuki Oshima, told me that as much as he enjoys the dancing, it is the audience that really energizes the *ren* and feeds the performance frenzy. "No audience, no Awa Odori," he said.

More than one hundred spectators sat in the auditorium that evening. Most were senior citizens, some looking old enough to belong to Japan's war generation. It was summertime, and each ticket holder was given a fan. Dozens of men and women whipped them back and forth like butterfly wings.

At 8:00 p.m., the musicians appeared. *Boom! Boom! Boom!* The drummers went first. Then other instruments joined in, layer by layer: the wooden flutes, the bells, and the shamisen, a traditional three-stringed lute. The dancers followed, Oshima among them, happily grinning and fully regaled: the women in peach-colored kimonos and half-lunar straw hats, the men in black and white headbands, shirts, and shorts. They moved around the stage with care, pulsating as one to the music: arms, legs, fingers, wrists, knees, and feet bobbing up and down, up and down.

The spectators screamed and clapped their approval.

"We will make the audience experience the pleasure of this dance!" the *ren* leader shouted. "There are many young people in the front seats!" he said, pointing to a row of gray-haired seniors. "Where are you all from?"

"Shizuoka! Nagoya! Niigata! Kyoto!"

"How many are seeing Awa Odori for the first time?"

Dozens of arms went up.

Oshima came onstage with a handful of *ren* performers, tasked with showing the audience how to dance. The group's leader broke down the fundamentals of Awa Odori. "Put your hands in the air," he said. "The higher they are, the more beautiful. Stand up and lean forward. Right leg forward first. Then your right hand. Then left foot, left hand, then back."

At the leader's invitation, some two dozen audience members ran onto the stage for a mini-seminar in dance. The music began. "Put your hands up as high as possible," the *ren* leader instructed. "Lean forward. Right foot, right hand, then back. *Ichi, ni, ichi, ni. One, two, one, two!*"

The musicians turned up the volume. Along with those on the stage, spectators in the auditorium rose from their seats and started dancing in the aisles. And on it went, until the music suddenly ended.

"Hooray!" people shouted.

"I can't believe you guys are not from Tokushima!" the leader told the novice dancers. "And maybe you in the audience who didn't dance felt the pleasure of Awa Odori nonetheless!"

An old man shouted, "Yes! I did!"

The stage cleared, and the show continued. *Ren* dancers moved through a handful of Awa Odori pieces at varying tempos, shouting and singing all the while. Oshima took part in a slower dance. His face was more serious, the music somber. Then, without warning, the pace doubled, and movements accelerated. Oshima and his colleagues, apparently enraptured, screamed. Some dancers left the stage to cajole the audience. A throng of spectators then joined the *ren*, swirling on the performance space in a counterclockwise mass, like pilgrims in Mecca circling the House of God.

Afterward, I asked Oshima how he felt. He was dripping with sweat. "It was very tiring," he said, "but tons of fun."

My Japanese interpreter, a twenty-four-year-old woman from Nagasaki, smiled. "All of this dancing and shouting by the audience," she said, "it is so unusual and uncharacteristic for Japanese." Tokushima's postwar renaissance through Awa Odori appeared to have altered a nation's personality, at least when it wore dancing shoes.

12

Fukuoka

In June 1945, thirteen-year-old Nobuko Komiya lived in Fukuoka, a port city on the north coast of Kyushu, the southernmost of Japan's main islands. Centuries before, great typhoons had twice thwarted attempts by invading armadas of Mongol ships to land there. The grateful Japanese called each storm kamikaze, or "divine wind," a term later used for the World War II suicide pilots.[1] On June 19, 1945, the winds over Fukuoka were less imposing. American bombers ripped through the nighttime skies and let fall incendiary ordnance.

"I saw a B-29," Nobuko Komiya told me. "Everybody was running away. The sky was painted red from the flames of firebombs," she said. "We later learned that one thousand people had died that night."[2] Her family survived, but the attack burned down her house, scattered her next of kin, and interrupted a small business enterprise that dated back more than three hundred years.[3]

I met Nobuko Komiya entirely by chance. She was the proprietor of Matsuya, a confectionery store situated in Hakata, Fukuoka's historic mercantile district.[4] I had serendipitously walked into her store one afternoon, only to learn that my visit coincided with the sixty-fifth anniversary of the day American B-29s had upended the family business.

"I had no idea," I told her, when she informed me what had happened there on June 19, 1945.

"I thought you knew, and that's why you came here," she said.

Komiya represented the thirteenth generation of her family to preside over the sweetshop. Her ancestors, she said, had been taught by Portuguese merchants how to craft European treats. In 1673, Matsue Riemon, first in her long line of great-grandfathers, mastered a confection the Portuguese call *fios de ovos* (egg threads), a sweet concoction made of egg yolks and sugar that resembles yellow angel-hair pasta. He called the dish *keiran somen*, or sweet chicken egg noodles. It was and is, Nobuko Komiya said, what Hakata ought to be known for. And it accounted for 60 percent of her business.

Komiya said Matsue Riemon supplied *keiran somen* to the local ruling samurai family, the Kuroda clan. Pleased with the arrangement, the clan allowed Riemon and his successors to display the official Kuroda *mon*, or coat of arms. The *mon* was still on display in Nobuko Komiya's shop when I visited, hanging prominently on the wall above the cash register.

Nobuko Komiya's ancestors were so good at what they did, and so proud of their confectionary skills, that each shop director, over the generations, bore the same honorific name: Matsue Riemon. The original was Matsue Riemon I, then Matsue Riemon II, and so on down the line, thirteen generations. The title belonged to Nobuko Komiya's brother at the time of my visit. Matsuya, the shop name, means "Matsue's store."

After the American bombers came and went, Nobuko Komiya said— after their shop was destroyed, after the war ended, and after enough eggs and sugar could be found to make yet again the Portuguese sweet treat— her father peddled *keiran somen* to anyone who could afford to buy it. Many people purchased the confection, she said, as a way to put the war behind them. Slowly, and on his own, she said, her father rebuilt the business, one sweet noodle at a time. "On his own," she emphasized.

Now, Matsuya makes its products by hand. No machines allowed, she stressed. The confections, *keiran somen* and others, are displayed behind glass cases, as if in a museum, many split in half to reveal their sweet stuffings. Pieces are smartly wrapped and neatly labeled by name and price. *Keiran somen* occupies the largest single sales space, right beneath the *mon*.

Komiya was seventy-eight years old when we spoke. She was talkative, friendly, and generous with her time. She offered up tastes of various sweets, including *keiran somen*, which she served with green tea. "It goes well with coffee, too," she said, "because the coffee bean's special mix of aroma and bitterness helps dampen the sweetness of the noodle."

There was no hostility in Nobuko Komiya at the unexpected presence of an American, whose country, within her lifetime, had turned her family's life upside down.

"Were you ever angry at the United States?" I asked.

"Back then, yes, I was," she said. "But now it is peaceful in Japan, and those feelings left with the passage of time."

Nobuko Komiya told me that Matsuya's original shop, the one destroyed in 1945, had been situated three blocks away, at the end of a street that B-29s had obliterated. I walked over to see the spot. A small, marble monument stood there, barely two feet high, commemorating Matsuya's World War II ordeal.

Part 4

HOLOCAUSTS

Sometime after my mother-in-law, Yoko, told me she had witnessed the fire-bombing of Kobe, my wife suggested I watch an animated film called *Grave of the Fireflies*. The movie came out in 1988 and was produced by Studio Ghibli, a Tokyo production house (roughly analogous to America's Walt Disney Studios) responsible for such well-known features as *My Neighbor Totoro* and *Spirited Away*.[1] Those films are lighthearted and charming. *Fireflies* has been called "the saddest movie ever made."[2]

It tells the wrenching story of a teenage boy and his young sister who, like Yoko and her mother, Koh, got caught up in the maelstrom of the Kobe raids. The *Firefly* children lost everything, forced by unforgiving circumstance to beg and steal to get by. Starvation, poverty, homelessness, and death eventually won out.

Based on a semi-autobiographical story by writer Akiyuki Nosaka, the film viscerally conveys, through the eyes of innocents, the harrowing consequences of armed conflict.[3] It is a haunting work of art, a tender but heartbreaking eulogy to the lost promise of youth due to war.

Seita and Setsuko, the fictional children of *Grave of the Fireflies*, call to mind another young war victim who, in real life, also died too young. Her name was Anne Frank. She was trapped by a tragedy of entirely different circumstances and proportions. Like Seita and Setsuko, however, she came to symbolize for her people the sorrows of war. And as I discovered, Anne Frank is well known in Japan, where her presence prompts questions about the comparability of Jewish and Japanese suffering.

13

Anne Frank in Japan

On a tree-laden mountain overlooking Hiroshima, on the grounds of an ancient Buddhist temple that sits amid maples and bamboo, two urns of ashes from Auschwitz lie buried. The remains remarkably made their way to Japan in two separate journeys, one in 1963 and one in 1972, each the result of outreach between Japanese peace activists and Polish emissaries, who found common purpose in remembering the not-long-past anguish of World War II.[1]

The Auschwitz urns rest beneath a weathered, rectangular stone marker, just down the path from the temple's bell and across the way from a Buddhist statue that says *kyuusei*, "salvation." Etched into the stone marker's face in both Japanese and awkwardly translated English are these words: "Here lie the souls of the sacrificed at Auschwitz Poland caused by the Nazism policy against the Jewish people during the World War II."

The temple, called Mitaki-dera, is more than twelve hundred years old. It is situated some two miles northwest of the Hiroshima hypocenter. A sign on temple grounds informs visitors that Mitaki "withstood the atomic bombing on August 6, 1945." The blast set the forest surrounding the temple on fire. A Hiroshima newspaper reported: "The waterfalls there, a symbol of the mountain, turned black from smoke and soot."[2]

The temple was used as a makeshift aid station in the days and weeks following the bombing. A mountainside cemetery near the temple now holds some three hundred graves of Hiroshima victims.[3] They lie not far from the Auschwitz urns, whose stone marker condemns what it calls the "avarice, rage and stupidity" that put all those souls underground, and pleads: "Never again."[4]

≋

I met Erika Kobayashi one summer afternoon in Tokyo's upscale Ginza district. She is a manga artist and writer, many years my junior, and decidedly offbeat. We had little apparent in common. But our fathers had served in World War II, mine for the US Army, and hers in a military aircraft plant in north-central Japan. Through them, we had each found links to the conflict that had shaped the lives of their generation. So seventy years after the war's end, Erika and I sat in the Shiseido Parlour Salon de Café, sipping tea, eating cakes, and, improbably, talking about the Jewish Holocaust.[5]

My interest in these issues was more direct than hers: I was Jewish; she was not. My dad had helped liberate a Nazi concentration camp. Hers was a sixteen-year-old high school student mobilized as a wartime laborer. But my father had left me a handful of photographs from Buchenwald. And hers had left her his wartime journal.

As a teenager, Erika had read Anne Frank's diary, the iconic account of a young Jewish girl trapped in Nazi-occupied Amsterdam from 1942 to 1944. Erika had found the book on her father's bookshelf. She studied it, and then read her father's journal. She was bothered by the moral disparity between her dad's wartime service and the victimization of innocent European Jews: Japan, she said, was "totally allied with the Nazis, and that was totally the opposite position from Anne Frank."

Troubled by the idea that "my father could have killed Anne Frank," Erika traveled to Europe, where she retraced Anne's life from the Frank family's hideout in an Amsterdam secret annex to the Bergen-Belsen concentration camp, where Anne died. Erika Kobayashi's account of the journey, which she called *Your Dear Kitty*, was later published in Japan.[6]

At our afternoon tea in the Ginza café, Erika told me a story that illustrates the surprising pull Anne Frank's diary had, and continues to have, on Japan.

In 2007, Erika was based in New York on a research fellowship. She was at a ramen restaurant in Midtown Manhattan when, as she put it, "Anne Frank came out of nowhere." The encounter, which transpired over bowls of Nagasaki noodles, began when an elderly man seated nearby struck up a conversation.

His name was Joel. He was seventy-three. His hair was white, his bearing large, and his demeanor introspective. He took a liking to Erika and, disarmed by the moment, revealed something he had never told anyone before.

"He was an American soldier in the Korean War," Erika recalled, "and he stayed in Japan sometimes because his army base was there. At that time he was really young, and he told me he played around with lots of women. Every night he slept with different Japanese girls."

It was 1953. The girls were prostitutes, and they wanted out. Life in Japan was hard as the country continued to tackle the arduous ongoing challenges of postwar recovery.

Joel told her that every time he slept with the girls they would cry in the middle of the night. "They would ask him 'why won't you become my boyfriend, why won't you bring me back to America?'" One particular woman, a tiny, plain-looking girl with glasses whom he indelicately described as "the ugliest of all," cried in the middle of the night, too. But Joel was fond of her.

"He treated her really carefully and kindly, but he didn't understand why she was crying," Erika said. "And he suddenly realized that in the bed next to him she was reading Anne Frank's diary, and that's why she was crying. That's the story he told. It was so shocking for me."

Joel's companion didn't explain why the diary had so deeply touched her. Erika wondered whether she had felt trapped by life's circumstances much as the Holocaust had trapped Anne Frank. Or maybe it was the familiar emotional pull of a young girl coming of age.

"It's an example of how popular the diary was and also how moving the diary is to every woman in any situation," Erika said.

Anne Frank's *The Diary of a Young Girl* was translated and published in Japan in 1952. Within a year it had become a bestseller. It is still widely read there, with total sales exceeding 5.9 million copies. Anne Frank's story has been told in Japan on other platforms, too—in manga and film, on television, and onstage in both dramatic and musical forms. The diary has also inspired a steady flow of Japanese tourists to Amsterdam, where some thirty thousand visit the Anne Frank House each year.[7]

The popularity of Anne Frank in Japan has little to do with interest in Judaism, let alone the Holocaust. It is Anne's personal story that draws most readers in, particularly young female readers. The diary's rich description of teenage emotions is a story that thirteen-, fourteen-, and fifteen-year-olds in Tokyo, Osaka, and Hiroshima relate to despite the wholly dissimilar circumstances of their lives.

"More than being Anne Frank the Holocaust victim, she's Anne Frank the teenager here," said Makiko Takemoto, a Japanese scholar who specializes in modern Germany history.[8] "The fact that Anne was killed as a result of the Holocaust is rather forgotten."

"Anne Frank is not even Anne Frank for most people," said Ran Zwigenberg, an Asian studies specialist at Penn State who has written about Japanese perceptions of the Holocaust.[9] "She's just 'Anne,' a figure of femininity and an early teenager, and everybody learns about her very private non-Holocaust-related life."

Zwigenberg told me that the diary was one of the first books in Japan to talk openly about menstruation. "And drawing on this image, a Japanese feminine hygiene company actually made a tampon called Anne's Day. Anne's Day became a euphemism for a woman's period."

I met with Zwigenberg at Hiroshima City University's Peace Institute, where he was a visiting scholar and where Takemoto was based. It was July 2015, just a few weeks before Japan would mark the seventieth anniversaries of the Hiroshima and Nagasaki atomic bombings and its surrender in World War II. These were hugely important events in Japan, where wartime misdeeds, suffering, guilt, and blame continued to affect government policy. For months, a planned anniversary statement by Prime Minister Shinzo Abe had preoccupied the Japanese media. At issue was whether and how Abe would ask forgiveness for his country's wartime aggression.[10]

Zwigenberg, an Israeli who speaks Japanese fluently, said there is "a culture of apology" in Japan, where expressions of remorse have real significance.[11]

Japan's relations with its Asian neighbors, particularly China and South Korea, would warm or chill on the strength of Abe's syntax. Would he say "deep remorse" and "heartfelt apology"? Would he acknowledge Japan's wartime "aggression" and "colonial rule"?

As it turned out, Abe used all those words, but he also suggested that after seventy years, enough was enough.

"We must not let our children, grandchildren, and even further generations to come, who have nothing to do with that war, be predestined to apologize," Abe said.[12]

Accepting responsibility for wartime behavior, articulating guilt and remorse—these are essentially ethical questions, and they have long nettled Japan's leaders. They also help explain the appeal of Anne Frank there.

"The Jews as a whole everywhere are usually a foil to talk about something else, especially in a place like Japan, where there are no actual Jews," Zwigenberg told me. "Anne Frank is a foil about how to talk or not talk about Japan as a war-aggression nation. It's about Japan's responsibility, an issue of morality, an issue of memory."

Zwigenberg and others have argued that by embracing Anne Frank, Japan, consciously or not, is soft-pedaling history. "Anne Frank's diary was popular in Japan precisely because it allowed the Japanese to relate to the Holocaust and World War II without tackling the hard historical realities" of the country's own wartime behavior, Zwigenberg has written.[13] "It has . . . helped the Japanese reconceive themselves as victims of the war," according to scholars David G. Goodman and Masanori Miyazawa. In their book *Jews in the Japanese Mind*, they write that "the popularity of Anne Frank's *Diary* in Japan has not necessarily translated into an understanding of the Jewish experience." Rather, it "has contributed to the tendency to generalize the war experience and avoid coming to terms with the specific problems of wartime responsibility and guilt."[14]

The influence of *The Diary of a Young Girl* in shaping Japan's feelings about its wartime behavior surely is limited. But according to Zwigenberg, this much can be said: when Japan reads Anne Frank, it feels better about itself.

Sayaka Hanamura is a Japanese actress who portrayed Anne Frank on-stage. She is a thoughtful woman who by vocation has reflected a lot on Anne Frank and Japan.

"It's complicated," she said, when I asked her about equating Jews and Japan as victims of World War II. "Japan was a victim of the atomic bomb, but Japan was also an ally of Germany. So when it comes to the topic of Jewish victims, it's very difficult."[15]

Hanamura said most Japanese understood Anne Frank's diary as a message of peace. In fact, according to Carol Ann Lee, a biographer of Anne's father, Otto Frank, the diary was originally marketed in Japan as a "protest against the great misfortunes brought by war."[16]

"We do share a common awareness with Jewish people that we don't want to repeat the war," Hanamura said. "But I do feel there are issues of Japan turning a blind eye to the war. So when I perform Anne Frank, I don't want to do so irresponsibly. Although Japan is the only country that experienced the A-bomb, that does not offset what the Japanese army did in World War II."

There are several organizations and even a church in Japan that honor Anne Frank and interpret her diary as a manifesto against the twin evils of war and intolerance. Akio Yoshida was deputy director of the largest of them, the Holocaust Education Center, located in Fukuyama City, not far from Hiroshima.

"Our center's main hope is for the Japanese people to know the story of the Holocaust," Yoshida told me. "We try to tell it to them through Anne Frank, the story of a girl who suffered so much just because she was born a Jew."[17]

The center is ground zero for Holocaust education in Japan. It features an exhibition hall where visitors pass beneath the words "Arbeit macht frei," the notoriously cynical Nazi concentration camp slogan, which declares: "Work will set you free." There is a somber remembrance space with the shoe of a child who perished in the gas chambers. Actual concentration camp barbed wire and crematorium bricks are on display, alongside a replica of Anne Frank's Amsterdam annex room.

Yoshida said the center took care not to equate the Holocaust with the atomic bombing of Hiroshima. "The two are different. Japan and the United States were at war. The atomic bomb was a result of the war. The Jews were not fighting. They were discriminated against because they were Jewish. It's not the same, and Japanese should know about the Holocaust so they can differentiate it from the Hiroshima event."

The center is affiliated with a Christian church that is situated along a winding road on the heights overlooking Osaka. Both center and church were founded by Makoto Otsuka, a clergyman who took an interest in Anne Frank after a chance meeting with Otto Frank during a 1971 visit to Israel. The church, which features a statue of Anne as well as a stained glass Star of David, is called Anne's Rose Church. A rose bush donated by Otto Frank grows in the facility's garden.[18]

I went there in July 2015 with high school student Karen Kanazawa and her mother, Mie. Both are Japanese (the family lived in nearby Kobe), and both had heard about Anne Frank in school. Together they had read *The Diary of a Young Girl* for the first time a few weeks before the visit.

"I researched Anne Frank and found out that she passed away when she was fifteen years and eight months old, which is exactly how old I am right now," Karen said.

Seiji Sakamoto, the church reverend, showed us around the sanctuary, which displays a model of Anne Frank's Amsterdam hideout, a silver baby spoon used by Anne that was contributed by her father, and a glass-enclosed first edition of the 1952 Japanese translation of the diary.

"When I read the diary, I feel like I'm reading the Bible," Sakamoto said.

After the tour, Karen and Mie sat down with Sakamoto and shared their thoughts about Anne.

For Mie, the diary was about "the growth of a bright teenage girl with a shining heart." She told Sakamoto she was particularly struck by diary passages about Anne's sometimes contentious relationship with her mother. "I wonder if Karen might have the same negative feelings about me," she said.

"No, no never," Karen assured her, "although I was curious about Anne's anger against her mother and her rebelliousness."

Karen said she admired the strength of Anne's personality. "Where did the confidence come from? Anne said she was never jealous of her sister, Margot, even though Margot was treated so well by the adults. If it was me, I would have felt jealous."

I was struck by the absence of questions or comments from Karen and Mie concerning the Holocaust. The psychology of Anne the teenage girl is what fascinated them, her emotions and angst and intelligence and strength of mind. Their perception of the diary is typical of the takeaway gleaned by most young Japanese readers.[19]

That kind of thinking bothered Machiyo Kurokawa, a survivor of the Hiroshima bombing who wrote about Anne Frank. I spoke with Kurokawa a year before her death from leukemia in 2011.[20] She died at eighty-one, the same age Anne Frank would have been had she, like Kurokawa, survived the war.

Machiyo Kurokawa was an impressive woman, stout of stature and of heart. When I first saw her, she was chugging to our meeting place like an old locomotive, a bit bent over, lugging a heavy backpack over her shoulders.

Kurokawa's passion for Anne Frank began in the early fifties when she first read the diary. She visited the Anne Frank House in Amsterdam and attended Anne Frank symposia. She also traveled to Bergen-Belsen, where Anne Frank died, and to Auschwitz. "I've been to Auschwitz many, many times," she said.

Her first visit was in 1981. "I was on a bus with a group of Japanese tourists, and we were talking about how horrible it was. Suddenly the bus driver stopped, turned around, and said, 'I was there in Auschwitz.' He rolled up his sleeve and showed us the number branded into his skin. We were all shocked. I was shocked. It was one of the biggest shocks of my life."

"I feel the Japanese people need to know about the Holocaust," she continued. "I think the sufferings of the Jewish people cannot be compared to what the Japanese people went through. Yes, we experienced the atomic bomb. But this was one event. The Jews have a long history of suffering."

Fumiko Ishioka, director of a Holocaust education center in Tokyo, was a good friend of Kurokawa's and delivered the eulogy at her funeral.

"Machiyo Kurokawa's work was important for letting people know *why* Anne Frank died," she told me. Kurokawa, she said, rejected sentimental readings of the diary. "She was critical of the way some Japanese almost 'beautified' Anne's death. Machiyo made sure young people understood Anne didn't die 'pretty.'"[21]

Machiyo Kurokawa's books were among three hundred or so Anne Frank–related volumes, including the diary, that were vandalized in Tokyo libraries in early 2014. The incident made international news and raised concerns that the nationalist policies of Prime Minister Abe had fostered prejudice and anti-Semitism. Police arrested a thirty-six-year-old unemployed man who was described as mentally unstable. The Japanese press reported that in a confession, the man said he was motivated by the belief that Anne Frank's diary was a hoax.[22]

The affair embarrassed the Abe government, and in March 2014, during a previously scheduled trip to The Hague, Abe visited the Anne Frank House to express his regrets.[23]

In January 2015, during a trip to Jerusalem, Abe visited Yad Vashem, Israel's memorial to victims of the Holocaust.

"Today I have learned how merciless humans can become when they single out a group of people and make that group the object of discrimination and hatred," Abe said. "In March, last year, I visited the Anne Frank House in Amsterdam. Today I find myself fully determined. *Ha-sho'a le'olam lo od*. The Holocaust, never again."[24]

14

The Holocaust of Hiroshima

Eighty-four-year-old Takato Kageyama, former submariner in the Imperial Japanese Navy, leaned on his wooden cane and stared at the large, six-paneled painting that dominated the wall of an exhibition room in the Hiroshima Prefectural Art Museum. The piece was stark, depicting an orange-red sky of swirling flames and dirty clouds that almost entirely filled the canvas. At the very bottom of the work, dwarfed by the conflagration and etched in black, were the skeletal remains of what once was a city. On the upper right, above a fiery cloud, sat Fudo Myoo, the Buddhist god of fire and wrath, looking down on it all. The painting was called *The Holocaust of Hiroshima*.

Ikuo Hirayama, one of Japan's most famous postwar painters, had created the work. If John Hersey's moving literary description of a devastated Hiroshima is what informed Americans about the city's dead and dying, then in Japan, it was Hirayama's canvas that memorialized the experience for a nation.

Kageyama, who grew up in Hiroshima, gathered his thoughts. Solemnly dressed in a dark gray suit, he had come to the museum to see this work of art and to pay respects to the memories it held. "My parents and two sisters died. All died," he said, stone faced.[1]

"Tell me what you think of the painting," I asked.

"Very sad."

Kageyama drew a breath.

"Your eyes are tearing up," I said softly.

He paused. "Yes, yes, yes, yes, yes. Yes."

The painting had visibly shaken Kageyama. It was not only the content that produced tears, but the unexpected presence of an American visitor alongside him that stirred his emotions.

"I hated America for more than thirty years," he told me. "It was a strong hatred." It took a long time for his anger to dissipate, he explained. "Now, there is only anguish and sorrow."

"How did you get over your anger toward Americans for what happened in Hiroshima?" I asked.

Kageyama explained that he was a baker, and some years ago he had the opportunity to travel to the United States on business. There, he met

FIGURE 11. Hiroshima atomic bomb survivor Takato Kageyama, standing in front of Ikuo Hirayama's painting *The Holocaust of Hiroshima*, November 2007. Photograph taken by author inside the Hiroshima Prefectural Art Museum.

an American sailor, also a baker, who had served on the battleship USS *Missouri* during World War II. The American described how a Japanese kamikaze had crashed into the ship during the Battle of Okinawa in 1945. Only then, Kageyama said, did he see the other side of the story. And then his anger began to wane.

Like Kageyama, the artist Hirayama was in Hiroshima when the A-bomb fell, a fifteen-year-old volunteer working at an army arsenal.

"On that day I saw a B-29 flying over my head," Hirayama told me.[2] "I went to a small house where my friends were and told them that something unusual was happening. And then it exploded. There was a strong flash right in front of me. I covered my ears. And there was a strong wind, and I squatted down and the wind went right over my head. And then I tried to escape through waterfalls of fire. Just fire everywhere. The sound of fire was extreme."

Hirayama grew ill from radiation sickness. His white blood cell count plummeted. He abandoned Hiroshima for Tokyo, where he recovered his health and studied art. He could not bring himself to return to Hiroshima for more than twenty years. "I did not go back there because so many people died," he said. "My friends died. And now I'm the only survivor among them who experienced the atomic bombing. I felt guilty and helpless."

By the time Hirayama finally visited the city in the 1960s, he had become well known as a painter of the great Silk Road, the ancient trade route that brought Buddhism to Japan. Buddhism had become Hirayama's artistic muse. He saw the religion as a spiritual salve for suffering, a well-intentioned and powerful set of beliefs to connect cultures and inspire humanity as the world tried to rebuild after World War II. "I picked Buddhism because it expresses the wish for peace, and also offers peace for the dead," he said.

Once back in Hiroshima, Hirayama went to Hiroshima Peace Memorial Park, where the hiss and flicker of a flame honoring the dead captured his attention. "I saw the color of the fire, which was orange, and it reminded me of the day of the bombing," he said. "I could not get rid of that color behind my eyelids."

The memorial flame stirred Hirayama's imagination. He immediately began sketching out ideas for what, in 1979, would become *The Holocaust of Hiroshima*.

≈

In autumn 2007, two years before his death in December 2009, Ikuo Hirayama welcomed me to his studio and home in Kamakura, about an hour south of Tokyo by train. We spoke in the residence tea room, an empty space covered with tatami mats overlooking a large patch of Tsubaki trees and bamboo. A burbling creek cut through the grove. "All kinds of animals come down here from the mountains to play around," Hirayama said. "Racoons, ferrets, squirrels, cats, pigeons. They all coexist here. I think they lived here before me."

He was proud of the tea room's unpretentiousness. "We in Japan keep it simple," he said. "Simplicity is an essential element of my art. Same for haiku in Japanese literature. Eliminating excess enables you to concentrate on work."

Hirayama specialized in an ancient painting technique called *nihonga*, in which colors are blended from ground-up mineral pigments and then attached to the canvas with glue.[3] His studio was a brightly lit space lined with hundreds of glass jars holding pigments of different colors, and tables filled with dozens of neatly stacked paintbrushes and palettes.

Several Silk Road canvases of desert caravans lay propped against a wall, still works in progress. Hirayama told me he had traveled the historic trade path, which ran from Asia to Europe, more than one hundred times, sketching pictures in China, Korea, Uzbekistan, Afghanistan, India, Syria, and elsewhere. "I stopped at every oasis," he joked.

In addition to his artwork, Hirayama devoted much time to collecting and preserving ancient Silk Road artifacts. His efforts earned him praise from UNESCO, which in 1989 named him a goodwill ambassador.[4]

I had met Hirayama a month earlier at a reception in Tokyo's National Museum of Modern Art, which was hosting a commemorative exhibition celebrating the artist's seventy-seventh birthday. It was there that I got a sense of Hirayama's standing in Japan. The elite showed up, including a former prime minister, the Chinese and Uzbek ambassadors, and one of

Japan's most prominent Buddhist priests.[5] Richard Dyck, a well-connected Tokyo-based American businessman, described the event as "extraordinary even by Japanese standards."[6]

The Holocaust of Hiroshima, on display that evening, was an unsettling exhibition outlier, its stark, fiery panels at odds with the many Silk Road landscapes, colored in soft blues and browns, that dominated the museum hall.

At his studio, Hirayama told me the Hiroshima painting was a one-off, his only canvas to address what had happened to him in his youth. He acknowledged that, given the subject matter, the piece had been interpreted darkly, but stressed that was not his intention. He said the painting offers a message of hope.

"You can see on the right of the painting the Buddhist god of fire, Fudo," Hirayama said. "He is there as a phoenix, telling everybody that

FIGURE 12. Artist Ikuo Hirayama in his studio in Kamakura, Japan, October 2007. Photograph by author.

even though Hiroshima was burned it was reconstructed afterward. I believe the arts can overcome hardships. That flowers can blossom from anguish and inhumanity. That art can encourage people to live. That is what I believe. So even though some people who do not use their imagination see sadness in the painting, I never thought about this work with such feelings."

Likewise, Hirayama never proposed the word *holocaust* for the English-language rendition of the painting's title, according to Masakata Kono, curator at the Hirayama Ikuo Museum of Art in Hiroshima Prefecture.[7] Instead, Kono told me, the use of *holocaust* was a linguistic anomaly: a translator (Kono said he did not know who) chose the word, thereby advertently or inadvertently equating the destruction of Hiroshima with the genocide of European Jewry.

If done on purpose, it was a bold move. Ran Zwigenberg, the historian I interviewed about Anne Frank, explained that the Japanese-language title of Hirayama's painting did not contain the word *holocaust* or any Japanese-language equivalent.

"In Japanese, it is called *Hiroshima Shohenzu* (広島生変図), which means a map or a view of Hiroshima's metamorphosis," Zwigenberg explained.[8] He said the written characters Hirayama selected for the title represent life, change, and map. He added that in 1979, when Hirayama completed the painting, the word *holocaust* "was not used in Japan at all." Zwigenberg said the term entered the Japanese lexicon only after 1985, when Claude Lanzmann's monumental, nine-and-a-half-hour Holocaust documentary, *Shoah*, was released with success internationally.[9] "So the question is," Zwigenberg asked, "who gave the painting the English title of *Holocaust*?"

Hirayama Museum curator Masakata Kono tried but could not find the answer. "I asked an editor of the company that published the *Complete Works of Hirayama Ikuo* about the English title," Kono wrote to me. "He said: 'Hirayama never decided to use the word *holocaust*. Someone else (maybe one of the editors) used it.'"

An investigation by the Hiroshima Prefectural Art Museum, the permanent home of Hirayama's painting, did not produce any additional information regarding the decision to use the word *holocaust* in the English-language title.[10]

I never asked Hirayama about this issue, which I became aware of only after the artist had died. At my request, Kono searched Hirayama's writings to see whether the painter had voiced an opinion, one way or the other, on the use of *holocaust* in the *Hiroshima Shohenzu* translation. Hirayama had not. "Hirayama seemed not to be nervous about English titles," Kono said.

The curator said he found only one reference to the Jewish Holocaust in Hirayama's papers, a comment about Auschwitz in the painter's account of a June 1998 UNESCO symposium in Tokyo: Hirayama noted that the Nazi concentration camp and the Hiroshima Atomic Bomb Dome (the iconic building that partially survived the blast) had both been designated UNESCO World Heritage sites, Auschwitz in 1979 and the Hiroshima Dome in 1996. Hirayama said the two sites carried "historical lessons," but were "different in content and quality."[11]

≈

In May 1987, Elie Wiesel—the Jewish writer who had suffered Hitler's concentration camps and was the world's most prominent chronicler of the Holocaust—went to Hiroshima.[12] Seven months earlier he had won the Nobel Peace Prize for having "made it his life's work to bear witness to the genocide committed by the Nazis."[13] Clyde Haberman, then the *New York Times* Tokyo bureau chief, called Wiesel's journey to Hiroshima "an unusual marriage of catastrophes—a survivor of the Auschwitz and Buchenwald death camps coming face to face with the city that witnessed the lethal dawn of the nuclear age."

Wiesel was sensitive to the issue of false equivalence. He warned his Japanese hosts against "cheap comparisons" between Hiroshima and the Jewish Holocaust. "Auschwitz," he said, "was meant to be the condemnation of the last Jew to death. Here, obviously, it wasn't meant to kill the last Japanese." According to Haberman, Wiesel also said Japanese should "remember it was their militarist past that had brought them to ashes at Hiroshima."

With Wiesel in Japan, it was hard to avoid comparing—cheaply or otherwise—Hiroshima with the Holocaust. This was not the nuanced association raised by the Japanese reading of *The Diary of Anne Frank*. The Nobel laureate's presence forced the same-breath utterance of these two twentieth-century tragedies, each with its narrative of horror and heartbreak.

Directly juxtaposing the miseries of Japanese and Jewish suffering is a "moral minefield," according to Zwigenberg, who has thought a lot about the issue.[14] True enough, the memories are "entangled," he said. In each tragedy, innocents died in unprecedented mass killings. That, presumably, was the unknown translator's rationale for calling Hirayama's painting *The Holocaust of Hiroshima*. But the rationale is shaky; the Hiroshima and Holocaust narratives are entirely different. That is something some thoughtful Japanese understood, such as Anne Frank scholar Machiyo Kurokawa and Akio Yoshida of the Holocaust Education Center. But, in Zwigenberg's view, it is a point that needs to be grasped more widely in Japan.

"The atomic bombing of Hiroshima was a deliberate mass killing of the civilian population of a Japanese city, but it was not genocide," Zwigenberg said. "The bombing should be understood in the context of Japan's aggressive role in the Asia-Pacific War and the US campaign of terror bombing of Japanese cities. The Jews, in contrast, were innocent and not participants in World War II." All this "does not mean that the comparison of mass killings is impossible," Zwigenberg said, "just that it requires prudence."

≈

Sometime after I interviewed Ikuo Hirayama, I spoke with Yoko Ono. I told her, as an aside, that I am Jewish, and that my grandfather's sister had died in the Holocaust.

"Oh, God," she replied.

I told her of my interest in Hirayama, and in particular his *The Holocaust of Hiroshima*. She was not familiar with the painting. I described it.

"It's really a stunning piece," I said, "and it was the first time I had seen the term *holocaust* used in Japan to describe what had happened in Hiroshima."

"Well, you don't own the word," she snapped.

On August 11, 2010, Yoko Ono and Elie Wiesel attended a Manhattan screening of *A Film Unfinished*, a Holocaust documentary by Israeli director Yael Hersonski. They came separately. Ono was there because "I think it's very important to show the truth. . . . We have to know about everything," she said.[15]

Newspaper coverage did not indicate whether Ono and Wiesel engaged in conversation at the screening, or whether they even met. But some years earlier, following his Hiroshima visit, Wiesel spoke some words that Ono would likely have embraced.

"I don't like to compare one atrocity to another; that would be demeaning to both," Wiesel said. "Every tragedy is unique, just as every human is unique. When a person loses someone dear to her, who am I to say that my tragedy was greater? I have no right. For that person, her tragedy is the greatest in the world—and she is right in thinking so."[16]

15

A Japanese Letter from Auschwitz

For Katsumoto Saotome, the Tokyo firebombings chronicler, it did not much matter whether Hiroshima could fairly be compared to the Jewish Holocaust. That was beside the point. What mattered was the unbearable human suffering, and the need to prevent it all from happening again. Saotome, like Elie Wiesel, believed in the power of bearing witness, particularly before young people. Tell the children the unsparing truth about military conflict, and maybe, as adults, they will renounce the battlefield. It is tragedy-of-war education, and Saotome discovered an effective classroom in Auschwitz.

"I have been to Auschwitz many, many times," he told me in our Hilltop Hotel interview. Saotome recounted one such trip in a book he wrote for young people called *Letter from Auschwitz*.[1]

He traveled there with a teenage boy named Masaru, an uncommonly thoughtful youth who was filled with curiosity and dismay about the troubled past: about Nazi Germany and its friendship with Japan; about concentration camps and the Jewish genocide; about what it was like back then, at home, growing up during the war.

"I can't believe something like this happened," Masaru said, referring to Hitler's death camps.

"You can't think that what the Nazis did was something that only happened far away in Europe," Saotome told him. "This is because Japan did something similar when it started its own aggressive war. At the time, Japan thought it was doing the right thing."

"Did everybody believe that?" Masaru asked.

"Yes," Saotome said, "that message was repeated almost daily, and everybody came to accept the worthiness of what we were doing. Fathers and sons and even neighbors all came back dead, and we believed they were fighting the devil."

"Now that I think about it," Masaru said, "that was a very scary society. It was as if humans had lost their humanity."

"Yes," Saotome said. "Our Japanese troops slaughtered innocent women and children across the sea in mainland China and in the countries of Southeast Asia. And when I think about it, here in Japan we were cutting off the heads of American troops who were coming down from B-29 parachutes. We all believed these to be patriotic acts on behalf of the country."[2]

"I would hope," Saotome wrote, "that after reading this book readers will be prompted to study why World War II happened and understand the great sadness that took place during that time." Enough sadness, he hoped, to forestall any new conflagrations.

Katsumoto Saotome devoted his adult life to humanizing that sadness; to giving voice, through his reporting and writing, to civilian war victims in Japan. At the same time, he aimed a razor-sharp pen at his homeland and wrote unflinchingly about Japan as an aggressor nation. His visits to Auschwitz, and consideration of Germany's decades-long postwar pursuit of Nazi war criminals, led him to conclude that Japan had inadequately handled its own dirty laundry. He articulated that opinion in another book, called *Auschwitz and Me*.[3]

Saotome was unsparing with his prose. "It is almost unthinkable," he wrote, that Japan would ever memorialize its war crimes in China or Southeast Asia with a museum like the one he saw in Auschwitz. German prosecutors pursued Nazi war criminals well into the twenty-first century, but "it is unthinkable that Japan would continue to investigate Japanese war crimes so many years after the war."[4]

Saotome objected to the enshrinement of Japanese war criminals in Tokyo's Yasukuni Shrine, the spiritual resting ground for Japan's fallen warriors, good and evil. The esteem reserved for war criminals there had long been a political controversy affecting Japan's relations with the rest of Asia, which suffered greatly under Japanese occupation. China and Korea, in particular, took offense whenever leading Japanese officials visited Yasukuni and bowed to the memories of malefactors sentenced to death by the International Military Tribunal for the Far East, which adjudicated Japan's wartime culpability.[5]

"Nazi war criminals are pursued throughout the world," Saotome wrote. "But here in Japan, in the Yasukuni Shrine, we honor Class A Japanese war criminals. If Joseph Mengele were to come to Japan," an exasperated Saotome concluded, "he could be safe here."[6] Mengele was Hitler's *Todesengel*, or Angel of Death, who performed nightmarish and deadly medical experiments on prisoners at Auschwitz.

Saotome was especially riled when he learned that a commemorative marker had been placed in the center of Tokyo in 1980 on the site of the demolished Sugamo Prison, where seven Class A war criminals were executed in December 1948. The men, including wartime prime minister Hideki Tojo, had been sentenced to death by the Tokyo tribunal.[7] The six-foot marker, which bore the words "Praying for Eternal Peace," seemed to honor their memories.

"When I heard about the monument it was as if fish bones had gotten stuck in my throat," Saotome wrote in *Auschwitz and Me*. "What a strange story. Europeans will shake their heads in disbelief and ridicule the marker, if they ever hear of it. Needless to say, Japanese Class A war criminals who had large responsibility in World War II are, like the Nazis, direct perpetrators of a war of aggression, no matter what." The memorial, Saotome wrote, reawakened the "ghosts of war."[8]

During our Hilltop Hotel interview, after Saotome had told me about his visits to Auschwitz, I mentioned that I had a personal connection to the Holocaust. The Nazis, I explained, had killed my grandfather's sister and her children during Hitler's campaign to exterminate European Jews.

"Ah, ah," he said, taken aback.

"I remember my grandfather telling me stories about the Jewish Holocaust in Europe. It's one of the reasons I was motivated to learn about what happened in Tokyo and Hiroshima and Nagasaki," I said. There was something broadly similar, I explained: the sheer enormity of the human suffering.

"I agree," he said.

We did not debate the propriety of talking about the Holocaust and Hiroshima. What struck me as remarkable, however, was that Saotome had found his own connection to Auschwitz, one that had sharpened his understanding of Japan's wartime actions. Visiting Auschwitz had been "a violent shock," he wrote.[9] It affected the way he thought about war and about victimhood, and moved him to look more critically at Japan's post-war reckoning with the past. In his book *Auschwitz and Me*, Saotome recalls how he felt when he first saw the death camp. "I'm here, I'm finally here," he wrote. "The largest killing field in the world! It broke my heart."[10]

Part 5

PRISONERS OF MEMORY

Elie Wiesel had been a prisoner in Auschwitz. Toward the end of the war, he was transferred to Buchenwald.[1] He was there when US troops arrived in April 1945. My father was one of the soldiers who entered the facility. I can't say for sure, but Wiesel and my father were probably in Buchenwald at the same time.

Years later, Wiesel, referring to himself with the third-person *he*, recalled the Americans' reaction upon entering the camp: "He remembers their rage at what they saw. And even if he lives to be a very old man, he will always be grateful to them for that rage, and also for their compassion. Though he did not understand their language, their eyes told him what he needed to know—that they, too, would remember, and bear witness."[2]

In Japan, I met two men who also had been held captive during World War II. Their experiences differed from each other's, and certainly from that of Wiesel. But the Japanese, like Wiesel, were profoundly affected by their wartime detentions, which left them in the postwar years, for better or worse, prisoners of memory.

16

The Gulag POW

The Renoir café, in the Kichijoji area of Tokyo's west end, was a popular hangout for Japan's gray-haired generation, the men and women who made it through the war, built families and careers, and now, in retirement, had the time to lounge with friends for a late afternoon coffee or tea. The café well suited its customer base. It was a safe, staid, and predictable place, conservatively upholstered with padded wooden chairs, potted plants, and a smoking-allowed sensibility. The design called up another era: a vintage prewar Tokyo wrapped with retro ambiance and a dash of European (*Renoir*) chic.[1]

On the afternoon at issue, the venue was packed. At a cramped table near the window sat a scholarly looking man, one of Japan's leading archaeologists. Now eighty-six, he was rumpled and soft spoken, with wispy salt-and-pepper hair, a moustache, and big, gold-colored glasses that covered half his face. He looked down when he talked, not (it seemed to me) out of shyness, but from self-effacement and introspection. Because of what he had been through, because of what had happened to him after World War II, he was cautious. He would only agree to be interviewed in this very public and noisy location.[2]

The man, Kyuzo Kato, reached into a satchel and pulled out a book. His hands, caressing the volume, were wrinkled and gnarly, having seen their share of shovels and dirt and, more recently, sand: in recent years he had trolled the deserts of central Asia, digging up Buddhist temples on the ancient Silk Road. His favorite spot was Old Termez, on the Amu Darya River in southern Uzbekistan at the Uzbek-Afghan border. Old Termez housed an archaeological site called Kara Tepe, once a hub of Buddhism.[3]

Kyuzo Kato leafed through the book, an account of his last Termez dig, with childlike enthusiasm, pointing to various photos and sketches of archaeological finds. Touching history, he said, gave him enormous pleasure.

He found the page he was looking for, raised his eyes, looked at me, and, without warning, began, unabashedly, to sing.

> Near the Pamir Mountains, the river Amu Darya flows,
> In and out of the desert Karakum,
> And along the river, ancient ruins stand,
> And a sad wildflower blooms.

Kyuzo Kato wrote those words. He was the sad wildflower, he said. But he sang cheerfully, with a certain gusto, and his voice cut through the din of café conversations. Taken aback, patrons turned their heads toward him. Kyuzo Kato paid no mind. Why would he? He had survived Joseph Stalin's notorious network of forced labor camps, the Gulag Archipelago.

In August 1945, when he was twenty-three years old, Kato was a soldier with the Japanese occupation army in Chinese Manchuria. Two days after the bombing of Hiroshima, and a week before Emperor Hirohito surrendered, the Soviet Union entered the war against Japan.[4] The Kremlin unleashed 1.5 million troops.[5] Soviet forces quickly overwhelmed Kato and his comrades in Manchuria, and others in northern Korea, forcing Japan to capitulate.

The Red Army took prisoner between five and six hundred thousand Japanese soldiers and civilians, including Kato. Many of the POWs were held for up to five years or longer, even though the war had ended. "The chaos of these numbers—hundreds of thousands of soldiers, sailors, and civilians simply disappearing overseas—suggests how essentially meaningless the formal dating of 'war's end' was for many Japanese," wrote historian John Dower.[6]

The prisoners toiled in draconian facilities in Siberia, Uzbekistan, and elsewhere across the USSR. One out of every five died.[7] The scheme was designed partially to offset Soviet workforce losses caused by the war and by Stalin's repression, whose combined military and civilian death toll approached forty million.[8]

The Japanese POWs constituted a postwar "army of slaves," said David Janes, a Japan expert formerly with the United States–Japan Foundation. "It was a giant workforce that Stalin used to build railways and harvest timber."[9] According to University of Hawaii historian John J. Stephan, "Japanese contributed five billion man-hours to postwar construction."[10]

The diplomacy required to unlock Gulag prison gates for the Japanese prisoners flowed between Moscow and Washington, DC. A nascent Cold War hindered the process.

"The Japanese internees were really part of the politics of the time," Janes explained. The United States controlled Japan after 1945, challenging Soviet interests in East Asia.[11] "Tensions between Washington and Moscow increased," Janes said, "making repatriation negotiations more difficult." The sheer volume of Japanese POWs added to the problem. There was postwar confusion, compounded by Kremlin obfuscation, about who and where the prisoners were and whether they were even alive.

Additional factors muddled the POW release. The Russians and Japanese had a track record. They had fought a war in 1904 and 1905, which Russia lost.[12] Bad feelings, inflamed by the most recent conflict, remained on both sides.[13] What is more, the Kremlin had a penchant for promulgating Marxist-Leninist ideology. "By 1948," Dower wrote, it had "become obvious that the Soviets were delaying repatriation in order to subject prisoners to intensive indoctrination, so that they might contribute to communist agitation on their return." The repatriation process, Dower concluded, was "excruciatingly prolonged."[14]

Kyuzo Kato told me he preferred not to speak of his years of internment in the Siberian Gulag. "If it was so bad," he said, "then I would not have survived." But Kato had written about it, in Russian, which he learned in the camps. His memoir was called *Siberia in the Heart of a Japanese Man*.[15] The book, for Kato, was cathartic. It described the indescribable: skin-freezing cold that never ended; inadequate housing; scant food and clothing. The worst moment, he said, was when he heard that three of his comrades had escaped into the Siberian winter. Only two were caught, while eating the flesh of the third. "When I found out about this, I wanted to stop being a human being," he wrote.[16]

Kato made his way back to Tokyo in 1950. He was twenty-seven and had been held in captivity for five years. He described the journey home circumspectly. It was difficult, "but nothing at all compared to Genjo Sanzo's travels," he said, referring to a seventh-century Buddhist monk who made an arduous sixteen-year-long journey from China to India across the Silk Road. "If I had the same strength of character as Genjo Sanzo, I'd be a happy man."[17]

Kato said he returned home in good health. He resumed study at Tokyo's Sophia University, where he had been enrolled prewar. He was interested in German and in philosophy. He went on to work as an editor, writer, and administrator with an encyclopedia publishing house. But it was hard going, he said. His Gulag years left him filled with "anger and agony." In 1957, at age thirty-five, Kato reached what he called a psychological "turning point," which changed, for the better, the way he thought about living.

"Everyone will remember both the bad and good about situations in life," Kato wrote in his memoir. "My years in captivity left not only grief, but also some warm memories about Siberia, its nature and people."[18]

"I wanted to hold on to what good things I derived from my years there, and make myself a better person as a result," he later told me. "It doesn't pay to remain angry in life."

Kato decided to steep himself in Siberian history, ethnography, and archaeology. He was inspired to do so, he said, by a Japanese fisherman called Dembei, who in 1697 had shipwrecked off Siberia's Kamchatka Peninsula and was captured by the Itelmens, an Indigenous people of Russia's Far East. Vladimir Atlasov, a Russian explorer, brought the castaway to the court of Peter the Great. There, Dembei (who had learned Russian) briefed officials about Japan and became the first person to teach Japanese in Russia.[19] In Dembei, Kato saw an alter ego who had turned captivity in Siberia into something better.

Kato's academic career took off. He joined the newly established Russian studies department of Tokyo's Sophia University.[20] In 1963, he published his first book, a monograph called *The History of Siberia*.[21] He eventually landed at the prestigious National Museum of Ethnology in Osaka, where he became professor emeritus of archaeology.

Kato's scholarly journey began in Siberia but matured elsewhere, farther south, along central Asia's historic Silk Road. "Siberia and central Asia are deeply interconnected," he explained. "Peoples from the north migrated south, and one of the northern Silk Road routes skirted Siberia."

He fell in love with Uzbekistan, which he first visited early in his career, in 1963 and again in 1965.[22] He would travel there more than fifty times for archaeological research. Shima Nobuhiko, a Japanese journalist, reported that Kato once told him: "My hope is to die while excavating."[23] In 2016, Kato passed away on a dig in Old Termez, of pneumonia. He was ninety-four.[24]

In his later years, Kato was widely acknowledged as the Japanese doyen of Silk Road studies. In 2002, the president of Uzbekistan awarded Kato the Order of Friendship for his archaeological work.[25] In 2010, the Ministry of Foreign Affairs of Japan recognized Kato for promoting cultural exchange with Uzbekistan.[26] In 2011, the Japanese government honored Kato with the Zuihoushou, or Order of the Sacred Treasure.[27] In 2015, Japanese prime minister Shinzo Abe called Kato a "noted archaeologist" who "braved the harsh sun" of central Asia to excavate ancient ruins.[28] At his death, Kato had written nineteen books on the Silk Road, central Asia, and Siberia.[29]

At the Renoir café interview, Kyuzo Kato likened archaeological sites to silk cocoons that shielded him from life's hardships and from his past. After his imprisonment in Siberia, he said, he had eschewed politics, preferring to stay aloof from the contemporary world. When he did allow himself to look back on his time in the Gulag, he did so gently and without bitterness. "It was like an educational exchange," he joked, "It was foisted on me, and I was an unwitting exchange student. But I came away with something positive from it all."

I asked him, in view of his positive spin on those years, whether he ever had fun in Siberia. "I was good at explosives," he joked. "I used to throw grenades into a lake in order to catch fish."

One day, Kato explained, he went out on a rickety boat, and the vessel tipped over. He fell into the icy waters and barely made it to shore. He lost consciousness from the cold. Once he came to, he shivered for hours and warmed up only after someone poured liquor down his throat. "That was fun," Kato chuckled. "Well, at least it seems pretty funny now."[30]

17

Cloth Man

Like Kyuzo Kato, Tatsuichi Horikiri served with the Japanese army during World War II. Whereas Kato fought in occupied Manchuria, Horikiri was based in Japanese-controlled China. Horikiri, like Kato, was a prisoner of war, albeit under wholly different conditions. He was held by his own people, by the Japanese army, and accused (falsely, he said) of treason. His experience in captivity was short lived but searing: it deepened his belief that for people like him, who had grown up in Japan's economic and social underbelly, injustice and suffering were fellow travelers.

Horikiri came from rural Japan. He was born in 1925 to a family of fishermen in an impoverished village in the south of Kyushu Island. "Since I was a small boy, I knew life is hard," he told me. "I couldn't get out of poverty. I was intent on knowing why, what social system causes us to be in this position."[1]

Before the war, Horikiri was educated in an industrial-technical high school. After graduation, in 1943, he moved to occupied China, where he worked for a private Japanese transportation company. His troubles began in the summer of 1944.

"I was in Beijing, where the army hired my company to do construction work," he said. "I was at an infrastructure building site. There was an accident that caused a communications cutoff. As a result, important information could not get through to the army, and a skirmish was lost. The army needed somebody to blame, and they came after me. They took me into custody and accused me of assisting the enemy. They ordered me to tell the truth, but I had nothing to tell because I hadn't done anything. So they tortured me. They threatened to shoot me. They hit me very hard. I wasn't wearing any clothing. My body was battered."

The army eventually released Horikiri but stripped him of his private citizen status and forced him to enlist in its ranks. Before deployment, however, he was sent back to his construction site quarters to regain his strength. Wracked by his ordeal, he lay down on a futon. There, Horikiri explained, he experienced an epiphany.

"The futon was wrapped in a cover that my mother had given me before I left home," he said. "She had stitched the cover together from old cloth with her own hands. As I lay there, I looked at the futon and remembered my mother. In the cover's design, I saw my mother's face. I cried all night and conversed with the futon as if it were my mother. It told me that I didn't do anything wrong. And at that point," Horikiri said, "my interest in old cloth arose."

≈

I met Tatsuichi Horikiri many years later, in his office at the Museum of Natural History and Human History in Kitakyushu, the northernmost city on Kyushu Island. He was eighty-four years old, had long ago retired from a postwar career in the construction industry, and had turned his passion for old cloth into a vocation. He had become a lay scholar of the threadbare, a prolific lecturer and essayist recognized, as one award put it, for his "remarkable achievements" in promoting society and culture.[2]

Horikiri believed that clothing could talk: that within each loop of thread lay the story of the garment's wearer or tailor. It was not a fool's endeavor, not anything of the sort. Horikiri was a self-made scholar determined to find, within old clothing, the inner being of Japan, that essence of humanity and wisdom he had discovered, long ago, in the fabric of his mother's handmade futon cover.

The rags of poor people interested Horikiri the most because, in his view, it was the poor who carried within them the history and soul of the nation. "For the masses," he once wrote, "those 'old days' were never good;

theirs were an incessant struggle for survival. We are shamefully ignorant of the past, all the more so when it comes to the lives of those at the very bottom. This is why I collect the clothes of ordinary folk."[3]

Horikiri traveled around Japan gathering the tattered garments and hand-me-downs of the common folk: the frayed kimonos, work clothes, and everyday wear of farmers and fishermen, of tradesmen and soldiers, of mill workers and beggars, of prostitutes and peasants. He had collected more than thirty-five hundred pieces of old fabric by the time I met him.

The Kitakyushu museum became their repository, where they coexisted with ancient fossils and dinosaur bones from the Paleozoic, Mesozoic, and Cenozoic eras. The juxtaposition tacitly acknowledged that relics of clothing, like fossilized animals and plants, can speak to earlier eras.[4] Horikiri, in effect, was an archaeologist of cloth.

"Seeing and holding these tattered garments used by farmers and villagers in times past," Horikiri wrote, "I cannot help but feel that they still exude the warmth and vigor of the bodies they once protected, and these scraps are trying to tell us their stories, provided that we only listen closely and with open hearts."[5]

Horikiri was an introspective man with thin gray hair and sad eyes. His work space was tucked deep inside the museum, an underground room cluttered with office bric-a-brac, cabinets, and specimens of cloth. On the day I met him, he was casually dressed in a long-sleeve purple shirt and dress pants, preparing the first major exhibition of what the museum called the Horikiri Collection. "I'm excited to talk with you," he said. "I don't often meet foreigners interested in cloth." We sat down over coffee, and Horikiri proceeded to explain his relationship to aged, weather-beaten clothing.

"When I look at cloth, what interests me is the way the cloth speaks to me, the energy that comes out of the material," he said. He picked up a blue, ragged piece of fabric. It was from a coal-mining region in Kyushu's Fukuoka Prefecture.

"This is a cloth that women wrapped around their waist," he said. The garment was rectangular in shape and tied around the back like an apron. The owner was probably a peasant, Horikiri said, and the item dated back to the 1920s or 1930s.

"It's hard to tell which is the front or rear of this piece. But it is a tapestry made from eighty-two different patches of tattered material stitched together as one. I know lots of poor people, but I think the owner of this cloth was the poorest of the poor."

Horikiri handed me the garment. "Robert-san, please touch it and feel the cloth," he said. He urged me to run my fingers over the tattered patches, which were the item's skin and bones, and to feel how they all came together. "It took a long time to stitch this, one piece at a time," he said. "It was sewn neatly and done with care. And that tells me the owner of this garment had a very healthy soul. I can read these emotions by looking at it."

Horikiri later described the cloth in an essay: "The fact that it was so meticulously mended, so thoroughly washed, and folded up with such care leads me to believe that the woman who owned this garment possessed a deep sense of human dignity, not defeated or uncaring, despite the daily hardship of her impoverished and challenging life."[6]

Horikiri brought out another garment, a dark, threadbare, hip-length jacket resembling a short kimono without the overlapping front. He found it in Izumi, a rural town in southern Kyushu. "This is a woman's field-worker coat," he said. "The middle part of the rear side is faded because the woman was carrying a baby on her back. At the bottom, you can see two areas where the material is very thin. That is where the baby's feet rubbed against the cloth. And on top, there are two discolored spots, one on each shoulder. That is where the baby's carrying sash hung."

The cloth was about eighty years old, he said. "When I visited the garment's owner, a very old lady came out of the house. She asked, 'Why are you taking it to the Kitakyushu museum? Maybe you are taking it to make people laugh at us poor folk.' And I said, no. The purpose is to show how difficult your life is."

Tatsuichi Horikiri was known in Kitakyushu as a researcher and historian interested in the lives of the working class.[7] He also struck me as part philosopher and part romantic, made thoughtful by wartime trauma and drawn to the downtrodden because of his upbringing. He was an ambassador for the vulnerable and the poor, and he claimed to have found, in their old pieces of cloth, something that in his view modern Japan had lost, something he described as "heart."

"What kind of heart? The sorrow and the hardship," he said. "Journalists often ask me is there anything happy in the clothes I collect and I say no. The happiness is very, very small when you compare it to the hardship of the people. I think that after the war, Japan developed quite rapidly and gained lots of wealth. But we threw away the experience, the heart of the people who wore those clothes. And that development is bringing the world in the wrong direction."

"How so?" I asked. "What impact has this loss of heart had on Japan?"

His response was explicit and unexpected, and had to do with murder.

The violent crime rate in Japan is very low. In 2009, the year I met with Horikiri, the US murder rate was more than twenty times higher.[8] But several months before I spoke with Horikiri some unsettling events had taken place in Japan. A thirty-six-year-old Japanese mother had received a life sentence for killing her nine-year-old daughter. Japanese media had widely reported the story.[9] Before that, reports of other horrific family-on-family crimes appeared in the press: an eighteen-year-old boy who had stabbed his grandmother to death; a seventeen-year-old boy who had killed and beheaded his mother.[10] For Horikiri, stories like these were hard to forget. Japan's postwar success, he believed, had stirred up humanity's worst instincts.

"The biggest impact is the mothers who kill their own children, and grandchildren who kill their grandparents," he said. "Back at the time these cloths were made, paths in the rice paddies were very dark, but women walked home safely. Nobody raped them. Today, even where the street is lit, women are attacked, even raped. This didn't happen back then."

At least that was Horikiri's perception. His collection of tattered clothing covered the first half of the twentieth century.[11] Violent crime did exist when those old cloths were made, but the absence of twenty-first-century information platforms meant that Horikiri may not have known about it. For instance, nationwide juvenile crime statistics published in 1952 by the National Rural Police Headquarters in Tokyo listed, for the years 1936–40, more than seven hundred homicides, seventeen hundred robberies, and approximately one thousand rapes.[12]

The serious crime rate hit a high in 1948, when an impoverished, postwar Japan was still struggling to arrange the basic necessities of life.[13]

"Aren't you overstating the case regarding crime in Japan?" I asked Horikiri. I reminded him that the rate of violent felonies in Japan is low. "Murders, like the ones you referred to, are rare. Isn't your assessment overly harsh?"

"You said it's a rare case to find such killings within families," Horikiri replied. "But for me it is shocking such a thing could even exist. It is not the rarity. It is the fact that it could happen at all."

Horikiri had been speaking calmly. But at this point in our conversation his tone changed. His voice grew purposeful, and louder. "I have one question for you, Robert-san. I have lived a long time and experienced war. There are many devils during wartime. But when I talk about these clothes, I talk about humanity. We can't forget that gods exist among the devils. What do you think?"

"I'm not sure I understand what you mean," I said.

"These clothes represent the love of the people. Today, in the news, only the devils get attention. I believe by talking about these clothes I can emphasize the humanity among us. Our wealth and abundance have ripped away that humanity and diminished the soul of the people. These old clothes may suggest poverty and hardship, but in my view people were happier back then."

≈

In one of his essays, Tatsuichi Horikiri explained that the working class of prewar Japan had the capacity, despite its poverty and low social standing, to find happiness in the simplest of things. "Oh, the wonders of those old, tattered clothes!" he wrote. "Even when they had become so threadbare that they were ready to be thrown out, they were still treated with extraordinary respect—being meticulously mended, washed, and folded. . . . Clearly, the people who wore these clothes had an outlook on life that we rarely see today—sound, industrious, and ultimately, full of hope."[14]

Horikiri came to that conclusion after having wandered around Japan for more than three decades, talking with common people often at length in their homes (all the while gauging their well-being and outlooks on life) and looking for truths.

"There are always those who are a little too creative in their storytelling," he noted, regarding his conversations with working-class folk. People tend to become the heroes of their own tales, he said, and he took care to verify everything he heard. "But regardless of whether or not I could authenticate every story," he wrote, "it became very important for me to try to find out about the lives of the underprivileged and to learn about the values and principles that guided their lives. And for this, the old clothes were invaluable."[15]

At the close of our conversation, I asked Horikiri, if he had to choose one piece of his own clothing to leave as his legacy, which would it be?

"None," he said. "The world is overly filled with things. Even the kimono is dwarfed by our abundance of wealth." He said Japan's most iconic garment had, in modern times, become devoid of meaning. "The kimono can no longer express the emotions of the people," he maintained. "The contemporary world has stifled even the kimono's ability to speak."

Tatsuichi Horikiri died in October 2019, at age ninety-four. Akiko Ueno, a curator at the Kitakyushu Museum of Natural History and Human History, told me Horikiri had worked on his archive of old cloth until three months before he passed away.[16] His family mourned his death quietly, and at their request, his death was not widely announced. Ueno, who had worked alongside Horikiri for many years, said she only told people who inquired about his well-being that he had died.

At the time of his death, there were 4,500 items in the Horikiri Collection. Nearly all were made from kimono cloth.[17]

Part 6

WAR CRIMES, REPENTANCE, AND APOLOGIES

There is in my household one old piece of cloth: a valuable item filled with tradition and dear to the family. It is my father's Jewish prayer shawl, or tallis. I discovered it after he died, inside a velvet pouch in a bedroom closet near his photographs of Buchenwald.

The prayer shawl is white, with blue stripes and traditional fringes, called tzitzis, which are meant to remind the wearer to obey the commandments of God.[1] The garment dates back to postwar Chicago. My dad acquired it from Rosenblum's bookstore on Roosevelt Road, near his childhood home. I found it stored in a red box filled with wartime souvenirs.

The box contained two other especially compelling keepsakes: a small, threadbare Nazi flag, its edges beaten and frayed; and a Nazi military belt buckle my father had somehow procured. In what I took to be a purposeful act, he had placed the tallis pouch on top of the buckle and flag, symbolically smothering the Nazi junk.

I acquired a tallis of my own when I was eight years old. It came from my grandfather Abe on the occasion of my entering Hebrew school. Abe, who was not a rich man, fully funded my formal Jewish education. He did so to increase the odds that his grandson would perpetuate the faith for future generations. For five long years I sat before my teacher, Rabbi Klein, and learned about the religion, history, culture, and language of my forebears.

Rabbi Klein taught us that repentance (*teshuvah* in Hebrew) is an important element of Judaism. For Jews, making amends and seeking for-giveness are central to living a principled life. Rabbi Klein called me Yerach-miel, my Hebrew name, which means "God shall have mercy."[2] I was, by Jew-ish moniker, an incarnation of forgiveness from the highest order.

In Hebrew school we studied Yom Kippur, the Day of Atonement, Juda-ism's repentance-dedicated holiday. It is the holiest day of the year and the last of the "Ten Days of Penitence" following Rosh Hashanah, the Jewish New Year. On Yom Kippur observant Jews (and considering the stakes, even less observant ones) pray and fast and ask God to forgive their sins.

In my childhood household the go-to book on penitence and other Jew-ish practices was Milton Steinberg's *Basic Judaism*.[3] Published in 1947 with a $1.75 price tag, it was a fixture of the family bookshelf. It now sits in my home, more than seventy-five years later.

Steinberg wrote that a Jewish wrongdoer can earn absolution through a spiritual act of repentance: "He must seek to bring home to himself an open-eyed understanding of the causes, nature, and effects of his misdeeds, so that his remorse may be deep-seated and his will for betterment firm."[4]

In Japan, repentance and remorse have been subjects of high-stakes po-litical discourse throughout the postwar years. Leaders from the emperor on down have struggled with whether, how, and how often to apologize for the country's wartime misdeeds. The Japanese-language version of Steinberg's *Basic Judaism*, by the way, came out in 2012. I doubt Tokyo's ruling elite con-sulted the volume for guidance. Had they done so, however, they would know that the Japanese word for *teshuvah* is *kuiaratame*.[5]

18

Atrocities and Dead Souls

All wars produce deaths. Dead soldiers. Dead civilians. Dead souls. Nations mourn these casualties for generations to come. For Japan, mourning the dead and injured from World War II—and judging its own role in waging that war—has always been complicated.[1] The associated questions are nettlesome and messy. Japan was an aggressor state that caused immeasurable cruelty and harm. Did its soldiers, however, even the most brutal, die honorably? Civilians, hundreds of thousands of them, lost their lives or suffered injuries in firebombings or atomic blasts. Can these casualties be labeled righteous, and therefore capable of diminishing Japan's culpability for its wartime behavior; or were they the unfortunate but necessary collateral damage of a justifiable US campaign to defeat the enemy that attacked Pearl Harbor and started the war in the first place?

Questions such as these have generated much analysis and debate among historians and others who consider such things.[2] The broad issues involve assessments of morality, victimhood, culpability, and justice.

These broad issues, however, become personal on the ground, where a war touches brick and mortar, skin and bone; and the questions raised there are visceral and pointedly specific: Was this or that behavior factually evil? Was such and such an act unadulteratedly and unambiguously wrong? Was it, therefore, an atrocity or war crime?

Katsumoto Saotome, the Tokyo air raid victim who chronicled the human toll of the American firebombing campaign, had also thought about wartime atrocities, about right and wrong, about assessing blame. "Whenever war happens," he concluded, "I cannot say that human beings do not turn into monsters."[3]

In our Hilltop Hotel interview, Saotome argued that monstrous acts occur on all sides of a conflict, among victors and vanquished. He pointed to the Americans, to former US defense secretary Robert McNamara, who in 1945 worked under Curtis LeMay, the general in charge of the US incendiary air campaign against Japan. After the war, LeMay said that had Japan defeated America, he would have been prosecuted as a war criminal for the Tokyo firebombings. McNamara agreed. "He, and I'd say I, were behaving as war criminals."[4]

"McNamara was exactly correct," Saotome told me. The United States had "killed without discrimination. It killed many civilians. But I must say," Saotome added pointedly, "that Japan did the same thing in many parts of Asia. I cannot say we were the only victims here."

≈

On May 5, 1945, some three months before the bombing of Hiroshima, a Japanese air force fighter rammed into an American B-29 bomber in the skies over northern Kyushu Island, not far from the city of Fukuoka. The B-29 was heading back to its base in Guam after having attacked an airfield elsewhere in Japan. Both planes crashed to the ground. Police captured at least nine surviving US airmen.[5]

Eight of the Americans wound up in Fukuoka's Kyushu Imperial University medical school, where they were subjected to horrific experimental procedures: doctors removed a lung from one man to measure the respiratory system's response to surgery; they injected another prisoner with seawater instead of sterile saline solution, just to see what would happen; they drilled through one captive's skull to determine whether removing part of the brain could control epilepsy. None of these or other procedures was medically necessary. All eight Americans died as a result of the medical assaults. In a callous postscript just hours after Emperor Hirohito had announced Japan's surrender on August 15, Fukuoka authorities beheaded more than a dozen other US POWs in their custody.[6]

John Dower, the Pulitzer Prize–winning American scholar specializing in Japan and World War II, neatly considered Japanese war crimes in his 1986 book *War without Mercy: Race and Power in the Pacific War*.[7] Dower's assessment is worth repeating, for he skillfully sketched out the issues.

"Japanese atrocities conformed to several broad categories: massacres of noncombatants, the maltreatment and killing of prisoners, routinized torture, forced labor, and institutionalized murder in the form of lethal medical experiments," Dower wrote. "Their atrocities frequently were so grotesque, and flaunted in such a macabre manner, that it is not surprising they were interpreted as being an expression of deliberate policy and a calculated exhibition of some perverse, 'national character.'"

What else, Dower asked, is to be made of this: "the 'friendly contest' between two officers in late 1937, avidly followed in some Japanese newspapers, to see who would be the first to cut down 150 Chinese with his samurai sword; or of the rape and murder of nuns in the streets of Hong Kong; or of the corpses of tortured Englishmen hanging from trees in Malaya, with their severed genitals in their mouths." Or of the Nanking Massacre, where Japanese troops killed and raped tens of thousands of Chinese noncombatants?[8]

Dower said it is impossible to determine exactly how many people were subjected to Japanese atrocities, or how many troops actively participated. "There can be little dispute about the wide range of conventional Japanese war crimes, however, or about the actual occurrence of certain shocking incidents which were singled out for special publicity in the Allied camp and contributed greatly to the effectiveness of propaganda depicting the Japanese collectively as an inherently savage race."

As for the US firebombing campaign, there was, among American officials, little in the way of LeMay and McNamara's postwar self-awareness and candor. American military planners, Dower said, "remained sensitive to the moral issue of bombing civilians" and worried about negative public opinion. A few military officials privately voiced concerns about "moral ambiguity." "When Tokyo was incinerated," however, "there was scarcely a murmur of protest on the home front."

Indeed, in the aftermath of Pearl Harbor, anti-Japanese rhetoric had stoked what Dower called "exterminationist" sentiment among Americans, where the aim was to kill as many Japanese as possible. Japanese were portrayed as subhuman, likened to monkeys, apes, cockroaches, or other vermin. Media depictions played up physical stereotypes about skin color or facial characteristics, which reinforced preexisting racial prejudices about a "Yellow Peril" that threatened the American way.

In America, hostile attitudes about Japanese were reinforced when the US government sent more than one hundred thousand Japanese Americans to wartime internment camps. Far fewer people of German ancestry living in the United States were similarly treated.[9] Americans understandably vilified their adversaries, both Japanese and German, whose aggression had caused the war and whose wartime atrocities were well known. But Japanese vilification had racial undertones that hostility toward Germans did not. As journalist Ernie Pyle put it, the Germans "were still people," whereas Japanese were "something inhuman and squirmy." That sentiment tinted the backdrop behind US policymakers as they made tactical military decisions regarding Japan.[10]

"The Allied air raids were widely accepted as just retribution as well as sound strategic policy," Dower concluded. "And when Allied prosecutors sitting in the gutted capital city of Japan in 1946 accused the country's leaders of promoting the indiscriminate destruction of 'men, women and children alike,' they still did so with little sense of irony. Japan had merely reaped what it sowed."

19

Repentance and Apology

The War Criminal's Son

The American air campaign in 1945 largely spared the city of Morioka in northern Japan. Two raids left three people dead. Property damage was minimal.[1] Among the surviving local residents: the Komai family, mother and son. They stayed in Morioka after the war, where the boy, Osamu, married and built his own home.

There was in that postwar Komai household an old kimono that Osamu treasured. It was a garment of consequence, a vintage piece of cloth filled with meaning and beloved by the family because it had crossed generations, from parent to child, through wartime and peace. The kimono belonged to Osamu's father, Mitsuo, and hung heavily on the son's shoulders and memory. Its fabric told a tender but terribly sad story.

I visited Osamu Komai one snowy November morning in 2009.[2] He was a gentle, fit, seventy-two-year-old retired "salaryman," the Japanese designation for white-collar worker. He lived on the outskirts of Morioka in a modest two-story postwar residence of stucco and wood. His front door opened onto a carpet of rice fields. An old volcano, Mount Iwate, rose in the distance. It last blew up in 1919.[3] Mitsuo Komai, the father, was a student in Morioka at the time and might have seen the eruption.

Mitsuo's kimono was striking: an utterly white summertime robe, or *yukata*, designed for comfort. Osamu said his father's garment was made of hemp, which fended off the August heat and kept Mitsuo cool. Its dazzling bright hue reflected the sun, and in the warm summer months the kimono glistened and stood out like snow.

There was a photograph on display in Komai's home, a portrait of a young Osamu wearing his father's *yukata*. The photo was monochrome black and white, taken in the late 1950s, when Osamu was some twenty years old. He struck a rakish pose, peering sideways over the kimono's collar and, with youthful arrogance, dragging on a half-spent cigarette.

"I do have bits and pieces of memory about my father," Osamu told me. "He liked to smoke cigarettes, so I smoked too."

Osamu said the original kimono, the one in the photo, no longer existed. He owned an exact duplicate, which his wife, Sachiko, stitched. "It was just after we married," Sachiko said. "He told me he wanted to wear a kimono just like his father wore. So I made it from scratch."

"What happened to the original kimono?" I asked.

"It's gone," Osamu answered. "It's burnt. I threw it away."

FIGURE 13. Osamu Komai in his father's kimono, Morioka, Japan, circa late 1950s. Courtesy of Osamu Komai.

"Why?"

"I was very young," Osamu said, "and I could not come to terms with how I felt about my father."

Osamu Komai spent a lifetime thinking about his father and grappling with the repercussions of what his father did. The ruminations were not simple, and did not concern the typical tussles a son may have with his dad. For the Komai men, the issues and consequences of their relationship were weightier, involving wartime, good and evil, and the question of whether or how a nation, or a person, should own up to bad deeds. For Osamu Komai, these were not abstract concerns. He was the son of a Japanese war criminal.

His father, Mitsuo Komai, was executed in 1946 for committing war crimes at Kanchanaburi, the forced labor camp in Thailand whose prisoners (primarily Allied POWs) built the famous bridge on the River Kwai.[4] Mitsuo was a high-ranking officer there, second in command of one of the main camp's branches. He ordered the torture of prisoners and participated in the beating deaths of two British POWs.

When Osamu Komai learned about his father's execution many years after the war, he initially thought it was an act of victor's justice, that the Allied powers had killed his father as an act of revenge. He discovered, however, that the accusations were true.

"It was inevitable, what my father did," Osamu told me. "It couldn't be avoided. I don't think he regretted it until the last minute, just before he was put to death."

Osamu spent much of his adult life making amends for his father's conduct. He traveled to England to apologize, in person, to Eric Lomax, a Kanchanaburi prisoner who was beaten and waterboarded on his father's orders.

"In Japan," Osamu said, "one family member is responsible for the actions of another."

Osamu Komai shared his life story with me over many hours and with unexpected candor and emotion. It was an intimate, complicated account of a son's unwanted inheritance, of a wartime phantom that did not die; a tale of bad acts that lingered and of a father's love for his son, and a son's affection for his father. It was a tangled and harrowing narrative that

Osamu Komai revisited whenever he put on his father's white kimono, the one refashioned by his wife.

≈

At its height, the Japanese labor camp in Kanchanaburi, Thailand (also known as Kanburi), held some sixty thousand Allied prisoners of war. Most came from former territories of the British Empire, primarily Brits and Australians who were captured after the fall of Singapore in February 1942, along with Dutch POWs from the Netherlands East Indies. A small group of Americans were there, some seven hundred, many of whom were taken after the Japanese had sunk their battleship, the USS *Houston*.[5] The Japanese also pressed into service more than two hundred thousand noncombatants to labor alongside these POWs: Asians (predominantly Indians) from occupied territories elsewhere in the region.[6]

Situated in Thailand's northern jungles, Kanchanaburi—its base camp and branches—supported a massive railroad construction project designed to fuel, feed, arm, and otherwise bolster Japanese expansionism.

"After its lightning conquest of most of Southeast Asia, the [Japanese] Empire was in danger of outrunning its supply lines," wrote railway historian W. L. Gwyer.[7] "It did not have enough ships to keep its far-flung military effort going." As a result, Gwyer said, in 1942, Japanese military planners set out to build a railroad connecting Thailand, then called Siam, with neighboring Burma (now Myanmar).

"The Imperial Japanese Army finished it in fifteen months, but at an appalling price," Gwyer wrote. Cruel treatment and punishingly harsh conditions, including tropical heat, malaria, poisonous snakes, and food shortages, ran up the death toll.[8] "No one really knows for sure, but guesses are that 100,000 Asians perished, along with 13,000 POWs. In human terms," Dwyer concluded, "it was probably the most costly railway adventure in history."[9]

The Thai-Burma line was known as the Railway of Death. It sits high on the list of Japanese wartime atrocities.[10]

Mitsuo Komai never set out for a military career, and, in his prewar years, Kanchanaburi was not an assignment he would have envisioned.

"My father was not a professional soldier," Osamu said. He was a college-educated businessman, caught up, like the rest of his compatriots, in the miasma of Japanese nationalism and wartime fervor.

According to Osamu, Mitsuo was blessed with a keen sense of order. "From what my mother told me, my father seemed to be not quite obsessive-compulsive, but he would take care of things very neatly. He was very, very well organized." He also was relatively fluent in English, thanks to university studies in literature. It was an unusual skill set the army found attractive, one well suited for a camp filled with English-speaking British and Australian prisoners. Mitsuo, who volunteered for the army, was sent to officer training school, then ordered to Kanchanaburi.

"What kind of man was your father?" I asked.

"I don't remember much," Osamu said. "Before the war I do recall going for walks with him, and he would hold my hand. On holidays he would sometimes take me to the amusement park. My mother said he was very kind, a gentle person who would not even kill a bug."

Osamu and I spoke in the living room of his house, a cluttered but comfortable space with a heater tempering Morioka's early wintertime chill. Osamu had brought out a heap of research paraphernalia for our conversation, an archive of notebooks and files stuffed with papers and photographs relating to his father's wartime years. He grabbed various documents as we conversed, extracting information with a fluency evidencing the many years he had put into considering his father's military service.

Osamu said his parents had met through literature. "They would write poems to each other. My father gave my mother a book of poetry titled *Hatsukoi*, or 'First Love.'" Osamu picked out an old gray volume from a nearby bookshelf. Published in 1925, it had a crumbling binding, and several loose pages fell out.

Pointing to an inscription on one of the pages, Osamu said: "My father wrote this." "It says, 'What does love mean?'"

"It sounds like your father was a romantic," I said.

"Mmm, yes," Osamu said. "My aunt told me later on that yes, he was a romantic person. He would take her, my aunt, to the Morioka castle and give her candy."

"My father really loved us children," Osamu added. "He would write very often." He dug into a nearby folder and retrieved an old postcard. It was a message Mitsuo had written to Osamu from Kanchanaburi after having received a letter from his young son. In the note, Mitsuo addressed Osamu by his nickname, "Ochan":

April 5, 1942

Ochan,

I know you're happy to start kindergarten in April. Good for you. You're going to have so much fun in your white school uniform. Please enjoy your time at school. Stay safe every day. Be careful on your way to class and watch out for cars and motorcycles. I insist you let mother or grandmother know if you don't feel well. I dreamt about you last night, Ochan, which made me very happy. Please remember to put out water and flowers for your late brother.

Sayonara.

≈

After the war, the victorious Allied powers convened military tribunals across Asia to prosecute Japanese accused of committing war crimes. There were three categories of transgression: Class A concerned "crimes against peace," regarding those who had planned and waged a war of aggression; Class B covered conventional war crimes such as mistreatment of prisoners and civilians; and Class C concerned "crimes against humanity," which were widespread and systematic atrocities including torture, murder, extermination, and enslavement.[11]

Some fifty tribunals were held, variously under Dutch, British, American, Australian, Chinese, French, and Filipino jurisdiction. An estimated 5,700 Japanese were prosecuted for Class B and C offenses.[12] Of these, more than 900 defendants were sentenced to death (the actual number executed was 920); 475 received life sentences; nearly 3,000 were sent to prison; and some 1,000 were acquitted.[13]

Class A defendants were tried in Tokyo at the International Military Tribunal for the Far East, a high-profile proceeding that lasted two and a half years. The accused were twenty-eight top Japanese military and civilian wartime leaders. Seven of them consequently were executed.

Osamu Komai's father, Mitsuo, was tried at a tribunal in Singapore and accused of Class B and C offenses. What follows are excerpts from that proceeding.[14] The content—a mix of legal documents and verbatim trial transcripts—describes, in stiff, no-nonsense yet engrossing language, what Mitsuo did at Kanchanaburi, the case against him, and the consequences.

From the official record of the Military Court for the Trial of Six War Criminals, among them Mitsuo Komai, in Singapore, February 1946:

CHARGE SHEET

1st Charge
Committing a war crime, in that they at Kanburi Camp between 29 Aug and 10 Sep 43 in violation of the laws and usages of war cruelly beat and maltreated Serjeant-Major Thew, at that time a prisoner of war in their custody in consequence whereof severe suffering and injuries were inflicted on the said prisoner of war.

2nd Charge
Committing a war crime, in that they at Kanburi Camp between 1 and 29 Sep 43 in violation of the laws and usages of war cruelly beat and maltreated Major Slater, Major Smith, Lieutenant Collins, Lieutenant Lomax and Lieutenant MacKay, at that time prisoners of war in their custody in consequence whereof severe suffering and injuries were inflicted on the said prisoners of war.

3rd Charge
Committing a war crime, in that they at Kanburi Camp on or about 29 Sep 43 in violation of the laws and usages of war cruelly beat and maltreated Captain Hawley and Lieutenant Armitage, at that time

prisoners of war in their custody in consequence whereof the said prisoners of war met their deaths.[15]

PLACE & DATE OF TRIAL	Singapore 5, 6, and 7 Feb 46.
ACCUSED	(2) Capt. KOMAI MITSUO
PLEA	1st charge—Not Guilty 2&3 charges—Guilty
FINDING	All charges—Guilty
SENTENCE	death by hanging.[16]

From the opening address by the prosecutor, Capt. J. F. Reilly (February 5, 1946):

This case, which has come to be known as the Kanburi Radio Case, arises out of happenings in or about September 1943 at the Kanburi POW camp of which the first accused was the Camp Commandant whilst the second accused [Komai] was his adjutant and the other four accused were the senior NCOs of his Camp Staff . . .

At the material time there was, as we are told by Capt. Komai (Accused No.2), considerable chagrin amongst the Japanese hierarchy that the Railway had not been finished by the end of August. This was due to causes which are irrelevant to the present case, but the Japanese put it down to sabotage, and in an attempt to combat this a search of all POW Camps was ordered. Evidence will reveal that the Japanese suspected that a Radio Set was being operated somewhere in the Area and that the spirits and morale of the Prisoners was being kept high by belief in an ultimate allied victory due to dissemination of the news of the American victories in the Pacific and the retribution being meted out to the enemy in the skies over Germany.

These Japanese suspicions were only too well founded. Towards the end of August or the beginning of September, a secret radio set concealed in a small coffee tin was found on the bed of Sergeant

Major Thew. . . . It was believed to have been made by Thew and Sergeant Smith and both of these men were on or about the 1st September 1943 taken to KANBURI Camp for interrogation. . . .

Capt. Komai carried out (this) task in a thorough fashion and assisted by his Senior NCOs and Camp Staff . . . inhumanly thrashed and beat Sergeant Major Thew to within an inch of his life, so much so that one witness will aver that in the Camp hospital a few days after this brutality Sergeant Major Thew was beyond recognition. This performance forms the subject of the first charge.

The next stage in this tragedy was reached when five officers suspected of disseminating Sergeant Major Thew's radio reports were brought into Kanhuri [sic] Camp for interrogation. They were: Major Smith, Major Slater, Major Knight (who later died in Singapore), Lt. McKay [sic], Lt. Lomax.

Again (with) Capt. Komai officiating, the same maltreatment was meted out to these officers until, as witnesses will testify, after the beating and over-night exposure, supervised and joined in by the principle [sic] who smelt of liquor, the area in front of the guard room resembled on the morrow a miniature battlefield with Major Smith almost dead from severe shock, another officer unconscious in a ditch, and youthful Lieutenant Lomax with both forearms broken, and the others severely mauled and bruised. . . . (This) incident . . . forms the subject of charge two. . . .

The investigation was resumed on the 23rd September when four other officers were brought into Kanburi Camp. . . . They were Capt. Hawley, Lt. Armitage, Capt. Gregg, Lt. Gilchrist. The cruel "murder" . . . of the two first named officers forming the subject of the third charge.[17]

From the address by defense counsel, Sq. Leader Brash:

Now as regards Captain Komai. The Captain has pleaded guilty to beating 5 British Officers until they were severely injured. He has pleaded guilty to the 3rd Charge causing the death of two British

Officers. . . . I cannot say anything in mitigation. I say this however: He has been perfectly frank right through. He submitted that he was responsible for what took place. . . . He has not put anybody into trouble, no matter how these confessions were obtained, and he has come forward and pleaded guilty and asked if it be possible that his frankness in admitting this brutality will be taken into consideration if the Court considers that is possible.[18]

From the closing address of the prosecutor, Capt. Reilly:

It is respectfully submitted by the Prosecution that the evidence before the Court speaks of a joint effort by the Camp officials of KANBURI POW Camp, who throughout the investigation into the secret Radio Set carried out the necessary interrogation punctuated with brutal maltreatment under the leadership of Capt. Komai who stands a self-confessed murderer.[19]

ALLIED LAND FORCES SOUTH EAST ASIA MILITARY COURT—WAR CRIMINAL DEATH WARRANT

TO: The Officer in charge of CHANGI JAIL Singapore Island.
WHEREAS one Captain KOMAI MITSUO (Name of condemned) was on the 7th day of February 1946 convicted by a Military Court at Singapore of a war crime and sentenced by such court to the penalty of death by judicial hanging and
WHEREAS in accordance with Army Order No. 81 of 1945, such sentence has come before me for confirmation and after due consideration and in exercise of the powers conferred upon me, I have confirmed the sentence of death by judicial hanging so imposed.
NOW THEREFORE I hereby order you to execute such sentence within 24 hours of receipt of this warrant by judicial hanging and for so doing this shall be sufficient warrant. . . .
    (Signed) L. H. Cox, Maj-General
    G.O.C. [General Officer Commanding]

SINGAPORE DISTRICT
DATE: 13th March 1946[20]

≈

My father beat two POWs to death, and for that he was hanged
on March 14, 1946, at Changi prison in Singapore.

—*Osamu Komai, letter posted to the online forum*
US-Japan Dialogue on POWs, January 23, 2005

Osamu Komai learned the details of his father's case well after the fact, in 1953. His mother had just died, at age forty-eight. Osamu was sixteen at the time, and still in high school. There had been whispers about what had happened: neighborhood murmurings that Osamu was the son of a war criminal; a remark from his uncle, cut short by his mother, that Mitsuo had been executed.[21] But the topic was out of bounds, not to be mentioned by Osamu or anyone else in the Komai household.

"I had heard stories from people around me," Osamu told me. "But after my mother died, we were going through her belongings and we found newspaper articles she had kept, articles about the execution and about my father being a war criminal. That's when I formally found out."

"How did you react when you found out?" I asked. "What effect did that knowledge have on your own life?"

"I wanted to become distant from my father. I wanted to forget about him. I got really depressed. There was a stigma around the words war criminal. I didn't like it at all."

"You've talked to me about how people who knew your father described him as a kind, gentle man who wouldn't hurt a bug. You've talked about how your father would give your mother books of poetry, that your father was a romantic. So what happened? What caused him to behave the way he did at Kanchanaburi?"

Osamu must have considered that question before, but its broaching appeared to have startled him. He paused to formulate an answer, then bit his lower lip.

"It was that place," he said. He bit his lower lip again. "The Kanchanaburi concentration camp. My father was very fluent in English so he was able to communicate with the officers, including the ones who died. He probably had befriended them before it all happened. Later on, I learned that my father had told one of his friends that he felt betrayed by the radio business."

"Just to be clear, you're saying that your father had a relationship in English with these POWs and felt betrayed by the fact that the POWs were building and using a radio behind his back?"

"Yes," Osamu said. "Soldiers have told me that spying activities during wartime is the worst thing you can do. So it couldn't be helped that the POWs were killed."

This time, I paused to consider my next question.

"Osamu-san, did you hate your father for what he did?"

"It's not that I didn't like my father. It was the war criminal issue that I was really sick and tired of. I kept on thinking, why was my father accused of being a war criminal? Was it really for things he did, or was it some kind of retribution? I thought maybe he was innocent. So I started looking into it and found out it was all true. When I actually tracked down the trial documents, I saw the names of the people he killed. And Mr. Lomax's name was there. So I thought that I really wanted to apologize to Mr. Lomax on behalf of my father. I wanted to apologize for my father having broken Mr. Lomax's arms. When I found out that Mr. Lomax was still alive, I had to go see him. And that is what happened in 2007."

≈

Eric Lomax, the young British lieutenant who had been so brutally treated in Kanchanaburi, survived the war and eventually returned to the United Kingdom. He studied personnel management in his native Scotland and taught at a university there. The passage of time did little to diminish the trauma of his wartime experiences. After retiring in 1982, Lomax set out to find the man he considered to be his chief tormenter at Kanchanaburi, an interpreter named Takashi Nagase. Even though Mitsuo Komai spoke English, Nagase, a more skilled linguist, was brought in to assist with the POW interrogations and punishments. In a memoir called *The*

Railway Man, Lomax wrote there was "no single dominant figure" from Kanchanaburi "on whom I could focus my general hatred, but because of his command of my language, the interpreter was the link; he was centre-stage in my memories; he was my private obsession."[22]

Lomax described Nagase as "the hateful 'American' interpreter who had supervised the beatings."[23] For Lomax, Nagase was the omnipresent face of Japanese brutality. Matsuo Komai was the director, pulling the strings behind the scenes.

Lomax eventually met with the interpreter Nagase. "The need to know is powerful," he wrote.[24] The encounter took place in 1993, in Kanchanaburi, on a terrace beneath a large, smiling Buddha statue, next to the River Kwai railway museum.

"I had forgotten how small he was, a tiny man," Lomax later recalled.[25] Nagase came to the meeting in "an elegant straw hat, loose kimono-like jacket and trousers. From a distance he resembled an oriental carving, some benign wizened demon come to life."

The interpreter approached the former prisoner. "He began a formal bow," Lomax said, "his face working and agitated, the small figure barely reaching my shoulder. I stepped forward, took his hand and said '*Ohayo go-zaimasu, Nagase san, ogenki desu ka?*' 'Good morning, Mr. Nagase, how are you?' He looked up at me; he was trembling, in tears, saying over and over 'I am very, very sorry.'"

Lomax saw that Nagase was filled with guilt, remorse, and humility. Improbably, the former enemies reconciled.

In his memoir (which was made into a movie), Lomax quoted Nagase at length. Nagase blamed Mitsuo Komai for Lomax's harsh labor camp treatment. It was Komai, according to Nagase, who had ordered the beatings. Nagase told Lomax that Komai had relatives who had survived the war: "I know his son lives in the north of Japan, having dishonour."[26]

Nagase, acting as an intermediary, later facilitated Osamu Komai's meeting with Eric Lomax. Osamu had written to Nagase requesting help with organizing the encounter. On June 30, 2007, Komai visited Lomax at his home in Berwick-upon-Tweed, England. At the time, Lomax was eighty-eight. Komai was seventy.

"I inquired very carefully whether Mr. Osamu Komai was aware that I was probably responsible almost single handedly for his father's arrest, conviction and execution," Lomax told Berwick journalist Nan MacFarlane, referring to war trial testimony against Mitsuo Komai. "I was assured that he knew." According to MacFarlane, Lomax also knew that Osamu's willingness to apologize for the sins of his father was "an extraordinary gesture."

"Apparently it is the equivalent of offering me his soul," Lomax said.[27]

When Osamu Komai finally met Eric Lomax, the war criminal's son was anxious and contrite. "I didn't know what to say to him," Osamu told me. "So he greeted me and told me, many times, thank you for traveling such a distance."

"What did you talk about?" I asked.

"In the beginning," Osamu recalled, "Mr. Lomax looked me in the face and didn't say a word. Then he said, 'You look exactly like him, like your father.' Then he asked if there were any questions I would like to ask about my father. He said he would answer as much as possible. When he said that to me, I was speechless. I had tears in my eyes."

"Did you ask him about your father?"

"I couldn't ask him anything. I didn't know what to say. So Mr. Lomax asked me what my father used to do in Japan, before the war. I told him he was a businessman. And interestingly enough, Mr. Lomax asked me if I knew anything about how the Japanese found out that the POWs had built a radio. He thought one of the POWs was an informer. But of course, I didn't know."

"I want to get a sense of why you felt the need to apologize to Mr. Lomax," I said. "Did you feel that you personally were somehow responsible for what your father did?"

"I think it probably has to do with the Japanese mentality," Osamu said. "What my father did, or something that I did, or something that my children might do, it is the same as if I had done it."

"After you apologized to Mr. Lomax, did you feel like a heavy burden had been lifted off your shoulders?" I asked.

"Yes. Absolutely. Although there was criticism here in Japan. Many people, former soldiers, said: 'Why do you have to go there and express regret. It was wartime. The responsibility was fifty-fifty. It's not your fault.' But I wanted to go and apologize. And I felt that I was forgiven."

Osamu Komai's meeting with Eric Lomax was an extraordinary act of atonement. It was not a onetime thing, however. Osamu devoted his senior years to learning as much as he could about his father; and he wore that apology to Eric Lomax like a badge of honor, explaining publicly, to anyone interested, that a son's repentance for the wartime immorality of his father was the honorable thing to do.

Osamu visited Changi Prison in Singapore, where his father was executed. He traveled to Kanchanaburi, where he and his wife "embarked on a memorial tour riding on the Thai-Burma railway."[28] He spoke to Japanese war veterans and their families. He made multiple pilgrimages to the Yokohama War Cemetery, a memorial and burial ground for some fifteen hundred British and Australian soldiers who had died in Japan as POWs. And he hosted the son of an American POW who had been imprisoned in Japan during the war.[29]

At the conclusion of their meeting, Eric Lomax gave Osamu Komai a memento. It was a fine art greeting card, hand addressed "to Mr. Osamu Komai," with an idyllic image on the front of smiling children at play. Inside, Lomax wrote some words from Henry Wadsworth Longfellow, the American poet.

"Look not mournfully on the past," the message said, "it will not come again; Wisely improve the present, it is thine; Go forth to meet the Shadowy future, without fear."[30]

Osamu Komai gave me a photocopy of that postcard, punctuating the end of our interview. But as I was preparing to leave, he offered up a final thought.

"Lomax invited me into his house," Komai said. It was a gesture Osamu took as an act of absolution. But Osamu, disheartened, told me he never actually heard the words he so desperately wanted Lomax to say: "I forgive you."

20

Repentance and Apology

The Wartime Emperor's Son

Hirohito, the emperor who led Japan through World War II, was never tried as a war criminal. The United States kept him out of the prisoner's dock and far from the hangman's noose. Washington figured the stability of Japan's postwar recovery, and America's interest, was better served with Hirohito (whom the Japanese worshipped and idolized) on the throne as a "symbol" of the nation, a defanged figurehead, constitutionally barred from engaging in politics. The emperor's powers, once supreme, would become almost entirely ceremonial in postwar Japan.[1]

Hirohito, who reigned until his death in 1989, was spared the fate of Mitsuo Komai, who died in 1946 at the end of a rope. But Hirohito, like Mitsuo, was a father. The emperor's son Akihito was born in 1933 and experienced the war as a child, much as Mitsuo's son, Osamu, did. While Osamu's father was branded a war criminal and Akihito's was not, both sons reckoned with what their fathers had done during the war and grappled with how to digest the consequences. Osamu Komai did so modestly, mostly unseen. Akihito, who succeeded Hirohito as emperor of Japan, was a public figure on a much larger stage. The questions he faced were easily posed but difficult to answer: whether and how to address the legacy of his father's wartime behavior; whether and how to make amends for his country's transgressions. Akihito's responses as emperor carried high stakes, for they affected Japan's foreign relations and the royal family's standing at home. His reckoning would be carefully choreographed by the palace and government officials, and each step would be scrutinized along the way, both inside Japan and abroad.

≈

General Douglas MacArthur, supreme commander for the Allied powers in postwar Japan, engineered Hirohito's immunity from prosecution for war crimes. A legal brief prepared by one of his aides set out the broad rationale: saving Hirohito would promote the "peaceful occupation and rehabilitation of Japan," and, with the Soviet Union turned adversary from ally, a stable Japan would foster the "prevention of revolution and communism."[2]

On January 25, 1946, MacArthur dispatched a "secret and priority" telegram to General Dwight D. Eisenhower, then US Army chief of staff. MacArthur claimed that "no specific and tangible evidence" had been uncovered connecting Hirohito "with political decisions of the Japanese Empire during the last decade." Hirohito's wartime role, MacArthur argued, "was largely ministerial and automatically responsive to the advice of his counsellors."

"His indictment will unquestionably cause a tremendous convulsion among the Japanese people, the repercussions of which cannot be overestimated," MacArthur added. "He is a symbol which unites all Japanese. Destroy him and the nation will disintegrate."[3]

MacArthur's insistence that Hirohito was a passive leader manipulated into war by others (the victim of an "overthrow from below" as Hirohito himself once put it) was controversial, and despite contrary evidence, the claim endured for many postwar years.[4] Writing in August 2000 in the *New York Times*, journalist and Japan expert Patrick Smith observed: "Scholars on both sides of the Pacific have long asserted that this version of events was a politically motivated concoction. But the orthodoxy has proved impervious. In Japanese and American schools alike, students still read of the indecisive fellow who preferred marine biology to politics and knew little of the world beyond his palace grounds."[5]

That same year, Harvard University historian Herbert P. Bix published

Hirohito and the Making of Modern Japan, a groundbreaking, Pulitzer Prize–winning study that convincingly debunked the notion of emperor as docile figurehead.[6] That interpretation of history, Bix argued, was sugarcoated nonsense.

Hirohito exercised "real power and authority independent of governments and the bureaucracy" and was "the leading participant in, and remains a key to understanding, the major political and military events of his nation in the twentieth century," Bix wrote. "During the last year of the war, Hirohito continued to exercise a direct, sometimes controlling, influence on military operations and to project his mythic presence into Pacific battles."[7]

"Hirohito was never a puppet," Bix said, in a 2014 article summarizing his research findings. Bix showed that Hirohito, from the start of his rule in 1926, was a dynamic, active, but conflicted monarch who operated behind the scenes, allowing his advisers "to later insist that he had acted only in accordance with their advice." Hirohito was behind Japan's efforts to build a colonial empire, Bix wrote. He "failed to prevent his army from invading Manchuria in 1931" and "sanctioned the full-scale invasion of China in 1937, which moved Japan into a state of total war." He "exercised close control over the use of chemical weapons in China and sanctioned the attack on Pearl Harbor in 1941. Even after the war, when a new, American-modeled Constitution deprived him of sovereignty, he continued to meddle in politics."[8]

"The official line that Hirohito only with tremendous unwillingness went along with plans for war and the war itself is just not true," affirmed Kenneth Ruoff, an American historian specializing in Japan's monarchy. "Even so, there was a massive campaign after the war to claim that Hirohito had always been a pacifist. And to a considerable extent, his son Akihito reinforced that when he had the chance."[9]

Hirohito died on January 7, 1989, at the age of eighty-seven, after suffering from intestinal cancer.[10] He had ruled for sixty-two years. He was, as a *New York Times* obituary headline put it, "A Leader Who Took Japan to War, to Surrender, and Finally to Peace."[11] Of the three leadership roles, it was the last, the monarch who presided over Japan's warless postwar recovery, that Hirohito, Akihito, and Japan clung to the most. Indeed, Hirohito's regime (despite the war) had formally been called the reign of Showa, which means "Enlightened Peace," and inasmuch as Japanese emperors are posthumously named after their eras, Hirohito, in death, formally and forever became known as Emperor Showa.[12]

Hours after his father died, Akihito signed a decree that perpetuated the peace motif. The new imperial era, he said, would officially be labeled Heisei, which means "Achieving Peace."[13] By the time he voluntarily abdicated in 2019 due to advanced age (he was eighty-five) and declining health, Akihito, turned emperor emeritus, had transformed the aim of "achieving peace" into something tangible, and had helped Japan reflect on the war years and heal.

≈

World War II was always there during the three decades Akihito sat on the Chrysanthemum Throne.[14] Its memories lurked in the back of Japan's collective mind; and for Emperor Akihito, its history never really faded.

When he turned eighty in 2013, Akihito was asked which events had shaped his life. "I would say that what stands out most in my mind is the Second World War."[15]

"The Emperor Emeritus was a child during the war and he saw large parts of Tokyo reduced to ashes," wrote Hashiguchi Kazuhito, imperial family correspondent for NHK, Japan's national broadcasting company. As an adult, Kazuhito said, Akihito wanted to confront Japan's wartime history. "His former aides say this firsthand experience of war was a large reason for his commitment to the cause during his reign."[16]

With words and actions and a gentle manner, Akihito repeatedly spoke to the war's legacy during his tenure on the throne, explaining how he thought it should be remembered and urging younger generations never to forget. In appearances at his annual birthday celebration and at memorial commemorations, Akihito offered contrite remarks "reflecting" on the past with "feelings of deep remorse over the last war."[17] Akihito also traveled widely on peace and reconciliation visits to nations and territories his father's army had assaulted, occupied, exploited, and victimized.

"So much of his reign was devoted to trying to console the people vic-timized by that war, both in Japan and outside of Japan," said Ruoff. "It's important to remember how much time he spent making the rounds and talking to them firsthand."

Among Akihito's destinations were China and the Philippines. Each country had suffered appallingly as a result of Japanese occupation. Max Hastings, the World War II historian, has written that "China's people paid a vastly more terrible price" than any other nation fighting Japan.[18] "All estimates are unreliable," Hastings said, "but it seems reasonable to accept the figure of 15 million Chinese wartime dead as a direct conse-quence of Japanese military action, starvation or plagues, some of these deliberately fostered by biological warfare specialists of the Japanese ar-my's Unit 731." Hastings put the estimated number of Filipino deaths at about one million. By comparison, Japan's losses by war's end "were esti-mated at 2.69 million dead, 1.74 million of these military."[19]

In Beijing and in Manila, Akihito acknowledged his country's past ag-gression: visiting China in 1992, he expressed "deep sadness" for the "great suffering" Japan had inflicted; and in a subsequent trip to the Philippines, he remembered "fierce battles" between Japan and the United States that resulted in the loss of innocent Filipino lives, "something we Japanese must never forget and we intend to keep engraved in our hearts."[20]

Accompanied by his wife, the Empress Michiko, Akihito also trekked to some of the war's most horrific and iconic battlegrounds, where thou-sands of soldiers and civilians had perished: Iwo Jima, Saipan, Peleliu, and also Okinawa, which they visited multiple times.[21] The excursions pro-duced striking photographic images of the two royals bowing in silent prayer toward jagged cliffs and ocean waters where combatants once fell.[22] The imperial couple also wrote poetry during these island tours, verses that mused on the past and showed that for Akihito and Michiko, these visits were personal, not the usual diplomatic show-and-tell.

> Water now fills, so calmly,
> The stone basin to the brim
> At this memorial site,

How you, who died in the war,
Must have thirsted for water then.

—Michiko, 1994, on Iwo Jima

At Saipan
An old man who had fought there,
Just as it had been,
Lying down on the sea-shore
Told us the whole sad story.

—Akihito, 2005, on Saipan

The imperial verse was thoughtful and eloquent, meant to console the souls of the fallen.[23] But Akihito's travels, ostensibly ceremonial, had a double edge, and their intent, never explicitly voiced, was political.

"Throughout his reign he gave the impression of doing all he could to unsettle complacent and forgetful attitudes to the war, and to discomfort those on the right who regarded [the war] as a just and heroic undertaking," wrote Richard Lloyd Parry, a correspondent and Asia expert at the *Times of London.* "Not even the most rabid militarist could have objected to his purpose: to offer prayers of 'consolation' to the dead of all sides. In practice though, the effect of such visits and the media coverage they attracted was to remind Japanese of the butchery and waste that characterized the last year of the war."[24]

≈

Osamu Komai, the son of Kanchanaburi war criminal Mitsuo Komai, confronted his father's war guilt unhesitatingly: he probed the historical record in search of the facts; he admitted, first to himself and then to others, that his father, undeniably, had performed and supervised evil acts at the Thai prison camp on the River Kwai; he apologized unambiguously for his father's crimes, undertaking a long, wrenching journey of contrition to meet one of his father's victims.

The paternal motivations behind Akihito's actions were less straight-forward, and his desire to atone for his father's wartime stewardship less clear. Herbert Bix, the Hirohito biographer, wrote that Akihito apologized "only for the suffering caused by Japan's wartime past." "Akihito avoided any acknowledgment of his father's war guilt," Bix said.[25]

Historian Kenneth Ruoff agreed. "I think Akihito saw his reign as making amends for the fact that Japan had been an aggressive imperial-ist, but I don't think he saw his father as having been the most responsible agent here," he told me.

Akihito himself publicly addressed his father's culpability on one oc-casion in 2009, twenty years after Hirohito's death. "It is my perception that the events that led to war must have been contrary to what he would have wished," Akihito said.[26]

That rare statement, cautiously framed as a "perception," was nonethe-less exculpatory. Akihito's public judgment regarding his father's role in unleashing a long, painful, and costly war was not guilty.

It is difficult to gauge the connection between that assessment and the penitent reconciliation campaign Akihito undertook in the wake of Hirohito's death: whether an altruistic faith in Heisei (Achieving Peace) motivated the son; or whether something else, some moral belief (in the manner of Osamu Komai) that a son, even the son of a divine emperor, is responsible for his father's actions; or both.

"It's tricky," Ruoff said, when I asked him what motivated Akihito. "We may never know what he felt privately about his father, whether he felt that his father should have atoned more for the war. What is clear is that he did do all sorts of things which his father did not do."

≈

One of those actions involved Korea, a benchmark of any Japanese post-war reconciliation endeavor. Irrespective of motivation, an imperial gesture toward Korea produced what Ruoff described as Akihito's most significant act of contrition.

Japan's postwar relationship with Korea presented a Gordian knot of issues.

Japan had annexed Korea in 1910 and ruled it as a colony until 1945.[27] One Western journalist who lived in Korea at the time wrote that "the aim of the Japanese was nothing else than the entire absorption of the country and the destruction of every trace of Korean nationality."[28] Alongside this attempt at cultural eradication, the Imperial Army conscripted millions of Koreans as slave laborers, resulting in the deaths of tens of thousands.[29] Moreover, tens of thousands of Korean women (the so-called comfort women) were forced to work for the Japanese military as sex slaves in Korea, China, and other Japanese-controlled territories, as well as in Japan.[30]

The postwar relationship between Japan and Korea has been described as a feud dating back more than a hundred years.[31] In 2015, a Japanese ambassador to South Korea tactfully observed: "I cannot say that this journey has always been smooth sailing."[32]

In December 2001, Akihito issued a remarkable expression of regret for Japan's wrongdoing. He did so from a familiar platform: his annual birthday press conference at the Imperial Palace in Tokyo. The event that year was held in advance of the 2002 FIFA World Cup, which Japan was cohosting with South Korea, in Seoul.

Imperial press conferences are carefully scripted affairs befitting an ancient and chary monarchy well set in its ways and well shielded from the spontaneity of White House press gatherings or British media scrums. Nothing is left to chance. All questions are provided in advance, and well-considered answers are put down on paper for the emperor to read.[33]

One journalist (customarily unnamed) posed what the official Imperial Household Agency transcript described as question 3: "As the tournament draws ever nearer, exchange on a person-to-person level between the two countries is intensifying. Could Your Majesty tell us of any interests or thoughts you have concerning the Republic of Korea, which both historically and geographically is Japan's close neighbor?"[34]

It was an inquiry the emperor easily could have swatted away with a polite response devoid of significant content. Instead, Akihito swung hard and made news.

"I, on my part, feel a certain kinship with Korea," Akihito said, explaining that one of his eighth-century imperial ancestors was Korean.[35] The assertion made headlines in Seoul, and implicitly took aim at the myth, favored by some in Japan's Far Right, that Japanese, and the imperial line, are racially pure.[36] Akihito also said Korea "contributed greatly" to Japan's development, especially in culture and technology. This was "truly fortunate," he said. "It is regrettable however, that Japan's exchanges with Korea have not all been of this kind. This is something that we should never forget."

Akihito did not explicitly describe the terrible damage Japan had inflicted on Korea. But diplomacy is often a business of nuance and understatement, and Akihito's words of regret were significant nonetheless.

"I thought this was the single most important moment in the entire reign," Ruoff said. "It was the most moving and emotional. It was an incredible history lesson that took aim at all the myths that helped the Japanese justify their rule over Korea."[37]

Akihito was expected to travel to Seoul for the FIFA World Cup. He did not, however, and would never step foot on Korean soil. The Japanese government held Akihito back, worried an imperial visit to South Korea would trigger opposition and even protests inside that country. Bad feelings were still high, despite the passage of time. Akihito's conciliatory words could not fully dampen wartime memories, which still felt fresh; his gesture of "kinship" could not adequately minimize tensions between the two countries. The emperor's failure to attend the FIFA World Cup opening ceremony in Seoul was all the more striking because the Koreans had invited him to be there.[38]

≈

Did Akihito's years-long peace campaign make a difference? From a broad perspective, yes. He did not vanquish history, but with conciliatory words and actions—a kind of soft diplomacy—the emperor did help Japan, at least in part, mend relations with some of the countries it had harmed during World War II.

But Akihito played a supporting role here: residents of *kantei*, home of the Japanese prime minister and his cabinet, wrote the script. The emperor produced optics, not policy. He headed a "symbolic" monarchy.[39] Japanese ties with its wartime enemies ebbed and flowed, as ties between nations do, but they ebbed and flowed without regard to Akihito.[40]

Nor did the emperor's diplomacy silence militant nationalist voices at home, voices that chafe at well-intentioned World War II apologies. The Far Right has a certain "nostalgia for a golden age of the nation," as one scholar observed: it is prone to proliferate anti-Chinese and anti-Korean attitudes; it fully embraces the controversial Yasukuni Shrine, situated in the middle of Tokyo, where fallen soldiers, including war criminals, are honored; and it believes that Japanese wartime atrocities have been overblown.[41]

It is clear, however, that Akihito's reconciliation campaign went down well with most of the Japanese public. At the time of his abdication in 2019, the imperial family was more popular than at any time since the end of the war.[42] "Wildly popular," is how one leading Japanese news agency described Akihito and his wife.[43]

Akihito's genial bearing, modesty, and grace were hard not to like. The touchy issues of Hirohito's war guilt and of Akihito's failure to censure his father did not really resonate inside Japan. What did matter, and mattered most to Akihito, was historical memory. If Akihito's reign had a single, overarching theme, that would be it.

"I was 11 years old when the war ended," he said in December 2018, at his last birthday press conference before abdication. "I have believed it is important not to forget that countless lives were lost in World War II . . . and to pass on this history accurately to those born after the war."[44]

This was an entreaty Akihito repeatedly articulated to a Japanese public he feared was growing increasingly indifferent to the country's wartime past.[45] If Heisei—Achieving Peace—was the name of Akihito's era, his imperial mantra was "please do not forget."

Part 7

FLASHBACKS

On January 17, 1995, at 5:46 a.m., a violent earthquake hit Kobe, my wife's hometown. More than six thousand people died. Many thousands were injured.[1]

Her childhood home was unscathed, and her parents, who still lived there, escaped unharmed. But her grandmother Koh, who lived nearby in a single-story wooden structure, was killed when the building collapsed on top of her. She was ninety-six.

Koh made a living sewing kimonos, and the house was her work space. "I loved to stay in that place," my wife recalled. "It had a wonderful garden with different kinds of fruit trees, oranges and persimmons, and the house had a very distinct smell. There was one room filled with drawers and needles and threads and measures. My grandmother used to sit in the middle with her eyeglasses on, leaning over her work, and I sat next to her, looking on."

The house sat near the earthquake's fault line. Rescue workers had trouble extracting Koh's body. Afterward, some of her kimonos were found strewn and tattered in the rubble.

"My grandmother once gave me a summer kimono, which she made in that Kobe house," my wife recalled. "It was blue, and I still use it. I remember the first time I wore it. Grandmother had forgotten to take out a needle, and it pricked me when I put it on."

21

Tsunami

Flattened Landscapes

On Wednesday, March 16, 2011, Emperor Akihito, solemnly dressed in a dark double-breasted suit and shadow blue tie, entered a reception room at the Imperial Palace and sat down behind a desk, his face looking grim. Two microphones stood before him, one to his left and one to his right.[1] At the appointed moment, the emperor gave a slight bow, then stared at the television camera in front of him. He picked up a sheaf of paper with both hands, gathered his thoughts, and commenced to read.

So began the first nationally broadcast address by an emperor since Akihito's father, Hirohito, announced Japan's surrender in a radio speech to his nation on August 15, 1945. Men and women who were alive back then remember that event, not only for its somber content: it was the first time they had ever heard Hirohito's voice.[2] It was high pitched; Akihito's was measured, with a medium-high timbre.

"I am deeply saddened," Akihito said, "by the devastating situation in the areas hit by the Tohoku-Pacific Ocean Earthquake, an unprecedented 9.0-magnitude earthquake, which struck Japan on March 11. The number of casualties claimed by the quake and the ensuing tsunami continues to rise by the day, and we do not yet know how many people have lost their lives. I am praying that the safety of as many people as possible will be confirmed."

The emperor paused, drew a breath, and continued: "My other grave concern now is the serious and unpredictable condition of the affected nuclear power plant. I earnestly hope that through the all-out efforts of all those concerned, further deterioration of the situation will be averted."

The snow that fell in Onagawa, Japan, on the day of the tsunami was wet and intermittent, its flakes mixing with the wind and chilling rain. This small fishing village in the Tohuko region on the eastern coast of Japan's main island thought little of the foul weather. It was, after all, still late winter, the eleventh day of March. Plum blossoms were blooming elsewhere in Japan, but in Onagawa the cold season lingered, and on this day, which would be remembered as 3/11, the snow and the wind and the chilling rain were unwelcome and unpleasant, but not unforeseen.[3]

Nature delivered two unexpected blows in rapid succession: a giant earthquake and then the tsunami, monstrous in countenance and demeanor. Onagawa survived the first strike. The second, with wave heights nearing fifty feet, decimated the village.[4] By the time it was over, 75 percent of Onagawa's buildings were washed away; 827 people were killed (one out of every twelve of the town's 10,014 residents); and some 80 percent of the population was left homeless.[5] Emergency responders would never find the bodies of more than 250 of the dead.[6]

Some one hundred miles south of Onagawa, also on the Tohuko coast, stood the remains of the Fukushima Daiichi Nuclear Power Plant. The earthquake and tsunami had shaken, battered, then overwhelmed the facility, resulting in a nuclear meltdown, radiation release, and evacuation of many tens of thousands of people from surrounding areas.[7]

The "triple disaster" (earthquake, tsunami, and nuclear catastrophe) left up to twenty thousand people dead or missing nationwide.[8] The Japanese prime minister, Naoto Kan, called it the worst crisis since World War II.[9]

It was hard not to think of the war during those horrible March days. The release of radiation at Fukushima evoked memories of Hiroshima and Nagasaki. But it was the videos, the widely disseminated televised images of the tsunami flattening Onagawa and other coastal villages, that perhaps even more strongly conjured up wartime recollections.

The images filled Japanese television screens, transmitted first in real time via helicopters deployed by NHK, then over and over again in video replays.[10] Viewers across Japan watched with fascination and horror as tsunami waves, endlessly long and interminably large, bullied their way over coastal sea walls and then crashed, almost effortlessly, through homes, offices, stores, and other buildings in the way. Once on land, the advancing waters scooped up cars and trucks and concrete and earth and human beings who had failed to reach high ground. This accumulated mass, this tsunami plunder, turned the waters black, and those black waters rolled inland until they were spent. Then the waters retreated back to the sea, battering victimized towns and villages one more time along the way.

Hour after hour, TV viewers absorbed these horrific images in the tsunami's wake, the shattered corpses of towns and villages. Then, on March 12 and 14, more unsettling broadcast pictures came: explosions at the Fukushima nuclear plant.[11]

Devastated landscapes. Radioactive plumes. Taken aback and whiplashed, Japan, and especially its elderly, revisited World War II.

Testimonies to that effect were easy to find.

Eighty-two-year-old Keijiro Matsushima, a Hiroshima survivor: "It seemed as though the Japanese people were experiencing the third atomic bombing."[12]

Seventy-three-year-old Hisako Kimura, also a Hiroshima *hibakusha*: "Only concrete buildings are still standing in the ruins, just like Hiroshima after the atomic bombing."[13]

Eighty-five-year-old Otoko Wada from Kamaishi, a Tohoku coastal town shelled by the US Navy in 1945 and heavily damaged by the 3/11 tsunami: "The distressing scene was the same as at that time."[14]

Seventy-five-year-old Hirosato Wako, who had fled Natori, one of the most badly hit tsunami enclaves, an hour's ride down the coast from Onagawa: "I lived through the Sendai air raids," referring to Allied wartime attacks on Tohoku's most populous city, "but this is much worse."[15]

"For the elderly who live in the villages lining Japan's northeastern coast, it is a return to a past of privation that their children have never known," wrote Martin Fackler, then Tokyo bureau chief for the *New York Times*. Fackler visited Natori in the days after 3/11 and spoke to Hirosato Wako and others. "As in so much of the Japanese countryside, young people have largely fled, looking for work in the city. The elderly who remained are facing devastation and possible radiation contamination, a challenge equal only to the task this generation faced when its defeated, despairing nation had to rebuild from the rubble of the war."[16]

Amid this mass of sorrow came the televised, calming presence and reassuring words of seventy-seven-year-old Emperor Akihito. The emperor's speech was watched in Tohuko refugee centers and in Tokyo metro stations.[17]

"It is my heartfelt hope that the people will continue to work hand in hand, treating each other with compassion, in order to overcome these trying times," Akihito said. "It is my sincere hope that those who have been affected by the disaster will never give up hope and take good care of themselves as they live through the days ahead, and that each and every Japanese will continue to care for the afflicted areas and the people for years to come and, together with the afflicted, watch over and support their path to recovery."[18]

"It definitely seemed like an appropriate moment for an emperor to take to the air," historian Kenneth Ruoff told me. And Akihito, Ruoff said, "unquestionably would have known" that by speaking to Japan during a national emergency he was walking in his father's shoes, under very different conditions. For Japan's war generation, the echo of Hirohito's radio address and the wartime memories it stirred up were the unspoken backstory to Akihito's speech on the triple disaster. It was March 2011, but for many, especially the elderly, it was also 1945.

≈

On the day Akihito addressed the nation (five days after the tsunami) it was snowing again in Onagawa. The gnawing winter threw misery at the already miserable task of searching the rubble for survivors. Japanese soldiers had arrived on the scene to assist. One hundred thousand soldiers had been deployed to stricken coastal towns, the country's biggest mobilization since World War II.[19]

The Onagawa village landscape was horrendous and unearthly; conditions were onerous. Tossed by giant waves, a snow-dusted car teetered upside down on top of a three-story apartment building. A mangled two-story structure, its guts exposed, sat prostrate on a heap of wreckage. A blue-rimmed fishing boat, also tossed, lay precariously on its side, its bow pushed nose down into a crushed building, its stern propped up high on the edge of a wall of debris. Melting snow was used for portable toilets. As for the emperor's speech, one Onagawa survivor, Shigeo Suzuki, later told me: "I'm sorry, I don't know whether the emperor made a speech on TV or not. I was staying at the evacuation center at that time. There was no electricity and no TV."[20]

Left somewhere in the tsunami's muddy detritus was the framed photograph of a little girl dressed in a ceremonial kimono. She posed standing, her dark hair styled just so, her eyes fixed forward, the slightest hint of a smile on her lips. Sand, silt, and clay partially covered the photo, like clumps of dirt on a coffin.

"The picture just grabbed me," said photojournalist Motoya Nakamura. "I said oh my god, it is what the nation is experiencing. It is all here. The instant of March 11. All the happiness of the people is gone, washed away. It signified the whole event."[21]

Motoya Nakamura grew up in Nagoya, 160 miles southwest of Tokyo. He moved to the United States when he was twenty-six, determined to become a photojournalist. He succeeded, eventually landing a job with the *Oregonian*, Portland's daily newspaper. Three weeks after the 3/11 triple disaster, the paper sent Nakamura, then forty-eight, to Japan to cover the aftermath, along with a colleague, journalist Richard Read, who had worked and lived there as a correspondent.[22]

They made their way to Onagawa, where Nakamura found the little girl's picture in a school gymnasium that had survived 3/11 because it was located on high ground. The facility was being used as a shelter for displaced people; it also housed hundreds of other mud-caked photos, all ripped from homes by tsunami waters and scattered, like shrapnel, into

FIGURE 14. The Onagawa girl, dressed in a holiday kimono. The framed photograph of the little girl had been retrieved from detritus left by the March 11, 2011, tsunami, which destroyed much of Onagawa, a fishing village on the northeast coast of Japan's main island. Photojournalist Motoya Nakamura found the picture in an Onagawa gymnasium and photographed it during a reporting trip there in April of that year.
Courtesy of Nakamura and the *Oregonian*.

the debris. These orphaned pictures of once-happy mothers, fathers, children, and grandparents rested side by side on the gym floor, like so many bodies in a morgue, placed there by caretakers who hoped surviving family members might find them and bring them home, if they still had homes to bring them to.

"I encountered pictures like that everywhere," Nakamura told me. "They looked like unfound bodies, begging me to recognize them."

Instantly, Nakamura saw something familiar in the little girl's photograph, something that brought him back to his own childhood. The girl was celebrating a hugely popular Japanese holiday called Shichigosan, which means Seven-Five-Three. Each year in November, the holiday honors the happiness and good health of three- and seven-year-old girls, along with five-year-old boys. Parents customarily dress their children in traditional Japanese clothing, often marching them off to shrines and local photography studios to memorialize the occasion.[23]

"When I was little, there was a photo of me wearing a kimono, and wearing a plastic samurai sword, too," Nakamura said.

He found the little girl's photograph underneath a gymnasium table, sitting on top of a bed of old newspapers. "It still hadn't been cleaned," he said. "The light was hitting it in an eerie way. It caught my attention because of the light." He snapped a picture of the photo.

In an essay published in the *Oregonian*, Nakamura said the Shichigosan portrait of the little girl looked as if it had come from the bottom of the ocean. "The photo paper is curled, damaged by the water. Under the mud-covered glass, she poses for the camera to show her growth. Her posture shows pride. The mud on the frame glass over the picture obscures her subtle smile and makes her appear sad."[24]

"That kimono the little girl is wearing is symbolic of a rite of passage," Nakamura told me. "And that signified to me what Japan was going through, also a rite of passage, like World War II."

Nakamura's parents lived through the war. Their hometown, Nagoya, a municipality of 1.5 million, was bombed repeatedly in 1945. Forty percent of the city was destroyed.[25] Nakamura said his father never talked about the war. But his mother did. "I remember she mentioned that during an air raid, she, as a little girl, ran from one bunker to another, holding her two younger brothers' hands. She also remembers the chocolate that American GIs gave to them after the war. They didn't have much to eat during that period."

Nakamura is a father of two. His connection to the little girl in the photo, he said, felt personal. "Both as a parent of 7- and 10-year-old children and as a native Japanese who went through the same ceremony as a child," he wrote, "my heart is filled with deep sorrow, wondering what happened to her. Did she and her family make it? They might be safe living at a shelter somewhere, or. . . . Tears fill my eyes as I photograph the picture, praying for her and her family's lives."

The photograph was published in the *Oregonian*. That is where I first saw it. In November 2018, I emailed a digital copy to Shigeo Suzuki, the Onagawa survivor who hadn't seen Emperor Akihito's televised speech. Suzuki showed the photo of the little girl to Tadashi Abe, an Onagawa town hall worker who looked after unclaimed tsunami family photographs. "More than ten thousand of them were found," Abe said. "I clean the pictures and scan them."[26]

Tadashi Abe showed the photo around, and his boss recognized the girl. "It's a small town," Abe noted. "Everybody knows everybody."

The little girl in the photo was Masako Abe (no relation to Tadashi).

When the tsunami came, Masako was not in Onagawa. Then eighteen, she had traveled to Ishinomaki, nine miles down the Tohoku coast, to attend a driving school. "It was my first day on the road," she said. "I was literally just leaving the school to go for a ride with my instructor, but I had forgotten something and had to return to the school to look for it. That's when the earthquake hit. If I hadn't forgotten it, we would have been heading for the road where the tsunami was coming. I was told that it was a close call."[27]

Masako survived the tsunami uninjured, but in Ishinomaki the waters destroyed more than fifty thousand homes and killed more than three thousand people.[28] It took Masako five days to get back to Onagawa. "We didn't have any means to communicate, so my mother and brother thought I had died."

The tsunami wrecked Masako Abe's house in Onagawa. Her parents and two older brothers were away at work when the waves hit. Her mother and brothers survived, but her father did not.

"He was a truck driver," Masako said. "He had driven the truck to the shelter at the Onagawa gymnasium after the earthquake, but when he realized that an elderly lady who had once looked after him wasn't in the gym, he got in his truck and went out to look for her. The tsunami came and swept him away when he was going to her house. My mother would later say things like, 'Why did he have to go save the lady?' But I think it's fine because it's just the kind of thing he would do. That is the person he was."

Before 3/11, the Shichigosan photograph hung on the living room wall of the Abe household, next to a certificate of commendation Masako had received in elementary school for not having any cavities. "In Onagawa, you get awarded for that," she said.

"I was three years old when the photo was taken," she recalled. "I had my picture shot at a studio, and afterward we went to show the Shichigosan photo to my father's grandfather, who was in the hospital. I was still wearing my kimono, and the head nurse wanted to show me off. I remember going around the rooms of the hospital one by one. I received a lot of pocket money and sweets."

It was an agreeable and reassuring recollection that bumped up hard against subsequent events. "More than half of my relatives died in the tsunami," Masako said: her father, maternal grandparents, aunts, and uncles, all elderly; and all had lived through World War II.

"Everyone who had experienced the war has passed away," Masako added. "There's no one left to talk about such things."

In Onagawa and elsewhere along the Tohoku coast, it was the elderly who were especially hard hit by 3/11. According to the Cabinet Office of the Government of Japan, in the entire affected Tohoku region (which includes Miyagi, Iwate, and Fukushima Prefectures) 46.5 percent of total deaths were people seventy years or older. This represented the largest single cohort of all 3/11 casualties.[29] This was Japan's war generation, people who had lived through the conflict and remembered what it was like. The tsunami silenced those memories. Thousands of Tohoku grandfathers

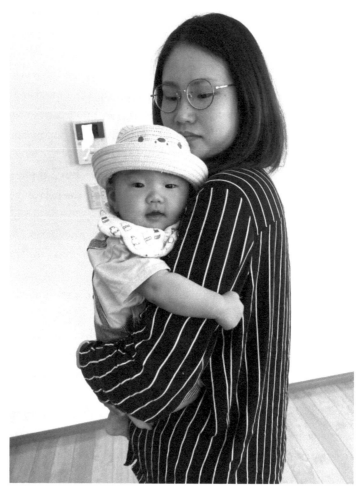

FIGURE 15. Masako Abe, age twenty-nine, with Shin, one of her two children, in Onagawa. November 2021. Courtesy of Masako Abe.

and grandmothers and elderly aunts and uncles could no longer pass down their stories, if they were inclined to do so. As Masako Abe put it, after the triple disaster there were far fewer men and women around to talk about such things.

22

Meltdown

Radiation Refugees

Kenichi Arita, a sixty-one-year-old medical doctor, was a cancer specialist at the Red Cross and Atomic Survivors Hospital in Hiroshima on 3/11. He treated men and women who had lived through the atomic blast, including his ninety-four-year-old father, Yoshiyuki.

"He has these pieces of glass under his skin," Arita said. "He was indoors when the A-bomb exploded, and the glass fragments were blown into his body. They are interesting. They move around sometimes and come to the surface. I remember when I was a small boy, I used to pick them out. My father can barely move now, but he's doing okay."

I spoke with Arita one month after 3/11.[1] He had just returned from Fukushima City, where he had gone to treat some of the thousands of people who had fled the area around the Fukushima Daiichi Nuclear Power Plant, some fifty miles away.

Four weeks earlier, on the afternoon of March 11, Arita was at work in the hospital. "The actual earthquake happened at 2:46 p.m.," he recalled with precision. It was barely perceptible in Hiroshima.[2] Word of the catastrophe, and of the seismic shake time, spread via the media.

"I was examining patients in my office. Other patients were waiting outside in a reception area. There were TV sets there for people to look at. Suddenly I heard a huge stir. I was surprised and wondered what was going on, so I went out and saw all these people in front of the TV, watching videos of the tsunami eating up these little towns on the coast. I realized that something extremely terrible had taken place. I didn't learn about the Fukushima accident until that evening, when I got home and turned on the news."

Within days, Arita had decided to go to Fukushima to care for evacuees. He also went there for a more nuanced objective: to counter unfounded speculation that they were radiation contagious.

"What started to happen was similar to the situation in Hiroshima after the A-bomb," he told me. "People in Fukushima and elsewhere were saying things like 'if you touch someone who has evacuated from near the nuclear plants, you too can catch radiation.' The TV news was even reporting this. For us here in Hiroshima, we know this is nonsense. But rumors like that are harmful. So I thought that I needed to go in there to see the evacuees and to assess their circumstances in a calm manner."

The Fukushima evacuees he examined would come to be known as the "new *hibakusha*."[3] They were a twenty-first-century group of radiation-distressed people whose lives were upended by an earthquake and tsunami; by a questionably constructed and managed nuclear plant; and by what an independent investigatory commission later concluded was "a profoundly man-made disaster that could and should have been foreseen and prevented."[4]

≈

For the original *hibakusha*, like Arita's father, the events of March 11, 2011, incited the past with a potency unlike anything they had experienced since the war. The televised images of tsunami-wrecked towns and villages, so reminiscent of the postatomic landscapes of their youth, were bad enough; the Fukushima nuclear meltdown and the release of radiation made it worse. There was, among A-bomb survivors and others of their generation, a feeling, unique to them, that the awful history they had experienced during the war was repeating itself.

It felt like a betrayal. "The explosions in those nuclear reactors are a disaster caused by technology growing into a monster that human beings can no longer control," said Kyoko Hayashi, a Nagasaki *hibakusha* and winner of numerous Japanese literary awards.[5] "It is as if we, the atomic bomb survivors, did not exist. It is as if the experiences of the atomic bomb survivors have never counted for anything."[6]

"Madness," is what Kenzaburo Oe, the 1994 Nobel laureate in literature, called the Fukushima crisis. Oe, who was ten years old when the war ended, wrote: "This disaster unites, in a dramatic way, two phenomena: Japan's vulnerability to earthquakes and the risk presented by nuclear energy. The first is a reality that this country has had to face since the dawn of time. The second, which may turn out to be even more catastrophic than the earthquake and the tsunami, is the work of man. What did Japan learn from the tragedy of Hiroshima?"[7]

Kyoko Hayashi and Kenzaburo Oe did what well-known authors often do in the face of tragedy: they tried (from a safe distance) to articulate and communicate, in writing, what it all meant. For the elderly of their generation directly affected by 3/11, there was scant possibility to reflect with pen on paper. Their concerns were visceral and more immediate. Within hours, the triple disaster had ended the lives of thousands and upended the lives of thousands of others, many of whom became displaced persons: 3/11 turned surviving victims, the old and the young, into refugees. Their homes no longer existed, and for some, an invisible shroud of radiation loomed over the horizon, posing unknown peril. They had to flee. For the younger among them, it was hard, but it was even harder for the elderly, whose bodies were less capable of bearing the physical burdens and whose minds grappled with a horrifying sense of déjà vu.

The triple disaster necessitated the evacuation of an estimated 185,000 people.[8] Multiple studies in the 3/11 aftermath have found, not unexpectedly, that evacuees suffered severe and often long-lasting psychological distress, and that psychological distress increased with age.[9] One study sketched a disturbing picture of the stressors some elderly Fukushima evacuees encountered:

> Evacuation of the inpatients and elderly residents of nursing care facilities was hurriedly carried out by buses shortly after the accident. No medical personnel accompanied the evacuees, who were laid down on the seats of the jam-packed buses with full protective

suits on. No medical care, even food or water, was provided for many hours during the evacuation. As a result, scores of patients died in an evacuation that was supposedly intended to minimize radiation exposure. The life-threatening risk to these people was not radiation, but discontinuation of daily medical care. A recent study indicated that the severe health risk associated with the rapid evacuation of elderly residents from nursing care facilities after the Fukushima accident was 30 times higher than the radiation risk.[10]

Andrew Buncombe, a British journalist, reported from tsunami-ravaged towns following 3/11. He spoke with elderly evacuees and found a surplus of anxiety and confusion. "In the days after the tsunami," Buncombe wrote, "older people have struggled. Countless thousands have been left homeless and forced to sleep in hastily established evacuation centers in schools and gymnasiums, eating whatever food is available and hoping they do not become ill. As temperatures plunge to around freezing at night, all they can do is to wrap themselves in blankets."[11] "It's more terrifying than wartime," said a one-hundred-year-old man, a dementia patient who was forced to relocate multiple times from the Fukushima exclusion zone."[12]

In 2012, less than a year after the nuclear meltdown, the "Fukushima Health Management Survey," overseen by Fukushima Prefecture's Medical University, was administered to approximately 40 percent of all evacuees. At issue was severe psychological distress. The elderly (over age sixty-five) made up nearly one-third of those surveyed. The study concluded that acute mental anguish "was markedly high, at 14.6 %," nearly five times greater than normal.[13] Another study examined suicides. It found that for some who had experienced World War II, the trauma of 3/11 was too much to bear: suicides and attempted suicides among all Fukushima evacuees older than seventy had increased strikingly, especially among males, following the triple disaster.[14]

≈

That was the psychological state of play when Dr. Arita arrived in Fukushima City, three weeks after the earthquake and tsunami. He had traveled with a radiation technical expert and a handful of dosimeters to measure radiation levels. They set up shop at an evacuation center housing twelve hundred evacuees.

Fukushima City was well outside the disaster site's twelve-mile-radius evacuation zone.[15] But people were on edge: The crippled nuclear complex was still releasing harmful amounts of radiation, and Tokyo Electric, the plant's operator, was dumping highly radioactive water into the ocean.[16]

At the evacuation site, Arita was hard to miss. He wore a red cap with a Red Cross logo, a bright red shirt, white pants, and a black-and-orange-striped emergency field jacket. He resembled a human emergency beacon. When evacuees saw him, they knew he was there to help.

"There were a lot of elderly people there," he later told me. "They only had what they were wearing on their backs. It was very crowded, and people had to sleep quite close to one another. They were in an incredibly fatigued state. Some were not feeling well. Some were anxious. But most were basically healthy."

Arita walked around the evacuation center chatting with people, with dosimeter in hand. "They were worried," he said. "On the walls they had left messages saying 'have you seen so and so? If yes, please call this number.' The same kind of thing happened in Hiroshima after the A-bomb.[17] And they were asking me when can they go home, what is happening outside, how long will the situation last? They also wanted to know what the current radiation dose was. We found that levels of radiation were really not different from what most of us are usually exposed to. I didn't notice a single person who had radiation damage at that time. I did not, however, have the opportunity to examine people who actually had been working inside the damaged nuclear plants."[18]

"Did you tell evacuees you were from Hiroshima and that your father was an A-bomb survivor?" I asked.

"Yes, I did. In fact, I actually used this as a way to encourage people, telling them that the situation there was not as bad as what Hiroshima went through, so don't get discouraged."

≈

Iitate, population six thousand, was located twenty miles east of Fukushima City and twenty-eight miles upwind from the Fukushima Daiichi Nuclear Power Plant. The village was outside the initially imposed disaster evacuation area. In the days after 3/11, Japanese authorities did not order residents to flee, thinking radiation did not pose a threat. A shift in wind direction changed that calculus, but by the time the evacuation order came, a month had passed and residents had been living in a fog of radioactive particles.[19]

"The first thing that came to mind was the atomic bombing of Hiroshima," Iitate native and evacuee Kenta Sato said. Twenty-nine years old on 3/11, he had lived in Iitate with his father and elderly grandmother. He had watched the Fukushima Daiichi crisis unfold on Japanese TV, and was shaken by images of the hydrogen explosions caused by the meltdown. "I immediately put on a mask," he said.[20]

Sato grew up reading *Barefoot Gen*, an iconic Japanese comic series first published in the 1970s that conveyed the Hiroshima bombing's impact on survivors.[21] "It left a great impression on me," Sato said. "In *Barefoot Gen*, the blast from the A-bomb melted people's skin. I wondered if the nuclear plant explosions were going to cause the same kind of injuries. I had a strong unarticulated anxiety about the symptoms of acute radiation exposure, such as skin being damaged, hair falling out, and so on. I guess that's when I started to have a sense of crisis and started taking action."

Sato became an advocate for Iitate residents. He borrowed a dosimeter from a professor at a nearby university and traveled around the region, recording locations with abnormally high radiation readings. "I also wanted to know what would happen in the future, in the second and third years after the nuclear accident, and what we could do about it," Sato said. "So I went to Hiroshima to learn more."

Akiko Matsumoto, a Hiroshima *hibakusha*, had read about Kenta Sato's visit in a local newspaper. She sent him a letter.

"When I saw the accident at the Fukushima nuclear power plant, I saw it in relation to my own life," she wrote.[22] "People forget things easily," she told Sato. "The people of Fukushima will forget what happened on March 11. That is why it is important to write down everything that has happened since that time, no matter how small it may seem to you."

Matsumoto said detailed record keeping would help Fukushima residents justify compensation claims for any injuries caused by the nuclear catastrophe. She said Hiroshima survivors had to present comprehensive information in order to qualify for medical care and other benefits.

Matsumoto and Kenta Sato eventually met in person. "She taught me the importance of keeping a record of your own life, and she told me that even though she was exposed to radiation she was still alive and has been well," Sato said. "She became my mentor. She was my connection to that generation and those times. We shared the same kind of anxieties, and I think she helped me believe that my life will turn out okay."

Sato would return to Iitate, where, after evacuation restrictions were eased in 2017, he joined the village council. He became known as a solar energy advocate.[23] No More Nukes was his manifesto. The nuclear catastrophe at Fukushima Daiichi, which painted his town with radiation, had made atomic power plants in Japan unviable, at least for the short term.[24] It also had sucked the life out of Iitate: its population in 2020 was one-fifth the size it had been on 3/11.[25]

≈

Like Akiko Matsumoto and Dr. Arita, others from Hiroshima and Nagasaki reached out to people affected by the Fukushima nuclear accident. A group of concerned citizens in Hiroshima sent locally produced miso and pickled plums to consumers in Fukushima Prefecture who worried that radiation had tainted their produce.[26] A nurse from Nagasaki University packed up her belongings and moved permanently to Kawauchi Village, about twenty miles west of the Fukushima plant, to provide health radiation advice.[27] Numerous other private citizen volunteers traveled to Fukushima to assist with decontamination and debris removal as well as the provision of relief supplies. At the governmental level, Hiroshima Prefecture officials established an aid corridor to the Fukushima region, an effort that in purpose, size, and largesse resembled something of a twenty-first-century Berlin Airlift. According to data compiled by the newspaper *Chugoku Shimbun*, Hiroshima University, a national institution, dispatched 1,180 medical specialists and scientists to supervise health checks and locate radiation hot spots. More than 900 police officers from Hiroshima Prefecture carried out road inspections, organized traffic control, and measured radiation. Some 80 technical experts were sent to support civil engineering and construction. And more than 500 Hiroshima-based military personnel went to Fukushima to construct bathing facilities, deliver relief supplies, and monitor irradiated areas.[28]

Among the most notable visitors to Fukushima was Masamoto Nasu, a Hiroshima survivor and one of Japan's best-known children's authors. He had written a book titled *Children of the Paper Crane: The Story of Sadako Sasaki and Her Struggle with the A-Bomb Disease.*[29] In July 2011, Nasu met with elementary school students in a town called Yabuki, situated about fifty miles west of the Fukushima Daiichi nuclear plant. Their school was preparing to remove topsoil from its playground because radiation had been detected there. Nasu spoke out against harmful rumors and misleading information regarding radiation exposure. "I hope you will not be irrationally afraid of radiation," he told the children. "I encountered the atomic bombing when I was three years old, but I am still living and healthy."[30]

Nasu's concern about radiation misinformation, which Dr. Arita shared, wasn't speculative. Misinformation can produce fear, and fear can cause people to behave badly. In the weeks, months, and years after 3/11, the Japanese press reported numerous instances of discrimination against Fukushima evacuees. Bullying of schoolchildren was especially prominent. One young Tokyo transplant from Fukushima was called "radioactive" by her schoolmates, and taunted with cries of "Radiation! Bang bang!" Students in an elementary school in Yokohama physically assaulted a boy from Fukushima, extorting money and calling him "germ."[31] In 2017, the Japanese government revealed that there had been at least 199 cases of bullying targeting young Fukushima evacuees. A 2018 study in the *Journal of Radiation Research* declared that bullying, stigma, and prejudice toward evacuees, including children, had become a genuine social problem in Japan. "This phenomenon may be associated with the fact that knowledge about radiation has still not reached the general public, and to a potential lack of motivation among Japanese citizens to learn about radiation and bullying."[32]

In September 2011—six months after the triple disaster—Japan's economy, trade, and industry minister, Yoshio Hachiro, visited the Fukushima Daiichi nuclear plant. Afterward, he was reported to have rubbed the sleeve of his protective clothing against a reporter. "Look out, radiation!" he joked. Hachiro's ministry was charged with regulating the nuclear power industry. He was forced to resign two days later.[33]

≈

I had just said goodbye to Dr. Arita at the conclusion of our interview, when he remembered something.

"There's a story I'd like to tell you," he said.[34]

It took place in April 2011. Arita had just returned to Hiroshima from Fukushima City, when an eighty-year-old woman, his mother's cousin, came to his office. She was a survivor of the atomic bombing. "She was a schoolgirl back in 1945, sixteen or seventeen, and she had lost her father and two sisters in the American attack. After the war, she lived with her mother. Just the two of them. My mother told me it was a real struggle for them. But the lady now has two fully grown daughters of her own and is leading a tranquil life."

Arita said that when he saw the woman, whom he knew well, he could tell something was off. "I asked her 'What's wrong?' She opened her mouth three times as if to speak, but no words came out. I asked her again, 'What happened?' Suddenly she cried out and said: 'I haven't been feeling well since the day of the earthquake.'"

Her statement initially puzzled Arita. The woman lived in Hiroshima. The earthquake, the tsunami, the Fukushima meltdown: all of these took place far away, on the other side of Japan. "I couldn't understand what her physical condition had to do with the earthquake, so I asked her again, 'What do you mean?'"

The woman gazed at Dr. Arita. Then she began to tremble. "She told me that the images she had seen on TV, the footage of all that destruction caused by the tsunami, it was exactly what she had witnessed as a young girl in Hiroshima. Everything was gone, she said. And there was something even worse. She saw TV images of people wandering around in search of missing loved ones, calling out their names. It was exactly what she went through in Hiroshima after the sixth of August so many years ago. 'When I saw this,' she said, 'I remembered my own loss and felt immense pain.' And she cried and cried, right there in front of me."

Arita could not take his eyes off the woman. He tried to muster words of comfort, something, anything to ease her traumatic flashbacks.

"So I said: 'Here's the thing, you can change the way you think about all this.'" He told the woman about his fieldwork in Fukushima, about all the good deeds he saw going on there, about the spirit of evacuees, about the volunteers and international support for Japan, about hope. There was, he explained, something positive and uplifting to be found in the triple disaster response. "I'm sure we all can overcome this sadness," he told her. "The world is reaching out to you with words of sympathy."

Arita said at that point in the conversation, his compassion for the woman got the better of him. His own tears overwhelmed him. "I was at a loss for any more words. We both sat there silently. And after a while, she looked up at me, and her mood seemed to have completely shifted."

"You're right," she told Arita. In fact, she admitted, all things considered, she wasn't faring too badly. She had a strong disposition, as many of her generation had. She had been making an effort to get out of the house recently, to move her body, to talk, to get away from all the misery on TV. She had even joined a support group. And she was lucky: she didn't live on the Tohoku coast, in the triple disaster zone.

"After overcoming so many painful experiences, she had learned how to persevere," Arita said. "She had learned, out of necessity, how to recover. She needed time, patience, and the love of her family to get to the point where she is now. But now she can think positively and sort out her feelings."

Arita had found a powerful mix of character traits in his mother's cousin: Tenacity. Patience. Love. Self-reflection. Those were the instruments that facilitated her long and, as 3/11 revealed, sometimes unsteady recovery from the trauma of World War II.

"We human beings are reminded every day that greater powers can destroy and rob us of our daily lives," Arita reflected. "There are many merciless moments in this world. If you dwell on them, it can feel like you're standing at the edge of a cliff, with nothing but loss in front of you. Yet what stretches ahead is peace."

There is optimism in Dr. Arita's observation, a faith in dawn following darkness, in the sun coming out tomorrow. It is good and indeed necessary, he maintained, to cling to those clichés; to look forward to peace, not backward to misfortune.

Arita's optimism is tempered, however, by the recognition that life is filled with minefields, illnesses, accidents, earthquakes, storms, tsunamis, and wars; that all of these "merciless moments" are elements in history's periodic table; and that from them, grim memories can emerge, memories that are prone to linger, as they did for his mother's cousin, and as they did for those elderly members of Japan's war generation who watched what transpired on 3/11.

I keep in touch with Kenichi Arita. When we last spoke, in Hiroshima in January 2023, he told me that he had retired, but was still doing volunteer work with *hibakusha*. He had written a book about the survivor community titled *Our Mind and Expectations*, examining, through *hibakusha* testimonies, what it means to live life one's own way. The book, he said, was inspired by the end-of-life care of his own relatives.[35]

Arita told me his mother's cousin was still alive, still flourishing in her midnineties. But his father, Yoshiyuki, had died in April 2012, a year and a month after 3/11. He was ninety-four. He had experienced pain in his life, having carried those glass shards beneath his skin. But all told, Arita said, "he did okay." Yoshiyuki had lived to see his son become a doctor, and had become, in his own right, an *ojiisan* (grandfather) to his son's two children.

"My father was very happy about the birth of his two grandchildren," Arita said. "I think he loved them very much."[36]

Yoshiyuki's peers—the war generation survivors I met in Japan—mostly "did okay" during the postwar years. They fared well and even thrived, despite their wartime memories, despite whatever particular shards of glass they may have carried within. They had the capacity and determination to stare down painful recollections and to build something meaningful from them.

My own grandfather, Abe, was a generation older than Yoshiyuki. Abe lived through two world wars and a Nazi-led genocide that took the lives of his sister and six million other Jews. That was Abe's shard of glass, which he carried inside, immutably. Yet Abe, like Yoshiyuki, did okay. He fared well and thrived. His two daughters married and gave him four grand-children, which made him very happy.

Abe, a self-professed poet and religious scholar, was fond of Jewish proverbs. He liked how a few of God's well-ordered words could convey life's truths. Among them: "He that cannot endure the bad will not live to see the good." It is a sentiment, I think, that Dr. Arita and his father would have liked; and it is as good an adage as any to apply to those in Japan who shared with me their stories, and who had endured the bad and lived to see the good.

Notes

Preface

1. "Americans, Japanese: Mutual Respect 70 Years after the End of WWII," *Pew Research Report*, April 7, 2015.

2. Robert Rand, "For Japanese Soldier, the War Went On," NPR, *Weekend Edition Sunday*, December 7, 2008. I write in depth about the soldier in part 5 of this book, "Prisoners of Memory."

Introduction

1. See Max Hastings, *Inferno: The World at War, 1939–1945* (New York: Vintage, 2011), 255; Philip Jowett, *The Japanese Army 1931–45* (Oxford: Osprey, 2002), 1:7.

2. US forces entered the Buchenwald concentration camp on April 11, 1945. Video footage can be seen online: "US Forces Liberate Buchenwald," *Holocaust Encyclopedia*, US Holocaust Memorial Museum (website), n.d.

3. "Buddhism and Cremation," Neptune Society (website), n.d.; Anna Hiatt, "The History of Cremation in Japan," *JSTOR Daily*, September 9, 2015. Hiatt notes that historically, cremation was not always uniformly accepted in Japan as the preferred means of burial, with opposition variously coming from adherents of Confucianism and Catholicism. The Japanese government also briefly banned cremation in the 1870s, citing public health considerations over burning bodies.

4. For more on Japanese funerals and *kotsuage*, see Elizabeth Kenney and Edmund T. Gilday, "Mortuary Rites in Japan: Editors' Introduction," *Japanese Journal of Religious Studies* 27, no. 3/4 (2000): 167–73; Ai Faithy Perez, "The Complicated Rituals of Japanese Funerals," *Savvy Tokyo*, October 21, 2015; Hikaru Suzuki, *The Price of Death: The Funeral Industry in Contemporary Japan* (Stanford, CA: Stanford University Press, 2000), 117–18.

Part I

1. The quote and military service information are from an interview my father gave to one of his grandsons in September 2010.

Chapter I

1. Lawrence Baron, "The First Wave of American 'Holocaust' Films, 1945–1959," *American Historical Review* 115, no. 1 (2010): 95.

2. "Reaction of Humans to Atom Bomb in Film," *New York Times*, August 8, 1946.

3. Censorship of A-bomb images is more fully discussed and sourced later in this chapter.

4. The newsreel footage was in black and white. The actual photo, as will be noted later in this chapter, was in color. The *New York Times* said the newsreel was part of a "Paramount News" production on the atom bomb. Paramount, also known as British Paramount, was one of a handful of newsreel production companies operating in the 1930s and 1940s. The newsreel referred to in the *Times* article was called "Atom Bombs!" It consisted of two parts: "Bikini (Bomb no. 5)," about an American underwater nuclear test on July 25, 1946, in Bikini Atoll in the Marshall Islands; and "Hiroshima (One Year After)." Both parts of this newsreel can be found online under the title "Atom Bombs! I. Bikini (Bomb no. 5) II. Hiroshima (One Year After)," issued August 1, 1946, 5:19 (part 1) and 3:35 (part 2), Reuters Archive, British Pathé (website). The woman with the dress design imprinted on her skin can be seen in part 2, at the fifty-eight-second mark. Universal, one of Paramount's competitors, also released newsreels in August 1946, using much of the same video footage, cut together in reverse order (Hiroshima first, Bikini second). The Universal newsreel can be found online under the title "Jap Films of Hiroshima," issued August 5, 1946, 7:13, Internet Archive (website). The dress-imprint woman is at thirty-five seconds into the video. Regarding that woman, the Paramount newsreel on Hiroshima asserts she "would die in a few days anyhow not from her burns or visible wounds but from radioactivity." That assertion is entirely unsubstantiated, likely scripted by newsreel producers based on assumptions and without factual basis (the Japanese footage from Hiroshima would not have had a narrative backstory with the woman's case history attached to it). What in fact may have happened to the woman is the subject of this chapter. For background on newsreels in the 1930s and 1940s, see Emily Rutherford, "Researching and Teaching with British Newsreels," *Twentieth Century British History* 32, no. 3 (2021): 441–61; Luke McKernan, "A History of the British Newsreels," 2000, British Universities Film and Video Council (website), uploaded June 2009.

5. I gathered information about the photo of the kimono-scarred woman presented in this chapter on a visit to the museum in November 2007.

6. What appears to be an English-language translation of the Japanese medical report can be found online in the digital collection of the National Institute of Health's National Library of Medicine. See Army Medical College, First Tokyo Army Hospital, "Medical Report of the Atomic Bombing in Hiroshima," November 30, 1945.

7. The two photos were also included in the English-language translation of the First Tokyo Army Hospital's "Medical Report of the Atomic Bombing in Hiroshima," 357. In typewritten text, the woman was identified there as "S. Ushio female."

8. The definition is from the online Japanese-English dictionary *Jisho*. For more on *muenbotoke*, see Jake Adelstein, "無縁仏 (Muenbotoke): Buddhas without Connections," Japan Subculture Research Center (website), posted September 23, 2014; and Thersa Matsuura, "The Unconnected Dead: Muenbotoke," *Uncanny Japan* (podcast), episode 106, August 15, 2022.

9. I visited both places in November 2007. A-bomb victims' librarian Ayako Inoue assisted me at the National Peace Memorial Hall; official Shinji Uemoto assisted at Hiroshima City Hall.

10. Interview with author, December 2007, Tokyo.

11. Kimura's account appears in Yoshito Matsushigi, ed., *Atomic Bomb Photo Testament: A Collection of Photographs by the Photographers Who Survived the Bombing in Hiroshima*, 4th English ed. (Hiroshima: Association of the Photographers of the Atomic Bomb Destruction of Hiroshima, 1997), 77–80.

12. Interviews with author, November 2007 and March 2008, Hiroshima.

13. The American group, headed by Colonel Stafford L. Warren, entered Hiroshima on September 8, 1945, and visited Ujina and other hospitals beginning September 9. Warren, a physician and radiologist, had served as the chief of the medical division on the Manhattan Project, which developed the atomic bomb. For the group members' visit to Ujina Army Hospital, see James L. Nolan Jr., *Atomic Doctors: Conscience and Complicity at the Dawn of the Nuclear Age* (Cambridge, MA: Harvard University Press, 2020), 97; see also "Coverage of the Atomic Bombing," section 5, "Information Control," Hiroshima for Global Peace (website), n.d.; "Surveys of Hiroshima and Nagasaki," Atomic Heritage Foundation (website), posted June 2, 2017; Frank W. Putnam, "The Atomic Bomb Casualty Commission in Retrospect," *Proceedings of the National Academy of Sciences* 95, no. 10 (May 12, 1998): 5426–31. A US Navy photographer, Wayne Miller, traveled to Hiroshima in September 1945, becoming one of the first Americans to capture images of the A-bomb aftermath, including relief stations. See *Hiroshima Atomic Bomb Damage and Restoration as Shown in Collections from Overseas*, special exhibition, Hiroshima Peace Memorial Museum (website), December 2019. In a 2001 interview, Miller confirmed that he had rolls of color film with him in Hiroshima. See Wayne F. Miller,

An Eye on the World: Reviewing a Lifetime in Photography, oral history interview by Suzanne B. Riess (Berkeley: University of California Bancroft Library, 2003), 42. It is not clear whether Miller himself used or passed on color film to Japanese counterparts. However, US military photographers did take color photographs of Hiroshima in the A-bomb aftermath, and those photos, considered more graphic than black-and-white prints, were hidden until the 1980s, according to journalist and researcher Greg Mitchell. See Mitchell, "Hiroshima Film Cover-Up Exposed, Censored 1945 Footage to Air," *Asia-Pacific Journal* 3, no. 8 (2005): article 1554.

14. Nanao Kamada was chairman of the board of directors of the Hiroshima Atomic Bomb Survivors Relief Foundation and director of the Genbaku Retirement Home. I interviewed him in March 2008, in Kurakake, outside Hiroshima.

15. See "Frequently Asked Questions about the Atomic-Bomb Survivor Research Program," Radiation Effects Research Foundation (website), n.d. For an analysis of the complexity in determining A-bomb death statistics, see Alex Wellerstein, "Counting the Dead at Hiroshima and Nagasaki," *Bulletin of the Atomic Scientists*, August 4, 2020.

16. See "Average Age of A-Bomb Survivors Now Exceeds 75," *Chugoku Shimbun*, July 24, 2008, Hiroshima Peace Media Center (website), posted July 31, 2008.

17. The *rad*, or radiation absorbed dose, is the unit of measurement used to describe the amount of radiation an object absorbs after exposure. According to the US government's December 2016 *Quick Reference Guide: Radiation Risk Information for Responders Following a Nuclear Detonation*, p. 4, a ten-rad dose of radiation carries a 0.6 percent increased lifetime risk of cancer.

18. According to the Radiation Effects Research Foundation, the US-Japanese organization studying radiation impacts on *hibakusha*, 80 percent of A-bomb survivors who were exposed before the age of twenty were alive in 2011; A-bomb survivors, however, had a higher-than-average risk of developing certain cancers, especially leukemia. See Evan Douple et al., "Long-Term Radiation-Related Health Effects in a Unique Human Population: Lessons Learned from the Atomic Bomb Survivors of Hiroshima and Nagasaki," *Disaster Medicine and Public Health Preparedness* 5, suppl. 1 (2011): S122–33; "Past Results and Future Studies," Radiation Effects Research Foundation Research Foundation (website), n.d.

19. Calls were made in February and March 2008.

20. Telephone call to a Mr. Kadota at the Hiroshima National Peace Memorial Hall for the Atomic Bomb Victims, February 2008.

21. For a history of Ninoshima, see "Ninoshima: War and Atomic Bombing," Hiroshima for Global Peace (website), n.d.; and Jen Woronow, "The Tragedy and Hope of Ninoshima," *Circulating Now* (blog), National Library of Medicine, posted March 17, 2022.

22. The Atomic Bomb Memorial Mound can be viewed online; see, e.g., Masami

Nishimoto, "Landmarks of Hiroshima: Atomic Bomb Memorial Mound," *Chugoku Shimbun*, Hiroshima Peace Media Center (website), posted June 6, 2011.

23. Interview with author in November 2007.

Chapter 2

1. Interview with author in November 2007.

2. Miyoko Watanabe's recollection of August 6, 1945, is based on her interview with me, confirmed in an account she wrote titled "The Unspeakable Tragedy of that Day," which was part of the exhibition *Hiroshima-Nagasaki: Images and Stories from Eyewitness Accounts*, which traveled the United States in 2008; see Jason Sandford, "Hiroshima Survivor's Account," *Mountain Xpress* (Asheville, NC), July 9, 2008.

3. The Japanese government began student labor programs in 1938. Initially, students were required to work periodically during summer vacations. By 1944, the authorities ordered students to work year-round at munitions plants and other sites. See "The Start of Student Mobilization," *Mobilized Students: The Lost Tomorrows of the Students*, special exhibition, Hiroshima Peace Memorial Museum (website), July 2004; Ben-Ami Shillony, "Universities and Students in Wartime Japan," *Journal of Asian Studies* 45, no. 4 (1986): 769–87.

4. See also the testimony of Kizuku Kuramoto, Memories of Hiroshima and Nagasaki: Messages from Hibakusha (website), Asahi Shumbun Company, n.d.

5. Masami Nishimoto, "Landmarks of Hiroshima: Atomic Bomb Memorial Mound," *Chugoku Shimbun*, Hiroshima Peace Media Center (website), posted June 6, 2011.

6. Author interview with Hiroshima City Hall official Shinji Uemoto, November 2007.

7. I visited the Mound in November 2007.

8. Miyoko Watanabe died in December 2015, at the age of eighty-five. See Miho Kuwajima, "Peace Ribbon Assembly That Passes on A-Bomb Victims' Wishes to Be Held Indoors on August 1, Avoiding COVID-19 Infection," *Chugoku Shimbun*, Hiroshima Peace Media Center (website), posted July 19, 2020. Saeki is quoted in Yoshifumi Fukushima, "The Atomic Bomb Memorial Mound," *Chugoku Shimbun*, April 16, 1995, Hiroshima Peace Media Center (website), posted August 1, 2012.

Chapter 3

1. Interview with author, November 2007, Hiroshima.

2. For this and more about Skokie, see my radio piece "Keeping the Memory Alive," broadcast on April 29, 2000, on Public Radio International's show *The Savvy Traveler*, whose transcript is available online. That story was excerpted from a longer documentary about Skokie I produced for WBEZ, the Chicago public radio

station, in April 2000. The half-hour-long program "Regarding Skokie: Hate and Free Speech" was part of the *Chicago Matters* series on the topic "Seeking Justice."

3. For background on MacArthur's censorship policies, see John Dower, *Embracing Defeat: Japan in the Wake of World War II* (New York: Norton, 1999), 405–40. Dower writes: "It was not until after the occupation, on the seventh anniversary of the bombings in August 1952, that the public was afforded a serious presentation of photographs from the two stricken cities" (415). Dower notes that censorship nominally ended in 1949 when the censorship oversight office (the Civil Censorship Detachment) was disbanded; however, "this easing of formal controls was misleading," and "censorship assumed new forms" that were "more stringent, arbitrary, and unpredictable" (432).

4. For more, see Janet Farrell Brodie, "Radiation Secrecy and Censorship after Hiroshima and Nagasaki," *Journal of Social History* 48, no. 4 (2015): 842–64; Robert Jacobs, "Domesticating Hiroshima in America in the Early Cold War," in *Images of Rupture between East and West: The Perception of Auschwitz and Hiroshima in Eastern European Arts and Media*, ed. Urs Heftrich, Robert Jacobs, Bettina Kaibach, and Karoline Thaidigsmann (Heidelberg: Universitatsverlag Winter, 2016), 83–96.

5. That was the date the Treaty of Peace with Japan, also called the San Francisco Peace Treaty, came into force. See "Truman Signs Japan Treaty Giving Sovereignty April 28," *New York Times*, April 16, 1952.

6. Shuntaro Hida, a Hiroshima survivor who ran a counseling center at the Japan Confederation of A- and H-Bomb Sufferers Organizations, estimated that up to 80 percent of survivors chose to hide their status, fearing discrimination in employment or difficulties in finding a spouse. See Sayuri Romei, "6 Years after the Fukushima Disaster, Its Victims Are Still Suffering," *Washington Post*, March 10, 2017.

Part 2

1. The Pale of Settlement covered areas of present-day Russia, Ukraine, Belarus, Moldova, Lithuania, and Poland. Lyubeshov (the Russian rendering) has been variously spelled as Lubieszów (Polish) and Lyubeshiv (Ukrainian). Modern Lyubeshiv is located in northern Ukraine, just south of the Belarus border, about fifty miles from the Belarusian city of Pinsk, where Abe was sent for Jewish studies. For background on the Pale, see John Klier, "Pale of Settlement," *YIVO Encyclopedia of Jews in Eastern Europe*, September 14, 2010.

2. See Dov Peretz Elkins, *Bialik: Israel's National Poet* (Jerusalem: Mazo, 2021); Matt Plen, "Hayim Nahman Bialik: The Jewish National Poet," My Jewish Learning (website), n.d.; Avner Holtzman, "Bialik, Hayim Nahman," trans. Jeffrey Green, *YIVO Encyclopedia of Jews in Eastern Europe*, Jue 29, 2017.

3. The quotes are from Abe Yellin's unpublished autobiography and other papers, which are in the author's possession.

4. Multiple Holocaust survivor oral histories in the US Holocaust Memorial Museum (available online) confirm the general outlines of Abe's story: there were Nazi massacres of Lyubeshov Jews in 1942; Jews did dig trenches before they were shot. Material in Yad Vashem, the World Holocaust Remembrance Center in Israel, also confirms Jewish massacres near Lyubeshov. One story in the Yad Vashem digital archive almost exactly tracks what Abe wrote: In August 1942, in an area on the outskirts of Lyubeshov near a neighboring village called Sudcze, German and Ukrainian police took a group of several hundred Jews "and shot all of them to death in pits that the victims had been forced to dig." See the pages for "Lubieszów (Community)" and "Murder Story of Lubieszów Jews in Sudcze (Murder Site)," Untold Stories Research Project, Yad Vashem (website), n.d.

5. As one Jewish writer glibly noted in a *New York Times* blog post, "aside from 'Christina,' perhaps, there's no name that shouts 'Jesus is my Lord and Savior' as much as Mary." Devorah Blachor, "My Jewish Daughter, Mary," *Motherlode* (blog), *New York Times*, September 13, 2013.

6. See "Mary Miriam Pickman," item 1240089, Central Database of Shoah Victims' Names, Yad Vashem (website), n.d.

7. I researched the question in connection with the writing of this book and discovered that Miriam and Mary have historical links. Miriam (or Miryam/Miryem) is a Hebrew and Old Testament form of Mary (Miriam was the sister of Moses). Additionally, other Jewish Miriams of my grandfather's generation (and later) have sometimes been nicknamed Mary. See Jason H. Greenberg, "From Rochel to Rose and Mendel to Max: First Name Americanization Patterns among Twentieth-Century Jewish Immigrants to the United States" (master's thesis, City University of New York, 2017), 49. Also see: "Alternative to Miriam," Imamother: Connecting Frum Women (website), "Baby Names" forum, posted April 29, 2014 ("We had a great-aunt who everyone loved, her English name was Mary and her Hebrew name was Miriam,"); "Are There Any Jews Who Name Their Daughter 'Mary'?," question posted to Quora (website), January 21, 2022; Philip Kosloski, "What Was the Virgin Mary's Real Name?," *Aleteia*, September 12, 2020. For a scholarly take on all this, see Ephraim Effie Shoham-Steiner, "The Virgin Mary, Miriam, and Jewish Reactions to Marian Devotion in the High Middle Ages," *AJS Review* 37, no. 1 (2013): 75–91.

Chapter 4

1. Telephone interview with Catholic Nagasaki survivor Shigemi Fukahori, September 2020.

2. The Japanese Agency for Cultural Affairs states that in 2020 there were

1,915,294 Christians in Japan, or 1.2 percent of the country's population; see *Shukyo Nenkan* [*Religious Yearbook*], Reiwa 3 (2021): 35. Similarly, the US Department of State's Office of International Religious Freedom estimated that there were 1.9 million Christians in Japan in 2020, or about 1 percent of the population. See "2020 Report on International Religious Freedom: Japan," US Department of State (website), May 12, 2021. See also Mariko Kato, "Christianity's Long History in the Margins," *Japan Times*, February 24, 2009; Akito Ishikawa, "A Little Faith: Christianity and the Japanese," Nippon.com, November 22, 2019.

3. See Mari Yamaguchi, "Nagasaki, the Center of Catholicism in Japan, Prepares to Welcome Pope Francis," *Diplomat*, November 20, 2019; Takao Kawasaki, "Christianity's Long History in Nagasaki Puts It First on Pope's Agenda for Japan Visit," *Japan Times*, November 20, 2019.

4. According to the Japanese Catholic Bishops' Conference, Japan's total population in 2020 was 127,138,033, of which 435,083 (0.34 percent) were Catholic; and Nagasaki's total population was 1,350,769, of which 59,161 (4.38 percent) were Catholic. See Secretariat, Catholic Bishops' Conference of Japan, Social Communications Division, "Statistics of the Catholic Church in Japan, Jan. 1–Dec. 31, 2020," Catholic Bishops' Conference of Japan (website), August 2021, 1.

5. In 1945, Nagasaki's estimated population before the A-bombing was 240,000, of which an estimated 15,000 (about 6 percent) to 20,000 (about 8 percent) were Catholic. See Susan Southard, *Nagasaki: Life after Nuclear War* (New York: Penguin Books, 2015), 9; and "Bombings of Hiroshima and Nagasaki—1945," Atomic Heritage Foundation (website), posted June 5, 2014; *Atomic Bombing in Nagasaki and the Urakami Cathedral*, Nagasaki Atomic Bomb Museum curated exhibit, Google Arts & Culture (website), n.d.; *The Nagasaki Atomic Bomb Damage Records*, part 2, "The Atomic Bomb," section 2, chapter 2, "Damage in the Hypocenter Zone," Nagasaki National Peace Memorial Hall for the Atomic Bomb Victims (website), posted March 2018.

6. The five-volume history of the atomic bombing and assessment of the devastation it caused is called *Nagasaki genbaku sensaishi* [*Records of the Nagasaki Atomic Bombing and Wartime Damage*] (Nagasaki-shi: Nagasaki Kokusai Bunka Kaikan, Showa 52–60 [1975–85]). The city of Nagasaki published the first volume in 1977. Volume 5 came out in 1983. A revised edition of volume 1 was published in 2006. An English-language translation of that publication was made available in full in 2018 under the title *The Nagasaki Atomic Bomb Damage Records*, at the Nagasaki National Peace Memorial Hall for the Atomic Bomb Victims website.

7. The bomber was named after Frederick C. Bock, who normally piloted the aircraft. Bock was in a different plane that day, carrying blast measurement instruments. See Ellen Bradbury and Sandra Blakeslee, "The Harrowing Story of the Nagasaki Bombing Mission," *Bulletin of the Atomic Scientists*, August 4, 2015.

8. *The Nagasaki Atomic Bomb Damage Records*, part 2, "The Atomic Bomb," section 1, chapter 2, "August 9." See also Sean Potter, "August 9, 1945: The Dropping of the Atomic Bomb over Nagasaki," *Weatherwise*, July/August 2009, 14–15.

9. Material in this chapter about Mrs. Yamada and Kio Tanaka is based on interviews conducted in March 2008 in Nagasaki, with Masahito Hirose and Yoshitoshi Fukahori, both Nagasaki A-bomb survivors, as well as on Hirose's writings and published news articles about Hirose and Fukahori. Hirose volunteered as a researcher, editor, and translator at the Nagasaki Atomic Bomb Museum. Fukahori headed the museum's photographic archive. Much of Hirose's account of his relationship with the Yamada family can be found in his book *Nagasaki no Shogen* [*Testimonies of Survivors of the Nagasaki A-Bombing*] (Nagasaki: Nagasaki-no Shogen no kai, 1973). Information about the Yamada family and Kio Tanaka is also drawn from the following publications about Yosuke Yamahata, the photographer who took their pictures: Yoshio Tokuyama, *Genbaku to Shashin* [*Atomic Bomb and Photographs*] (Tokyo: Ochanomizu Shobo, 2005); Rupert Jenkins, ed., *Nagasaki Journey: The Photographs of Yosuke Yamahata, August 10, 1945* (Rohnert Park, CA: Pomegranate Artbooks, 1995); *Nagasaki Yomigaeru Genbaku Shashin* [*Nagasaki Journey*] (Tokyo: NHK, 1995).

10. The American mission's primary target was Kokura, an industrial city northeast of Nagasaki with one of the largest arsenals in Japan. A mix of smoke, heavy ground haze, and antiaircraft fire forced *Bockscar* to abandon Kokura and proceed to a secondary target, Nagasaki.

11. For bombing details, see "Hiroshima and Nagasaki Bombing Timeline," Atomic Heritage Foundation (website), posted April 26, 2016.

12. For estimated distances from the target point, see Alex Wellerstein, "Nagasaki: The Last Bomb," *New Yorker*, August 7, 2015 (three quarters of a mile off); Southard, *Nagasaki*, 41 (a mile and a half off).

13. *The Nagasaki Atomic Bomb Damage Records*, part 2, "The Atomic Bomb," section 1, chapter 3, "11:02 a.m."

14. Southard, *Nagasaki*, 47.

15. Southard, 36; *Atomic Bombing in Nagasaki and the Urakami Cathedral*.

16. For the Nagasaki Atomic Bomb Museum numbers, see the "Mini Atomic Bomb Exhibit" handout titled "An Outline of Atomic Bomb Damage," Nagasaki Peace (website), n.d. For the city's total population, see Southard, *Nagasaki*, 9; "Damage Caused by the Atomic Bombing," Kids Heiwa Nagasaki (website), n.d. On the Catholic figures, see *Atomic Bombing in Nagasaki and the Urakami Cathedral* (estimating that 10,000 of 15,000 Catholics were killed); *The Nagasaki Atomic Bomb Damage Records*, part 2, "The Atomic Bomb," section 2, chapter 2, "Damage in the Hypocenter Zone" (estimating 10,000 dead of a population of "approximately 20,000" Catholics); Southard, *Nagasaki*, 128 (estimating 8,500 Christian A-bomb victims).

17. For a map of Nagasaki in 1945, see Southard, *Nagasaki*, xiii.

18. For medical college fatalities, see *The Nagasaki Atomic Bomb Damage Records*, part 3, "Rescue and Medical Relief," section 4, chapter 3, "Atomic Bomb Disaster Investigations and Research." For death rate curve, see Masao Tomonaga, "The Atomic Bombings of Hiroshima and Nagasaki: A Summary of the Human Consequences, 1945–2018, and Lessons for *Homo sapiens* to End the Nuclear Weapon Age," *Journal for Peace and Nuclear Disarmament* 2, no. 2 (2019): 491–517.

Chapter 5

1. For Yamahata's actions see Rupert Jenkins, ed., *Nagasaki Journey: The Photographs of Yosuke Yamahata, August 10, 1945* (Rohnert Park, CA: Pomegranate Artbooks, 1995), 15–22.

2. Yosuke Yamahata, "Photographing the Bomb, a Memo (1952)," Japan Peace Museum (website), n.d. Yamahata wrote: "I had been directed to photograph the situation in Nagasaki so as to be as useful as possible for military propaganda."

3. On elf fires, see Yamahata; Henry Allen, "The Gate of Hell," *Washington Post*, October 21, 1995.

4. Jenkins, *Nagasaki Journey*, 55.

5. Jenkins, 45.

6. A large selection of Yamahata's photographs is reproduced in Jenkins, *Nagasaki Journey*.

7. See Jenkins, 49.

8. Kio Tanaka's story is told by Masahito Hirose in *Nagasaki no Shogen* [*Testimonies of Survivors of the Nagasaki A-Bombing*] (Nagasaki: Nagasaki-no Shogen no kai, 1973).

9. The location and timing of both the Yamada and Kio Tanaka photos are recorded in Yoshio Tokuyama, *Genbaku to Shashin* [*Atomic Bomb and Photographs*] (Tokyo: Ochanomizu Shobo, 2005), vii–viii.

10. *Nagasaki Yomigaeru Genbaku Shashin* [*Nagasaki Journey*] (Tokyo: NHK, 1995), 233.

11. The sequence can be seen in *Nagasaki Yomigaeru Genbaku Shashin*, 228–29; and Jenkins, *Nagasaki Journey*, 92–93.

12. Email to author, May 2022. Fraser is an associate professor in the Department of Art and Architecture at the University of San Francisco.

13. See Cecilia Dorger, "Maria 'Lactans' in Depictions of the Holy Family," *Marian Studies* 66 (2015): article 9; Anne M. Ashton, "Interpreting Breast Iconography in Italian Art, 1250–1600" (PhD diss., University of St. Andrews, 2006), 42–101.

14. Email to author, September 2020. Milliner is an associate professor of art history at Wheaton College.

15. Email to author, May 2022.

Chapter 6

1. For Dr. Akizuki and the First Urakami Hospital, see Susan Southard, *Nagasaki: Life after Nuclear War* (New York: Penguin Books, 2015), 76–78, 88–89; Committee for the Compilation of Materials on Damage Caused by the Atomic Bombs in Hiroshima and Nagasaki, *Hiroshima and Nagasaki: The Physical, Medical, and Social Effects of the Atomic Bombings* (New York: Basic Books, 1981), 528. For Dr. Akizuki's own account, see Tatsuichiro Akizuki, *Nagasaki 1945: The First Full-Length Eyewitness Account of the Atomic Bomb Attack on Nagasaki*, trans. Keiichi Nagata (London: Quartet Books, 1981), 24–85 (quote on p. 47).

2. See James Brodrick, *A Biography of St. Francis Xavier (1506–1552)* (New York: Wicklow, 1952); "Saint Francis Xavier and the Roots of Christianity in Japan," Nippon.com, August 27, 2015.

3. Andrew Gordon, *A Modern History of Japan: From Tokugawa Times to the Present*, 2nd ed. (New York: Oxford University Press, 2009), 5.

4. For a detailed recounting of the rise of Catholicism in Nagasaki, see Carla Tronu Montane, "Sacred Space and Ritual in Early Modern Japan: The Christian Community of Nagasaki (1569–1643)" (PhD diss., University of London, 2012).

5. See Jay Copp, "The Nagasaki Martyrs," Catholic Culture (website), July/August 1997; Gordon, *A Modern History of Japan*, 5 (three hundred thousand converts); Yvette Tan, "The Japanese Christians Forced to Trample on Christ," BBC News, November 24, 2019 (five hundred thousand).

6. João Paulo Oliveira e Costa, "The Brotherhoods (Confrarias) and Lay Support for the Early Christian Church in Japan," *Japanese Journal of Religious Studies* 34, no.1 (2007): 77; Neil Jopson, "The Rome of Japan," *Catholic Stand*, October 23, 2021; Tan, "The Japanese Christians Forced to Trample on Christ."

7. Shusaku Endo, *Silence* (1969), trans. William Johnston (New York: Taplinger, 1980), 257. Scorsese's film adaptation was released in 2016.

8. "The Edict of 1635 Ordering the Closing of Japan: Addressed to the Joint Bugyō of Nagasaki," in *Japan: A Documentary History*, ed. David J. Lu (London: Routledge, 2015), 1:221.

9. For background on Dutch-Japanese relations, see "Dutch-Japanese Relations: First Contact," The Netherlands and You (website), Kingdom of the Netherlands, n.d.; and "Japan-Netherlands Exchange in the Edo Period," National Diet Library of Japan (website), December 16, 2009.

10. See "Virgin Mary & Kannon, Two Merciful Mothers," *A-to-Z Photo Dictionary of Japanese Religious Sculpture and Art*, Onmark Productions (website), n.d.

11. Michael Hoffman, "Seeking Independence through Civilization," *Japan Times*, January 17, 2015.

12. Tan, "The Japanese Christians Forced to Trample on Christ."

13. "Urakami Parish History," section 8, "Construction of the Main Shrine," Urakami Cathedral (website), Archdiocese of Nagasaki, n.d.

14. Nagai is most well known for his controversial 1949 book *The Bells of Nagasaki*. In it, Nagai argued that "it was the providence of God" that dropped the bomb on the city. Nagai maintained that those who died in Nagasaki were chosen to "burn on the altar of sacrifice to expiate the sins committed by humanity in the Second World War." Thanks to that sacrifice, the war ended and "many millions who would otherwise have fallen victim to the ravages of war have been saved." "How noble, how splendid," he maintained, "was that holocaust of August 9, when flames soared up from the cathedral, dispelling the darkness of war and bringing the light of peace!" See Takashi Nagai, *The Bells of Nagasaki*, trans. William Johnston (Tokyo: Kodansha International, 1984), 106–10. For an evaluation of Nagai's view, and an introduction to contrary arguments that Nagai's theory of divine retribution justified the use of nuclear weapons, see Yuki Miyamoto, "Rebirth in the Pure Land or God's Sacrificial Lambs? Religious Interpretations of the Atomic Bombings in Hiroshima and Nagasaki," *Japanese Journal of Religious Studies* vol. 32, no. 1 (2005): 131–59. Nagai never saw the rebuilt cathedral. He died in 1951 from leukemia, at the age of forty-three. For a contemporaneous obituary, see "Dr. Nagai, Survivor of Nagasaki Bomb: His Books and Analyses on the Effects of Atomic Blast, as His Life Ebbed, Brought Fame," *New York Times*, May 2, 1951.

15. Quoted in Chad R. Diehl, "Resurrecting Nagasaki: Reconstruction, the Urakami Catholics, and Atomic Memory, 1945–1970" (PhD diss., Columbia University, 2011), 123 (Virgin Mary), 215–18 (overcoming hardship; flowers). There was a long debate in Nagasaki over whether to remove the ruins of the old Urakami Cathedral before building its replacement. Diehl covers this in detail. Nagai and the Catholic community wanted the ruins gone, maintaining they were a painful reminder of the crimes of their generation. Nagasaki's non-Christian residents wanted to preserve the ruins to commemorate the bombing and to symbolize the tragedy, much as Hiroshima retained its iconic Atomic Dome. The Catholics prevailed. For the American role in the controversy—the United States wanted the ruins gone—see Tomoe Otsuki, "The Politics of Reconstruction and Reconciliation in U.S.-Japan Relations: Dismantling the Atomic Bomb Ruins of Nagasaki's Urakami Cathedral," *Asia-Pacific Journal* 13, no. 32/2 (2015): article 4356.

16. For information on these and other activities, see Urakami Cathedral (website), Archdiocese of Nagasaki, n.d.

17. In 2016 there were an estimated 48,000 *hibakusha* living in Nagasaki; by March 2021, the number had fallen to 24,054, with an average age of about eighty-four. See Motoko Rich, "Survivors Recount Horrors of Hiroshima and Nagasaki," *New York Times*, May 27, 2016; "Number of A-Bomb Survivors and

Average Age," Japanese Ministry of Health, Labour, and Welfare (website), up-dated March 2021.

Chapter 7

1. Interview with author, March 2008, Nagasaki.

2. For Fukahori praying in Urakami, see Hiroaki Ono, "In Japan, Remembering August 9, 1945, and Praying for Peace," *Japan News (Yomiuri Shimbun)*, August 6, 2015.

3. The speech can be seen online: "Pledge for Peace, the 72th Nagasaki Peace Ceremony, City of Nagasaki (August 9th, 2017)," YouTube video, uploaded August 28, 2017, by prmvlibrary, 8:54.

4. See Melissa Miles and Robin Gerster, *Pacific Exposures: Photography and the Australia-Japan Relationship* (Canberra: Australian National University Press, 2018), 126–28. They write, "MacArthur's administration prohibited the publica-tion of ground-level photographs capturing the horror of the immediate atomic aftermath, including the handful of pictures . . . of Nagasaki taken by Yosuke Ya-mahata. These harrowing images were not published in the US until *Life* maga-zine presented them in a photo spread in September 1952" (128). See also Mike Ives, "After Atomic Bombings, These Photographers Worked under Mushroom Clouds," *New York Times*, August 6, 2020. More background on the censorship of A-bomb photos is in part 1 of this book, on Hiroshima.

5. Yosuke Yamahata and Munehito Kitajima, ed., *Genbaku no Nagasaki: Kiroku shashin* [*Atomized Nagasaki: The Bombing of Nagasaki—A Photographic Record*] (Tokyo: Daiichi, 1952).

6. Philbert Ono, "Tanaka Kio, Nagasaki Bomb Survivor Dies," *Photoguide.jp* (blog), December 14, 2006.

7. *Nagasaki Yomigaeru Genbaku Shashin* [*Nagasaki Journey*] (Tokyo: NHK, 1995), 237.

Chapter 8

1. Masahito Hirose, *Nagasaki no Shogen* [*Testimonies of Survivors of the Nagasaki A-Bombing*] (Nagasaki: Nagasaki-no Shogen no kai, 1973), 186.

2. Masahito Hirose, "Surviving Nagasaki," BBC News, August 5, 2005.

3. For Hirose speaking in English, see "Atomic Bombing Survivor Masahito Hirose, English Presentation," video recorded in 2010, uploaded August 4, 2016, 19:21, Nagasaki Atomic History and the Present (website), Colgate University.

4. *Voices of the A-Bomb Survivors: Nagasaki* (Nagasaki: Nagasaki Atomic Bomb Testimonial Society, 2009).

5. "English Compilation of A-Bomb Stories to Be Re-Launched, Fulfilling Late Hibakusha's Wish," *Mainichi*, January 31, 2016.

6. Interview with the author in March 2008.

7. Hirose's recollection of his conversations with Mrs. Yamada appear in Hirose, *Nagasaki no Shogen*, 183–88.

8. I visited the church and its cemetery in March 2008.

9. "Celebrating Spring: Two Japanese Customs That Honor the Changing of the Seasons," *Rikumo Journal*, March 28, 2022.

Chapter 9

1. Noguchi recounts his story in an online encyclopedia called *All about Mary*, published by the University of Dayton. See the article "Urakami Bombed Mary Statue," n.d.

2. Cited in Pino Cazzaniga, "Nagasaki's Wounded Madonna and Catholics' Mission of Peace," PIME AsiaNews (website), August 16, 2010.

3. Telephone interview with Fukahori from his Nagasaki home, September 2020.

4. Meilan Solly, "Nine Eyewitness Accounts of the Bombings of Hiroshima and Nagasaki," *Smithsonian Magazine*, August 5, 2020; Ayano Shimizu, "Hiroshima Marks 75th Atomic Bomb Anniversary with Call for Unity in Pandemic," *Japan Times*, August 6, 2020; "Atomic-Bomb Survivors Seek New Ways to Keep Their Memories Alive," *Economist*, August 1, 2020.

5. "Nagasaki Asks Japan Gov't to Push Nuke Ban amid Leadership Vacuum," *Kyodo News*, August 9, 2020.

6. The survey was administered by NHK, Japan's national broadcasting company. See Miki Masaki, "70 Years since the Atomic Bombing: How to Pass Down Waning Memories," NHK Broadcasting Culture Research Institute (website), November 2015.

7. "Atomic-Bomb Survivors Seek New Ways to Keep Their Memories Alive."

8. Excerpts from Fukahori's Pledge for Peace can be found in Hikaru Yokoyama, "Nagasaki Atomic Bomb Survivor Hopes to Pass Baton for Peace," *Asahi Shimbun*, August 10, 2020; "Remembering Atomic Bomb Victims in Nagasaki," News on Japan (website), August 9, 2020.

9. A video of the pope's Hypocenter Park appearance, uploaded November 23, 2019, 25:28, appears with the article "Pope in Nagasaki: We Cannot Repeat the Mistakes of the Past," Vatican News (website), November 24, 2019.

10. For Pope Francis's remarks, see "Apostolic Journey to Japan: Message on Nuclear Weapons," Activities of the Holy Father Pope Francis (website), Vatican, November 24, 2019.

11. Video of the mass can be seen here: "Pope Francis-Nagasaki-Holy Mass 2019-11-24," YouTube video, uploaded November 24, 2019, by Vatican News, 1:52:28.

Part 3

1. The first firebombing of Kobe took place on February 4, 1945. See "Summary," Kobe-shi mojokan [Kobe City Archives] (webpage), n.d.; "War Damage Situation in Kobe City (Hyogo Prefecture)," Ministry of Internal Affairs and Communications (website), n.d.; Alvin D. Coox, "Strategic Bombing in the Pacific, 1942–1945," in *Case Studies in Strategic Bombardment*, ed. R. Cargill Hall (Washington, DC: Air Force History and Museums Program, 1998), 314; "B-29's Hit Plans at Kobe in Daytime," *New York Times*, February 5, 1945.

2. US Strategic Bombing Survey, *Field Report Covering Air-Raid Protection and Allied Subjects in Kobe, Japan*, February 1947, 2; US Strategic Bombing Survey, *Effects of Air Attack on Osaka-Kobe-Kyoto*, June 1947, 162.

3. The February 5, 1945, *New York Times* article put the plane's altitude at more than twenty-five thousand feet.

Chapter 10

1. Quotes here and below on the bomb shelter are taken from Katsumoto Saotome with Richard Sams, "Saotome Katsumoto and the Firebombing of Tokyo: Introducing the Great Tokyo Air Raid," *Asia-Pacific Journal* 13, no. 10/1 (2015): article 4293.

2. Saotome, email exchange with author, December 2020.

3. For a history of napalm, see Robert M. Neer, *Napalm: An American Biography* (London: Belknap Press, 2015).

4. Quoted in John Dower, *War without Mercy: Race and Power in the Pacific War* (New York: Pantheon, 1986), 40–41.

5. Comment is from flight engineer Richard Baile; see "Richard Baile," YouTube video, uploaded March 6, 2020, by National WWII Museum, 2:38.

6. For "Great Tokyo Air Raid," see Asahi Shimbun Culture Research Center, "The Great Tokyo Air Raid and the Bombing of Civilians in World War II," *Asia-Pacific Journal* 8, no. 11/2 (2010): article 3320; "Legacy of the Great Tokyo Air Raid," editorial, *Japan Times*, March 15, 2015; Kirk Spitzer, "A Forgotten Horror: The Great Tokyo Air Raid," *Time*, March 27, 2012. The description of the Tokyo raid in this chapter is drawn from Dower, *War without Mercy*, 40–41; Seth Paridon, "Hellfire on Earth: Operation MEETINGHOUSE," National WWII Museum (website), March 8, 2020; Tony Long, "March 9, 1945: Burning the Heart Out of the Enemy," *Wired*, March 9, 2011; C. Peter Chen, "Bombing of Tokyo and Other Cities, 19 Feb 1948–10 Aug 1945," World War II Database (website), n.d.; William W. Ralph, "Improvised Destruction: Arnold, LeMay, and the Firebombing of Japan," *War in History* 13, no. 4 (2006): 495–522.

7. Interview with author, May 2008, Tokyo.

8. Among these writers was novelist and poet Yukio Mishima, who in 1970

committed seppuku, or ritual suicide, after participating in a failed right-wing insurrection; see Thomas Graham, "Yukio Mishima: The Strange Tale of Japan's Infamous Novelist," BBC (website), November 24, 2020. For more on the Hilltop Hotel, see Burritt Sabin, "The Parnassus of Surugadai," *Japan Times*, September 5, 2008; "Hilltop Hotel Story," Hilltop Hotel (website), n.d. ("Through the decades, many famous writers and novelists stayed here."); and "Yama-no-ue Hilltop Hotel—Edo-Style Tempura in Classic Style," *Exploring Old Tokyo* (blog), January 27, 2018.

9. William W. Ralph, "Improvised Destruction: Arnold, LeMay, and the Firebombing of Japan," *War in History* 13, no 4 (2006): 514.

10. "Largest Cities in Japan: Population from 1890," Demographia (website), Wendell Cox Consultancy, n.d. US air raids left Kyoto, the second largest city in Japan, largely untouched, due to its value as a world cultural heritage site.

11. Numbers are drawn from Max Hastings, *Retribution: The Battle for Japan, 1944–45* (New York: Vintage Books, 2009), 314; Dower, *War without Mercy*, 41, 325; Tony Reichhardt, "The Deadliest Air Raid in History," *Air and Space Magazine*, March 9, 2015.

12. The 1957 A-Bomb Survivors Medical Treatment Law said that *hibakusha* were entitled to "biannual health examinations for better health management, detailed health examinations in the event that any abnormality was found, and medical compensation if they were certified as eligible by the Minister of Health and Welfare." A subsequent piece of legislation was adopted in 1967: the Law Concerning Special Measures for the Atomic Bomb Exposed. In 1994, the Atomic Bomb Survivors Support Law integrated previous legislation. This law broadly "stipulates that the Japanese government should assume the responsibility of implementing comprehensive relief measures for the health, medical care and welfare of the atomic bomb survivors." See, respectively, the glossary entries "A-Bomb Survivors Medical Treatment Law" and "Atomic Bomb Survivors Support Law," Radiation Effects Research Foundation (website), n.d.

13. The primary advocacy group representing the interests of A-bomb survivors is Nihon Hidankyo, the Japan Confederation of A- and H-Bomb Sufferers Organizations, which was founded in 1956; see Nihon Hidankyo's website. The Association of Bereaved Family Members of Tokyo Air Raid Victims represents the Tokyo firebombing survivors; see Cary Karacas, "Fire Bombings and Forgotten Civilians: The Lawsuit Seeking Compensation for Victims of the Tokyo Air Raids," *Asia-Pacific Journal* 9, no. 3/6 (2011): article 3474; "Centenarian Woman Demands Compensation for Air Raid Civilian Victims," *Mainichi*, December 9, 2015. Material on military and civilian compensation in this chapter is drawn from Ryuichi Kitano, "War Victims Still Pushing for Compensation 75 Years after WWII," *Asahi Shimbun*, August 17, 2020; Philip Brasor, "Civilian Casualties of WWII Left

Out in the Cold," *Japan Times*, December 26, 2015; "Relief for Air-Raid Survivors?," editorial, *Japan Times*, August 15, 2010. On *hibakusha* legislation and litigation, see She Lin Loh, "Defining Hibakusha in Postwar Japan: The Boundaries of Medicine and Law," *Zinbun* 49 (2019): 81–92; Akiko Naono, "The Origins of 'Hibakusha' as a Scientific and Political Classification of the Survivor," *Japanese Studies* 39, no. 3 (2019): 333–52; "Survivors of Hiroshima and Nagasaki," Atomic Heritage Foundation (website), posted July 27, 2017; Tomohiro Osaki, "Supreme Court Rules Hibakusha Overseas Are Entitled to Full Medical Expenses," *Japan Times*, September 8, 2015; Eric Johnston, "Japan to Fight Ruling Recognizing Hiroshima 'Black Rain' Victims," *Japan Times*, August 12, 2020.

14. Robert J. Smith, *Ancestor Worship in Contemporary Japan* (Stanford, CA: Stanford University Press, 1974), 41.

15. Robert Trumbull, "Honor to LeMay by Japan Stirs Parliament Debate," *New York Times*, December 8, 1964.

16. Author Justin Aukema puts the number at more than 150. See Aukema, "The Need to Narrate the Tokyo Air Raids: The Literature of Saotome Katsumoto," in *Routledge Handbook of Modern Japanese Literature*, ed. Rachael Hutchinson and Leith Morton (London: Routledge, 2016), 198–210.

17. Justin Aukema, "Author Sees Parallels between Prewar, Nuclear Indoctrination," *Japan Times*, March 20, 2012.

18. Phil Davison, "Katsumoto Saotome, Chronicler of Tokyo Firebombing, Dies at 90," *Washington Post*, May 12, 2022; Mari Yamaguchi, "Japanese Writer Who Documented WWII Tokyo Firebombing Dies," *Mainichi*, May 12, 2022.

19. This and subsequent quotes from Ono on the Tokyo bombing are from the album sleeve of Yoko Ono's album *Rising* (Capitol Records, 1995). Ono's referenced songs are also from this album.

20. Murray Sayle, "The Importance of Yoko Ono," Japan Policy Research Institute Occasional Paper no. 18 (November 2000).

21. For readers with a bent toward linguistics, the literal (*romaji*) transliteration of the word from Japanese to English would be *kurushii*, with two *i*'s, reflecting a long pronunciation of the vowel cluster at the end. Ono's album simplifies things by using a single *i*. See "Word: 苦しい (Kurushii)," *Japanese Words and Phrases* (blog), Tumblr, September 10, 2013.

22. Interview with author, November 2009. Information about the Hotel Okura is available at its website.

23. For more on Sadako's life, see Sue DiCicco and (Sadako's brother) Masahiro Sasaki, *The Complete Story of Sadako Sasaki and the Thousand Cranes* (Tokyo: Tuttle, 2020). Sadako completed folding one thousand cranes in August 1955 (115). DiCicco and Sasaki explain the significance of the thousand-crane milestone: In Japan "the crane is considered a mystical creature and, in folklore, is said to live for

one thousand years. An ancient Japanese legend promises that anyone who folds one thousand cranes, one for each year of a crane's life, will be granted a wish" (100). Sadako's wish was to survive her illness.

24. For a profile of Sadako Sasaki, see "Death of an A-Bombed Girl," *Victims and Survivors*, permanent exhibit, Hiroshima Peace Memorial Museum (website), n.d.

Chapter 11

1. Austin Smith, "Tokushima Air Raids Digital Archive," *Impressions of East Asia* (blog), WordPress, n.d.

2. Smith.

3. For information about Awa Odori, see the tour guide item "Awa Odori: Very Popular Dance Festival during Obon," Japan-Guide.com, last updated June 17, 2022.

4. "Dancing at Japanese Festivals," Kids Web Japan (website), n.d.

5. Telephone interview, December 2020, Tokushima.

6. For references to Awa Odori as the dance of peace, see "Awa Odori Master Seijuro Shinomaya Dies," *Asahi*, September 16, 2019; Seijuro Shinoyama obituary, *Mainichi*, September 17, 2019.

7. "Dancing at Japanese Festivals." A Japanese newspaper reported that the Awa Odori festival in August 2022 became "a COVID-19 superspreader event among participants." It was the first time the full-scale festival had taken place since the onset of the coronavirus pandemic in March 2020. See Takashi Azuma, "More Than 800 Participants in Awa Odori Report Getting COVID-19," *Asahi Shimbun*, September 23, 2022.

8. The visit to Okamoto's shop and the interview with Tanaka took place in June 2010.

9. Hal Atwood, "Buddhist Monk Raises Awareness about the Swastika's Original Meaning," *Lion's Roar*, February 18, 2019.

10. Brian Ashcraft, "The Buddhist Swastika Becomes Popular Slang in Japan," *Kotaku*, January 25, 2018.

11. Okachu.com offers a *manji* kimono for sale. It is in springtime shades of salmon and white, layered with two horizontal rows of cherry blossoms (in white and red), with scattered, encircled *manji* appearing in the same two shades as the cherry blossoms.

12. "Dancers to Forgo Swastika in Germany," *Japan Times*, May 21, 2006.

13. For video of the group dancing in Taiwan, "AwaOdori in Kaohsiung, Taiwan at Japanese Gourmet Food Fair 2016—The Hachisuka-Ren from Awa Japan," YouTube video, uploaded November 6, 2016, by dm_jpop, 0:33.

14. Justin McCurry, "Japan to Drop Swastika from Its Tourist Maps," *Guardian*, January 20, 2016.

15. This visit took place on June 23, 2010. For video of Uzuki-ren in

performance, see "Awa Odori 'Uzuki-ren,'" YouTube video, uploaded August 6, 2019, by IKEKITA Minoru, 2:27.

Chapter 12

1. Kerry Emanuel, *Divine Wind: The History and Science of Hurricanes* (Oxford: Oxford University Press, 2005), 4–5.

2. Japanese sources put the death toll at 953. For background on the Fukuoka raids, see Mark Ealey and Yoshimura Akira, "One Man's Justice," *Asia-Pacific Journal* 3, no. 2 (2005): article 1884.

3. The visit and interview with Nobuko Komiya took place on June 19, 2010.

4. Hakata is a ward in Fukuoka City. However, it was once the name used to describe the entire Fukuoka area. Even today the two labels are used interchangeably. For instance, Hakata is the official name of the Fukuoka bullet train (*shinkansen*) station. See "The Difference between 'Hakata' and 'Fukuoka,'" *Finding Fukuoka* (blog), WordPress, March 2, 2011.

Part 4

1. *Grave of the Fireflies* (*Hotaru no Haka*) was directed by Studio Ghibli's Isao Takahata, based on a semi-autobiographical story by Akiyuki Nosaka. The film was released in the United States in 1993, with English-language subtitles. See "Grave of the Fireflies," IMDb.com, n.d.

2. See, e.g., "Grave of the Fireflies/Release," Ghibli Wiki (website), last updated October 17, 2020; "How Sad Is Grave of the Fireflies (1988 Movie)?," question posted to Quora (website), n.d.; James Gates, "Why 'Grave of the Fireflies' Is the Saddest Japanese Movie Ever Made," Culture Trip (website), December 10, 2022; Norberto Briceño, "I Just Watched the Saddest Movie Ever Made and Now I'm Ugly Crying," Buzzfeed, November 25, 2016.

3. On how the film reflected author Akiyuki Nosaka's real life, see Teresa Marasigan, "Here's the Heart-Wrenching True Story behind *Grave of the Fireflies*," *Esquire*, October 16, 2021; Masako N. Racel, "*Grave of the Fireflies* and Japan's Memories of World War II," *Education about Asia* 14, no. 3 (2009): 56–59.

Chapter 13

1. For the story behind the transfers of the Auschwitz ashes, see Ran Zwigenberg, *Hiroshima: The Origins of Global Memory Culture* (Cambridge: Cambridge University Press, 2014), 249–58. On maple and bamboo trees, see Gail Cetnar Meadows, "O-susume desu! Marvelous Fall Foliage at Mitaki Temple," *Hiroshima JETs* (blog), WordPress, November 8, 2009.

2. "Peace Seeds: Teens in Hiroshima Sow Seeds of Peace (Part 31)," *Chugoku Shimbun*, Hiroshima Peace Media Center (website), posted April 21, 2016.

3. "Peace Seeds."

4. The full English-language text of the Auschwitz stone marker reads: "Here lie the souls of those sacrificed at Auschwitz, Poland, caused by the Nazism policy [*sic*] against Jewish people during World War II. Together with that of Hiroshima, this utterly inhumane tragedy shall never again be repeated. We should ponder over ourselves of the avarice, rage and stupidity that are deeply infiltrated in the hearts of each and all and cultivate the integrity that all human shares [*sic*]." Zwigenberg, *Hiroshima*, 255. The newspaper *Chugoku Shimbun* put the number of Hiroshima graves at "roughly 200 to 300"; see "Peace Seeds."

5. Interview by author, July 2015.

6. Erika Kobayashi, *Shin'ai naru Kitty tachi e* [*Your Dear Kitty*] (Tokyo: Little More, 2011). Kitty was Anne's imaginary friend, whom she wrote to in her diary.

7. The publication statistics were reported in an email to the author, July 2015, by Susumu Shimoyama, editor at Bungei Shunju publishing company, which put out the original Japanese edition of Anne's diary. Worldwide, the book has sold more than thirty million copies in more than sixty countries and seventy languages. See "Anne Frank in Translation," Atlas Translations (website), posted March 7, 2019. For more on the publishing history in Japan, see Angela Coutts, "Remembering Anne Frank in Japan: Akazome Akiko's *Otome no Mikkou / The Maiden's Betrayal*," *Contemporary Women's Writing* 8, no. 1 (2014): 71–88. Coutts writes: "First published in Japan under the title *Hikari Honokani: Anne no Nikki / A Light Ever So Fragile: Anne's Diary*, it was reprinted 13 times in its first year of publication, selling over 100,000 copies. In 1986, it was republished as *Anne no Nikki / Anne's Diary*, in a new translation by Fukamachi Mariko, and it is estimated to have sold some 5 million copies. Its popularity was revived in 1995 when the animated film version by Nagaoka Akinori was released" (74). The book topped Japan's best seller list in 1953 and is still popular today; see "Japan Arrest over Anne Frank Book Vandalism," BBC News, March 14, 2014; Julian Ryall, "Japanese Retain Fascination with Anne Frank," Deutche Welle, March 2, 2015 ("bookshops still sell a steady number of copies"). On manga, film, and television adaptations, see Twwk, "Manga of a Young Girl: Anne Frank in Japan," *Beneath the Tangles* (blog), July 30, 2012; Akinori Nagaoka, dir., *Anne no nikki* [*The Diary of Anne Frank*] (Madhouse Productions, 1995), and the film's IMDb.com page, n.d. On the topic of stage adaptations, actress Sayaka Hanamura, who has played Anne Frank in Japanese productions, told me in a November 2009 interview in Tokyo that she was the fifteenth Japanese actress to portray Anne onstage in Japan. The first Japanese-language stage production took place in Tokyo in October 1956, and its audience was "moved to tears"; see "Anne Frank in Tokyo, Japanese-Language Version of Play Well Received," *New York Times*, October 6, 1956. On Japanese visitors to Amsterdam, see "Why Are the Japanese So Fascinated with Anne Frank," *Haaretz*, January 22, 2014.

8. Interview with author, July 2015, Hiroshima.

9. Interview with author, July 2015, Hiroshima.

10. Justin McCurry, "Japanese PM Shinzo Abe Stops Short of New Apology in War Anniversary Speech," *Guardian*, August 14, 2015; "'Sincere Condolences': Full Text of Shinzo Abe's Statement on World War II," *Washington Post*, August 14, 2015. For background, see John Swenson-Wright, "Why Is Japan's WW2 Surrender Still a Sensitive Subject?," BBC News, August 14, 2015. The issue of Japan apologizing for its World War II aggression is explored later in this book, in part 6, "War Crimes, Repentance, and Apologies."

11. One scholar writes that in Japan, apologizing is a "broadly shared social behavior that is a mix of habit, expectations, and underlying values." John O. Haley, "Comment: The Implications of Apology," *Law and Society Review* 20, no. 4 (1986): 500. Another scholar maintains that "Japanese life is a constant stream of apology, although how much of this is sincere and how much ritual apology is a moot point"; Chris Burgess, "Soft Power Is Key to Japan Reshaping Its Identity Abroad," *Japan Times*, September 2, 2008. Others note that in Japan, unlike the United States, civil and criminal defendants "are called upon to express personal apology to those they have injured or to the society whose rules they have violated"; Hiroshi Wagatsuma and Arthur Rosett, "The Implications of Apology: Law and Culture in Japan and the United States," *Law and Society Review* 20, no. 4 (1986): 462.

12. "Sincere Condolences."

13. Ran Zwigenberg, "Never Again: Hiroshima, Auschwitz and the Politics of Commemoration," *Asia-Pacific Journal* 13, no. 3/3 (2015): article 4252.

14. David G. Goodman and Masanori Miyazawa, *Jews in the Japanese Mind: The History and Uses of a Cultural Stereotype*, exp. ed. (Lanham, MD: Lexington Books, 2000), 168.

15. Interview with author, November 2009, Tokyo.

16. Quoted in Gillian Walnes Perry, *The Legacy of Anne Frank* (Barnsley, UK: Pen and Sword History, 2018), 333.

17. I visited the Holocaust Education Center and interviewed Yoshida in November 2009.

18. Anne's Rose Church in Nishinomiya has a Facebook page under the username @annesrosechurch.

19. Yoko Ogawa, one of Japan's most well-known writers and an International Booker Prize nominee, recalled in a newspaper interview how she reacted to Anne's diary when she read it in high school: "I became intrigued by the realistic feelings she expressed, like her rebelliousness toward her mother and defiance toward the other adults around her. I sympathized with the specific woes she felt as an adolescent girl, because when I read it, I was also trying to push back against my mother's image of me as the 'perfect daughter.' Anne's diary showed me a suitable

way to express my frustrations." See Yuji Yamamoto, "Writer Yoko Ogawa on the Significance of Anne Frank and Her Famous Diary," *Chugoku Shimbun*, Hiroshima Peace Media Center (website), posted May 26, 2015.

20. Interview with author, November 2009, Tokyo. Kurokawa's best-known book is *Anne Frank* (Tokyo: Tankoban, 2009).

21. Email to author, July 2015.

22. "Unemployed Man Says He Ripped Books on Anne Frank," *Asahi Shimbun*, March 13, 2014; "Tokyo Library Sends Message of Hope with Display of Donated Anne Frank Books," *Asahi Shimbun*, May 3, 2014; Mitsuru Obe, "Suspect Arrested in Anne Frank Book Vandalism," *Wall Street Journal*, March 14, 2014; "Tokyo Police Make Arrest in Anne Frank Vandalism," *Times of Israel*, March 13, 2014. In a July 2015 email to me, the press office of the Israeli Embassy in Tokyo, citing Japanese news reports, said that the suspect was released by police "after going through a psychiatric examination which stated that he is ineligible to stand trial and does not bare [*sic*] criminal responsibility."

23. "Japan PM Shinzo Abe Visits Amsterdam's Anne Frank Museum," BBC News, March 24, 2014.

24. "Remarks by Prime Minister Shinzo Abe at Yad Vashem," Prime Minister of Japan and His Cabinet (government website), January 19, 2015.

Chapter 14

1. I spoke with Kageyama inside the Hiroshima Prefectural Art Museum in November 2007.

2. Interview with author, October 2007, Kamakura, Japan.

3. For a detailed description of the *nihonga* technique, see "What Is *Nihonga?*," Yamatane Museum of Art (website), n.d.

4. UNESCO named Hirayama a goodwill ambassador for both his artistic work and his advocacy for the preservation and restoration of world heritage sites; see "UNESCO Mourns Loss of Japanese Painter and Goodwill Ambassador," UN News, December 4, 2009.

5. Yoshiro Mori was the former prime minister (in office 2000–2001); and in a nod to Hirayama's interest in Buddhism, the chief priest of the Yakushiji temple in Nara, Japan, attended. Hirayama's career was inexorably linked to the temple, a UNESCO World Heritage Site: in an achievement reminiscent of Michelangelo's Sistine Chapel, Hirayama had completed a series of paintings on Yakushiji's interior walls depicting the seventh-century travels of the Chinese monk Xuanzang, known in Japan as Genjo Sanzo, who brought the Hosso school of Buddhism to China and—later, through a disciple—to Japan. Hirayama had retraced much of Genjo Sanzo's journey to gather material for the temple paintings. One of the Yakushiji panels is 164 feet long. The series is one of Hirayama's best-known

works. For Genjo Sanzo's story and photographs of the panels, see, respectively, "15. Genjo Sanzoin Complex" and "17. Wall Paintings of Genjo's Travels," Yajushiji (website), n.d.

6. Interview with author, September 2007, Tokyo National Museum of Modern Art.

7. Kono, email exchange with author, April 2021.

8. Email to author, March 2021.

9. See Richard Brody, "Claude Lanzmann Changed the History of Filmmaking with 'Shoah,'" *New Yorker*, July 6, 2018.

10. Yuri Jinnai at the museum, email to author, April 2021.

11. Kono, email exchange with author, April 2021.

12. This account of Wiesel's visit, and all related quotations, is based on Clyde Haberman, "In Hiroshima, Wiesel Finds New Horror," *New York Times*, May 23, 1987.

13. "Elie Wiesel: Facts," Nobel Prize (website), n.d.

14. Ran Zwigenberg, "Entangled Memories: Israel, Japan and the Emergence of Global Memory Culture," *Asia-Pacific Journal* 13, no. 32/4 (2015): article 4354.

15. See Julie Platner, "An Unfinished Story," *Wall Street Journal*, August 13, 2010.

16. From "Oprah Talks to Elie Wiesel," interview by Oprah Winfrey, O, *The Oprah Magazine*, November 2000.

Chapter 15

1. See Katsumoto Saotome, *Aushubittsu kara no tegami* [*Letter from Auschwitz*], illus. Kazu Okano (Tokyo: Nihon Tosho Senta, 2001).

2. See Saotome, 73. On the beheadings of the American aircrew, see Timothy Lang Francis, "'To Dispose of the Prisoners': The Japanese Executions of American Aircrew at Fukuoka, Japan, during 1945," *Pacific Historical Review*, 66, no. 4 (1997): 469–501; Ken Aoshima, "Residents Recall the Day in 1945 When a Tokyo Suburb Came Out to Beat a US Airman," *Mainichi*, August 14, 2020.

3. Katsumoto Saotome, *Aushubittsu to watashi* [*Auschwitz and Me*] (Tokyo: Soudobunka, 1980).

4. Saotome, 120–21. For examples of active German prosecutions as recently as 2021, see Toby Axelrod, "Germany Seeks to Prosecute Over a Dozen More Nazi War Criminals," *Times of Israel*, August 5, 2021; Justin Huggler, "Germany's 'Nazi Hunter' Aims for Last 11 Prosecutions as Lifetime of Work Draws to a Close," *Telegraph*, December 24, 2020.

5. "China and South Korea Protest as Japan Honours War Dead at Yasukuni Shrine," *South China Morning Post*, August 15, 2017.

6. Saotome, *Aushubittsu to watashi*, 126.

7. On the Sugamo commemorative stone, see "Monument for Tojo Execution

Site Stirs Japanese," *New York Times*, March 16, 1980; Kit Nagamura, "The Sun Shines in Spiritland," *Japan Times*, May 4, 2007; Reid Knight, "The Sugamo Prison 'Memorial,'" *In Search of Modern Japan* (blog), Beloit College, November 11, 2022. On the memorial's silence regarding the Sugamo war criminals, Knight wrote: "Japanese discourse regarding the war has a tendency to gloss over certain factors regarding their culpability for war atrocities, and instead focus on themes such as preserving peace now rather than addressing past destruction."

8. Saotome, *Aushubittsu to watashi*, 223–24.

9. Quoted in Matthew Penney, "'The Most Crucial Education': Saotome Katsumoto and Japanese Anti-War Thought," *Asia-Pacific Journal* 3, no. 12 (2005): article 1640.

10. Saotome, *Aushubittsu to watashi*, 17.

Part 5

1. For key facts on Wiesel, see "Elie Wiesel," *Holocaust Encyclopedia*, US Holocaust Memorial Museum (website), last updated April 9, 2021.

2. Elie Wiesel, "The Perils of Indifference," speech delivered at the White House, April 12, 1999, American Rhetoric (website), last updated December 6, 2021.

Chapter 16

1. For background on the chain of Renoir cafés in Tokyo, see "Ginza Renoir—A Taste of 1960s Tokyo," *Exploring Old Tokyo* (blog), April 1, 2018.

2. Interview with author, October 2007, Tokyo.

3. "Uzbekistan Life: The Buddhist Legacy of Termez," Euronews (website), March 30, 2021. For an overview of Termez and Buddhism, see Atsushi Iwamoto, "A Study on the Prosperity and Decline of Buddhist Sites in Northern Bactria: Kara Tepe and Zurmala," *Rissho International Journal of Academic Research in Culture and Society* 2 (2019): 151–78.

4. The Soviet invasion was set in play at the February 1945 Yalta Conference, where Joseph Stalin promised US president Franklin Delano Roosevelt that the Soviet Union would declare war on Japan soon after the defeat of Germany. In return, the United States agreed to cede to Moscow territory the Kremlin had eyed since the czarist days: the Kuril (or Kurile) Islands, north of Japan. Yalta tossed aside a defunct 1941 nonaggression pact between the Soviet Union and Japan that had allowed Moscow and Tokyo to focus war efforts on their primary adversaries (Germany and the United States, respectively) and not on each other. For background on the nonaggression pact and Yalta, see Tsuyoshi Hasegawa, "Soviet Policy toward Japan during World War II," *Cahiers du Monde russe* 52, no. 2/3 (2011): 246; Louis Morton, "Soviet Intervention in the War with Japan," *Foreign Affairs* 40, no. 4 (1962): 653–62; Charles G. Stefan, "Yalta Revisited: An Update on the

Diplomacy of FDR and His Wartime Summit Partners," *Presidential Studies Quarterly* 23, no. 4 (1993): 755–70.

5. Hasegawa, "Soviet Policy toward Japan," 263.

6. John Dower, *Embracing Defeat: Japan in the Wake of World War II* (New York: Norton, 1999), 52. According to Dower, "Japanese authorities estimated that between 1.6 and 1.7 million Japanese fell into Soviet hands" (52). Regarding the numbers, historian John J. Stephan wrote: "In the final days of World War II, two and a half million Japanese fell into Soviet hands as Red Army units swept across Manchuria, northern Korea, and southern Sakhalin and as Pacific Fleet forces seized the Kurile Islands. . . . Meanwhile, 450,000 soldiers and 125,000 civilians were removed to the USSR and interned at 700 labor camps between Kharkov and Kamchatka." Stephan, review of *Behind a Curtain of Silence: Japanese in Soviet Custody, 1945–1956*, by William F. Nimmo, *Journal of Japanese Studies* 15, no. 2 (1989): 526–28.

7. Information on Japanese captives held in the USSR is drawn from Stephan, review of *Behind a Curtain of Silence*; Yokote Shinji, "Soviet Repatriation Policy, U.S. Occupation Authorities, and Japan's Entry into the Cold War," *Journal of Cold War Studies* 15, no. 2 (2013): 30–50. For a comprehensive list of material on Japanese captives, see Haruko Sakakibara, "Bibliography," Japanese Interned in Siberia (website), University of California, Davis, posted June 15, 2020.

8. Dower, *Embracing Defeat*, 52. Of the forty million who died, an estimated twenty million perished in labor camps, or from forced collectivization, famine, and executions. See Bill Keller, "Major Soviet Paper Says 20 Million Died as Victims of Stalin," *New York Times*, February 4, 1989. Keller cites estimates put forward by the historian Roy Medvedev in the Russian paper *Argumenti i Fakti*. Under Soviet leader Mikhail Gorbachev's policies of restructuring and openness (perestroika and glasnost), *Argumenti i Fakti* was an important platform for reporting fresh information about the Stalin years. Max Hastings, the British journalist and military historian, put the total wartime number of Soviet dead at twenty-seven million, including an estimated eleven million soldiers. See Hastings, *Inferno: The World at War, 1939–1945* (New York: Vintage Books, 2012), 152.

9. Interview with author, October 2008, New York.

10. Stephan, review of *Behind a Curtain of Silence*, 527.

11. For the Soviet view, see Igor A. Latyshev, "Soviet-U.S. Differences in Their Approaches to Japan," *Asian Survey* 24, no. 11 (1984): 1163–73.

12. For overviews of the Russo-Japanese War, see Richard Connaughton, *Rising Sun and Tumbling Bear: Russia's War with Japan* (London: Cassell, 2003); Raymond Esthus, *Double Eagle and Rising Sun: The Russians and the Japanese at Portsmouth in 1905* (Durham, NC: Duke University Press, 1988).

13. "The defeat of Russian troops during the Russo-Japanese war left bitter memories in the minds of people," Stalin said in a speech on September 2, 1945,

justifying the USSR's war against Japan. "It left a black spot on our country. Our people nourished hopes for the day when Japan would be defeated and the stain would be removed." Quoted in Dmitry Streltsov, "Russian views of Japanese History," *Asan Forum*, August 29, 2016. Stalin did not mention the Yalta Conference in the speech, skirting over the secret quid pro quo with Roosevelt. For Stalin's speech, see "Obrashchenie k narodu: 2 sentiabria 1945 goda," in *Sochineniia*, by I. V. Stalin (Moscow: Pisatel', 1997), 15:240–42, Stalin Archive (website), Centre for 21st Century Humanities, University of Newcastle, n.d.

14. Dower, *Embracing Defeat*, 52.

15. Kyuzo Kato, *Sibir' v serdtse Iapontsa* [*Siberia in the Heart of a Japanese Man*] (Novosibirsk: Nauka, 1992).

16. Kato, 74. In her history of the Gulag, Anne Applebaum wrote that one of the "standard methods" Gulag prisoners used during escapes involved cannibalism: "Pairs of criminals would agree in advance to escape along with a third man (the 'meat'), who was destined to become the sustenance for the other two on their journey." That appears to have been what happened in the story Kyuzo Kato tells. Anne Applebaum, *Gulag: A History* (New York: Doubleday, 2003), 398.

17. Genjo Sanzo is the Japanese name for the Chinese monk Xuanzang. For more on him, see note 5 in chapter 14. Also see: Der Huey Lee, "Xuanzang (Hsüan-tsang) (602–664)," *Internet Encyclopedia of Philosophy*, University of Texas at Martin, n.d.; Matthew Z. Dischner, "Xuanzang," *The Sogdians: Influencers on the Silk Roads*, digital exhibition, Freer Gallery of Art and Arthur M. Sackler Gallery, Smithsonian Institution, n.d.

18. Kato, *Sibir' v serdtse Iapontsa*, 3.

19. See "About the Department," Department of Japanology, St. Petersburg University (website), posted March 1, 2017. For more on Dembei and early contacts between Japan and Russia, see Boris Egorov, "How the Japanese First Appeared in Russia," Russia Beyond (website), March 30, 2022; George Alexander Lensen, "Early Russo-Japanese Relations," *Far Eastern Quarterly* 10, no. 1 (1950): 2–37; George Alexander Lensen, *The Russian Push toward Japan: Russo-Japanese Relations, 1697–1875* (Princeton, NJ: Princeton University Press, 1959). On Japanese castaways, see Curtis Ebbesmeyer and Eric Scigliano, "Borne on a Black Current," *Smithsonian Magazine*, June 15, 2009.

20. S. I. Kuznetsov, "Vspominaia professora Kato Kiudzo" [Remembering Professor Kyzuo Kato], *Izvestiia Irkutskogo gosudarstvennogo universiteta, Seriia "Istoriia"* 18 (2016): 72. I draw details of Kato's career from Kuznetsov's article.

21. Kyuzo Kato, *Shiberia no Rekishi* [*The History of Siberia*] (Tokyo: Kinokuniya, 1963).

22. R. Shagaev, "Kato-san byl vliublon v Uzbekistan" [Kato-san Was in Love with Uzbekistan], *Novosti Uzbekistana*, September 16, 2016.

23. Shima Nobuhiko, "70 Years after the Siberian Internment: The Passing of a Cultural Anthropologist," *Hatena Blog*, September 21, 2016. Nobuhiko worked as Washington correspondent for the newspaper *Mainichi Shimbun* and later became a commentator for TBS, the Tokyo Broadcasting System. In 1998, he founded the Japan-Uzbekistan Association, a nonprofit organization fostering ties between the two countries. See Japan-Uzbekistan Association (website), n.d.

24. Kato died on September 12, 2016. Shagaev, in "Kato-san byl vliublon v Uzbekistan," put the number of Kato's visits to Uzbekistan at sixty.

25. The Order of Dustlik (Friendship) was signed by President Islam Karimov. See *Vedomosti Olii Mazhlisa Respubliki Uzbekistan*, no. 4–5 (May 3, 2002): 91.

26. "Foreign Minister's Commendations FY2010 (Individuals)," Ministry of Foreign Affairs of Japan (website), posted July 2010.

27. Kuznetsov, "Vspominaia professora Kato Kiudzo," 74; Kusuke Kato obituary, Tokyo National Research Institute for Cultural Properties (website), September 11, 2016.

28. Shinzo Abe, "Speech by Prime Minister Abe on Japan's Foreign Policy toward Central Asia," on visit to Kazakhstan, October 28, 2015, Ministry of Foreign Affairs of Japan (website).

29. These books were released across half a century, from 1963 to 2020, and included notable titles *Shiberia no Rekishi* [*The History of Siberia*] (Tokyo: Kinokuniya, 1963); *Shiruku Rodo Jiten* [*Silk Road Dictionary*], coauthored with Shinji Maejima (Tokyo: Fuyo Shobo, 1993); *Kokogaku ga Kataru Shiruku Rodo Shi: Chuo Ajia no Bunmei, Kokka, Bunka* [*The Story of the Silk Road That Archaeology Tells: The Civilization, Nation, and Culture of Central Asia*], coauthored with Edvard V. Rtveladze (Tokyo: Heibonsha, 2011); and *Shiberia Ki: Haruka Naru Tabi no Genten* [*Siberia Records: Origins of a Faraway Journey*] (Tokyo: Ronsonsha, 2020).

30. For more on Kato, and to hear him sing, see Robert Rand, "For Japanese Soldier, the War Went On," NPR, *Weekend Edition Sunday*, December 7, 2008.

Chapter 17

1. Except where noted, all information and quotations from Horikiri came from my interview with him, November 2009, Kitakyushu, Japan.

2. Horikiri received the Fukuoka Prefecture Culture Award in 2010 in honor of his "remarkable achievements"; see "List of Fukuoka Prefecture Cultural Award Winners," Fukuoka Prefecture (website), 2010. Horikiri was also honored by the Japanese Museum Association in 2001; see "Horikiri Shinichi Profile," HMV&Books (website), n.d. Many of Horikiri's essays were translated into English and published in Tatsuichi Horikiri, *The Stories Clothes Tell: Voices of Working-Class Japan*, ed. and trans. Rieko Wagoner (Lanham, MD: Rowman and Littlefield, 2016); see p. xvi for information on the original, Japanese-language publications.

3. Horikiri, *The Stories Clothes Tell*, 5.

4. For a sampling of the collection, see the museum's catalog: Tatsuichi Horikiri, *Kolekushon Jidaifuku Mokuroku: Boro, Zokuhen Dai Ikkan* [*Rags: the Horikiri Tatsuichi Collection—Cataloging Cloth across Time*] (Kitakyushu: Kitakyushu Museum of Natural History and Human History, 2014). For a museum video featuring the Horikiri collection, see "Ranru shomin seikatsushi kenkyuka Horikiri Tatsuichi shi nitsuite" [Rags. about Tatsuichi Horikiri: Researcher of the Life History of the Common People], YouTube video, uploaded September 4, 2020, by user-rl9fu5gf9u, 2:44.

5. Horikiri, *The Stories Clothes Tell*, 7.

6. Horikiri, 8.

7. Yuko Tanaka, president of Tokyo's Hosei University and one of Japan's leading experts on cloth, said that Horikiri was known in Kitakyushu as a "common life history researcher." Email to author, May 2021.

8. For a cross-national comparison of violent crime statistics in 2009, see "Crime > Violent Crime Stats: Compare Key Data on Japan & United States," data year 2009, NationMaster (website), n.d.

9. "Life Term Upheld for Akita Mom Who Killed Daughter, Neighbor Boy," *Japan Times*, March 26, 2009; "Akita Child Serial Murder Case, Sentencing Reasons for Second Trial Judgment," *Asahi Shimbun*, March 25, 2009; "Demolition of Hatakeyama Inmates' Parents' House," *Mainichi Shimbun*, April 11, 2009; "The Unfortunate Mother Who Lost Her Daughter Was a Murderer! Published Letters from Thugs," TV Tokyo (website), May 9, 2009; "Akita Child Serial Murder Case: The Killer Who Killed His Daughter Talks about His 'True Feelings' at the Detention Center," Friday Digital (website), July 23, 2009.

10. "Troubled Yamagata Boy Admits Killing Grandma," *Japan Times*, October 19, 2007; "Japan Teen Took Mom's Head to Internet Café," Reuters, May 16, 2007.

11. Horikiri, *The Stories Clothes Tell*, xvi.

12. Walter A. Lunden, "Juvenile Delinquency in Japan: Pre-War, War and Post-War Years," *Journal of Criminal Law and Criminology* 44, no. 4 (1954): 430.

13. Doug Struck, "Japan's Violent Turn: Economic Malaise, Social Changes Spur Soaring Crime Rate," *Washington Post*, February 10, 2000.

14. Horikiri, *The Stories Clothes Tell*, 160.

15. Horikiri, 159.

16. Ueno, email to author, May 2021.

17. Ueno, email to author, June 2021. For three months in 2020, the Kitakyushu museum staged a posthumous exhibition in Horikiri's memory. The collection is not on permanent display, but Akiko Ueno told me that the museum planned to hold a small exhibition about once a year. Videos of the posthumous exhibition can be seen on the website of the Kitakyushu Museum of Natural History and Human History.

Part 6

1. For those who may be interested in the theological backstory to tzitzis (also called tzitzit): in the fourth of the Old Testament's Five Books of Moses, God tells Moses to instruct the Israelites to make fringes on the corners of their garments, to look at them "and recall all the commandments of God and observe them, so that you do not follow your heart and eyes in your lustful urge. Thus you shall be reminded to observe all My commandments and to be holy to your God" (Numbers 15:38–41). The translation is from *The Contemporary Torah, a Gender-Sensitive Adaptation of the Original JPS Translation* (Philadelphia: Jewish Publication Society, 2006).

2. See Shraga Simmons, "163 Hebrew & Jewish Names for Boys (and Their Meanings)," Aish.com, n.d.; "Jerahmeel (Yerahmiel, Yerahmi'el)," HebrewName. org, n.d.

3. Milton Steinberg, *Basic Judaism: A Book about the Jewish Religion—Its Ideals, Beliefs, and Practices—Written for Both Jews and Non-Jews* (New York: Harcourt, Brace, 1947).

4. Steinberg, 88.

5. The Japanese-language edition of Steinberg's *Basic Judaism* is called *Yudayakyo no Kihon*, trans. Mariko Yamaoka and Kazumitsu Kawai, ed. Izaya Teshima (Tokyo: Myrtos, 2012). The material on repentance (*kuiaratame*) is in section 5, chapter 10, "Shimin to shite no ningen" (Man as a Citizen).

Chapter 18

1. For two academic works on how Japan addressed its wartime culpability, see Philip A. Seaton, *Japan's Contested War Memories: The "Memory Rifts" in Historical Consciousness of World War II* (London: Routledge, 2007); and Jane W. Yamazaki, *Japanese Apologies for World War II: A Rhetorical Study* (London: Routledge, 2006). Japanese prime ministers have expressed variously worded "heartfelt apologies" and feelings of "deep remorse" for the country's wartime behavior; see "List of War Apology Statements Issued by Japan," Wikipedia, last edited October 20, 2022. At the same time, government officials have honored the souls of Japanese soldiers, even the most brutal, at the Yasukuni Shrine, situated in the heart of Tokyo—often to the ire of the rest of Asia. See, e.g., "Defiant Koizumi Visits Yasukuni," *Japan Times*, August 16, 2006; "China and South Korea Protest as Japan Honours War Dead at Yasukuni Shrine," *South China Morning Post*, August 15, 2017. A detailed discussion of Japan's wartime culpability and the morality of US actions is beyond the scope of this book, but see the preliminary bibliography in the next note.

2. A sample bibliography would include: "Debate over the Bomb: An Annotated Bibliography," Atomic Heritage Foundation (website), posted May 17, 2016;

Michael Bess, *Choices under Fire: Moral Dimensions of World War II* (New York: Alfred A. Knopf, 2006); Herbert P. Bix, *Hirohito and the Making of Modern Japan* (New York: Perennial, 2001); Herbert P. Bix, "War Responsibility and Historical Memory: Hirohito's Apparition," *Asia-Pacific Journal* 6, no. 5 (2008): article 2741; John Breen, ed., *Yasukuni: The War Dead and the Struggle for Japan's Past* (London: Hurst, 2007); John Breen, "Popes, Bishops and War Criminals: Reflections on Catholics and Yasukuni in Post-War Japan," *Asia-Pacific Journal* 8, no. 9/3 (2010): article 3312; Ian Buruma, *The Wages of Guilt: Memories of War in Germany and Japan* (New York: Farrar, Straus and Giroux, 1994); John Dower, *Embracing Defeat: Japan in the Wake of World War II* (New York: Norton, 1999); John Dower, "Japan Addresses Its War Responsibility," *Journal of the International Institute Online* 3, no. 1 (1995): n.p.; Richard H. Minear, *Victors' Justice: The Tokyo War Crimes Trial* (Princeton, NJ: Princeton University Press, 1971); B. V. A. Röling and Antonio Cassese, *The Tokyo Trial and Beyond* (Cambridge: Polity Press, 1993) (Röling was one of eleven judges in the Tokyo War Crimes Tribunal); Sebastian Swann, "Democratization and the Evasion of War Responsibility: the Allied Occupations of Japan and the Emperor," discussion paper no. IS/99/370, London School of Economics and Political Science, October 1999; Yuki Tanaka, "Crime and Responsibility: War, the State, and Japanese Society," *Asia-Pacific Journal* 4, no. 8 (2006): article 2200; Yuma Totani, *The Tokyo War Crimes Trial: The Pursuit of Justice in the Wake of World War II* (Cambridge, MA: Harvard University Asia Center, 2008); Sandra Wilson et al., *Japanese War Criminals: The Politics of Justice after the Second World War* (New York: Columbia University Press, 2017).

3. Katsumoto Saotome, *Aushubittsu kara no tegami* [*Letter from Auschwitz*], illus. Kazu Okano (Tokyo: Nihon Tosho Senta, 2001), 78–79.

4. Quoted in *"Fog of War* Director Remembers McNamara," NPR, *All Things Considered*, July 6, 2009.

5. For details on the capture of the Americans and on subsequent events, see Thomas Easton, "A Quiet Honesty Records a World War II Atrocity," *Baltimore Sun*, May 28, 1995; Justin McCurry, "Japan Revisits Its Darkest Moments Where American POWs Became Human Experiments," *Guardian*, August 13, 2015.

6. On the medical experiments see Easton, "A Quiet Honesty"; McCurry, "Japan Revisits Its Darkest Moments"; Rose Troup Buchanan, "US Prisoners of War Had Parts of Their Brains and Livers Removed during WWII, New Japanese Exhibit Shows," *Independent*, April 7, 2015. On the Fukuoka decapitations, see Justin McCurry and Timothy Lang Francis, "'To Dispose of the Prisoners': The Japanese Executions of American Aircrew at Fukuoka, Japan, during 1945," *Pacific Historical Review* 66, no. 4 (1997): 469–501. For a book-length examination of the Kyushu atrocities and resulting war crime trials, see Marc Landas, *The Fallen: A True Story*

of American POWs and Japanese Wartime Atrocities (Hoboken, NJ: John Wiley and Sons, 2004).

7. All quotations in this section are from John Dower, *War without Mercy: Race and Power in the Pacific War* (New York: Pantheon, 1986), 41–42.

8. Dower (43) notes that the total number of deaths in the Nanking massacre, also known as the Rape of Nanking, is controversial, but he puts the middle range estimate at two hundred thousand. See also Dower, 326n26.

9. Dower (79) writes that "the US government incarcerated Japanese-Americans en masse, while taking no comparable action against residents of German or Italian origin." Approximately eleven thousand Germans and three thousand Italians were detained in the United States. See "German and Italian Detainees," *Densho Encyclopedia*, last updated July 29, 2015; and Dan A. D'Amelio, "A Season of Panic: The Internments of World War II," *Italian Americana* 17, no. 2 (1999): 160.

10. Pyle is quoted from John J. Contreni, "'A Story That Can't Be Printed': Ernie Pyle's Ie Shima Memorial Dedication, Dealing with Men, and Military Journalism in the Mid-Pacific during World War II," *Indiana Magazine of History* 111, no. 3 (2015): 290. For racism and anti-Japanese sentiment, see Dower, *War without Mercy*, 81, 184–87 (references to monkeys and apes); 29, 37, 53–54 (exterminatioinist sentiment), 88, 182–87 (Japanese as subhuman); 155–63 ("Yellow Peril"). Dower (54) wrote: "Knowledgeable observers who followed American attitudes at the levels where opinions were shaped and policies made certainly concluded that support for an annihilationist policy against the Japanese was extremely strong." See also Dower, 155–63. Hannah Miles, "WWII Propaganda: The Influence of Racism," *Artifacts Journal*, no. 6 (March 2012): n.p.; "Propaganda Poster 'Jap Trap,'" c. 1941–45, ID ddr-densho-37-498, Densho Digital Repository (website); "Introduction to WWII Incarceration," Densho (website), n.d. (an illustrated history of the incarceration of Japanese Americans); "Anti-Japanese Exclusion Movement," *Densho Encyclopedia*, last updated October 8, 2020 (on the "Yellow Peril"). Densho is a grassroots nonprofit dedicated to preserving the history of Japanese Americans.

Chapter 19

1. The Japanese Ministry of Internal Affairs and Communications additionally reported a handful of injuries and damage to 155 households, affecting more than six hundred people. See its postwar summary of Morioka's wartime experience: "War Damage Situation in Morioka City (Iwate Prefecture)," Ministry of Internal Affairs and Communications (website), n.d.; "Air Raid Damage in Iwate Prefecture," Yahoo! Japan (website), n.d.

2. Except where otherwise noted, all material in this chapter about Osamu Komai and his father, Mitsuo, is from my 2009 interview with Osamu, as well as family archival material and other documents he provided to me.

3. Malcome Larcens, "Hiking Mount Iwate," Japan Travel (website), posted November 7, 2014.

4. See the 1957 Academy Award–winning movie *The Bridge on the River Kwai*, directed by David Lean and starring Alec Guinness. Allied POWs actually built two bridges on the River Kwai. Both were destroyed postwar. The film, a piece of historical fiction, was shot in Sri Lanka, not Thailand. Lean had a new bridge erected for the movie, using five hundred Sri Lankan workers and nearly three dozen elephants. Back in Thailand, the state railway authority built a new bridge on the River Kwai in 1955–56. The structure became a popular tourist destination. See W. L. Gwyer, "The Bridge That Never Was: But the Death Toll from Building Japan's Military Railroad Was All Too Real," *Railroad History*, no. 191 (2004): 107–11.

5. Information on Kanchanaburi POWs is drawn from "Burma-Thailand Railway and Hellfire Pass 1942 to 1943," Australian Department of Veterans' Affairs (website), last updated May 13, 2021 (see especially "The Workers"). Brits made up the largest group of Allied POWs at Kanchanaburi, some thirty thousand; there were also some eighteen thousand Dutch, thirteen thousand Australians, and the seven hundred Americans. See Michael Ray, "Burma Railway," *Encyclopedia Britannica*, last updated October 20, 2020. About half the Americans had served aboard the USS *Houston*, sunk by the Japanese in February 1942. See Chris Woolf, "A New Book Recalls the Japanese 'Railroad of Death' from World War II," review of *The Narrow Road to the Deep North*, by Richard Flanagan, *World*, October 15, 2014; Eric Niderost, "Working on the Railway of Death: A POW's Story," Warfare History Network (website), November 11, 2016.

6. Thomas Fuller, "Seeking Recognition for a War's Lost Laborers," *New York Times*, March 16, 2008; "Indian Labourers, the Unsung Heroes behind Death Railway," *Times of India*, December 27, 2018.

7. Gwyer, "The Bridge That Never Was," 108.

8. Alvin Smith, "The Kwai Bridge: The Reel and the Real," *New York Times*, December 17, 1972.

9. Gwyer, "The Bridge That Never Was," 108–9.

10. See Kirsten Magasdi, "Remembering Victims of the 'Death Railway,'" BBC News, November 8, 2003; "Blue Plaque for Bridge on River Kwai Hero," BBC News, July 29, 2017.

11. For definitions of Classes A, B, and C, and background on the military tribunals, see John Dower, *Embracing Defeat: Japan in the Wake of World War II* (New York: Norton, 1999), 443–84, especially 456; Higurashi Yoshinobu, "Yasukuni and the Enshrinement of War Criminals," Nippon.com, November 25, 2013; Philip R. Piccigallo, *The Japanese on Trial: Allied War Crimes Operations in the East, 1945–1951* (Austin: University of Texas Press, 1979).

12. Allied soldiers who may have committed war crimes were largely the beneficiaries of "victors' justice." In his book *Inferno: The World at War, 1939–1945* (New York: Vintage Books, 2012), 648, Max Hastings wrote: "Some British and Americans, and many Russians, were guilty of offences under international law, the killing of prisoners notable among them, yet very few faced even courts-martial. To have been on the winning side sufficed to secure amnesty; Allied war crimes were seldom even acknowledged."

13. Statistics are from Dower, *Embracing Defeat*, 447.

14. Osamu Komai gave me a copy of the proceedings of his father's military trial. All quoted material is taken verbatim from that document, with citations referring to reference numbers stamped on the original pages. I refer below to this document as the "trial transcript." Mitsuo Komai faced three counts of war crimes. The court rejected his not guilty plea to the first count. He pleaded guilty to counts two and three.

15. Trial transcript, 4.

16. Trial transcript, 3.

17. Trial transcript, 16–17.

18. Trial transcript, 66.

19. Trial transcript, 72.

20. Trial transcript, 5.

21. Osamu Komai, "Remembering My Father: My Post-War Life as a Child of a War Criminal," US-Japan Dialogue on POWs (online forum), posted January 23, 2005 (website since discontinued).

22. Eric Lomax, *The Railway Man* (London: Vintage Books, 1996), 225–26.

23. Lomax, 230.

24. "Eric Lomax," Forgiveness Project (website), n.d.

25. Lomax described his meeting with Nagase in *The Railway Man*, 262–69.

26. Lomax, *Railway Man*, 256. The film, directed by Jonathan Teplitzky, was released in 2013. Colin Firth played Eric Lomax. Nicole Kidman played his wife, Patti.

27. Nan MacFarlane, "Sorry: Son of Japanese War Criminal Travels to Berwick to Apologise; Extraordinary Act of Reconciliation," *Berwick Advertiser*, July 4, 2007.

28. Komai, "Remembering My Father."

29. See "Yokohama War Cemetery," Commonwealth War Graves Commission (website), n.d. Osamu's visit there in August 2005, for the sixtieth anniversary of Japan's surrender, received national coverage; see "Chichi no keishini Gimon" [Doubts about Father's Execution], *Yomiuri Shimbun*, August 16, 2005. Another national paper reported on Osamu's meeting with James Nelson, the son of an American POW who labored in a copper mine in Sendai, Japan; see "Horyo datta chichino sugata ou" [Searching for My Father, Who Was a Prisoner of War], *Asahi*

Shimbun, June 1, 2008. NHK, the Japanese public television network, also covered that meeting in a four-minute news story that day. The segment was called "POW and War Criminal: Meeting of the Sons of Japanese and US soldiers." In its August 3, 2008, issue, *Asahi* printed a photograph of Osamu speaking about his father at a Morioka history museum: "Heiwa no mirai he 'chichi no tsumi'" ["Father's Sins" toward a Peaceful Future]. On October 2, 2008, *Asahi* carried a story about Osamu's meeting in Morioka with Kan Duon, also the son of a war criminal. Kan's father, who was Korean, joined the Japanese military in 1942. *Asahi* reported that the two men prayed in front of Mitsuo Komai's grave in Morioka; see "Heiwa omou kokoroni kokkyo nashi" [No Borders for Peace], *Asahi*, October 2, 2008.

30. The quotation is slightly different in Longfellow's original text, where it appears as an inscription in a cemetery chapel: "Look not mournfully into the Past. It comes not back again. Wisely improve the Present. It is thine. Go forth to meet the shadowy Future, without fear, and with a manly heart." See Henry Wadsworth Longfellow, *Hyperion: A Romance* (Boston: Ticknor, Reed and Fields, 1853), 357.

Chapter 20

1. A postwar constitution was drafted in 1946 by the US occupation and presented to the Japanese government for approval. It went into effect in 1947. Article 1 erased any prewar semblance of divinity that the emperor once had and reduced it to something conceptual and emblematic: "The Emperor shall be the symbol of the State and of the unity of the People." Subsequent articles further stripped the emperor of power. Article 3 said: "The advice and approval of the Cabinet shall be required for all acts of the Emperor in matters of state, and the Cabinet shall be responsible therefor." Article 4 declared: "The Emperor shall perform only such acts in matters of state as are provided for in this Constitution and he shall not have powers related to government." Article 7 spelled out which imperial acts were constitutionally permitted:

The Emperor, with the advice and approval of the Cabinet, shall perform the following acts in matters of state on behalf of the people:

Promulgation of amendments of the constitution, laws, cabinet orders and treaties.
Convocation of the Diet.
Dissolution of the House of Representatives.
Proclamation of general election of members of the Diet.
Attestation of the appointment and dismissal of Ministers of State and other officials as provided for by law, and of full powers and credentials of Ambassadors and Ministers.

Attestation of general and special amnesty, commutation of punishment, reprieve, and restoration of rights.

Awarding of honors.

Attestation of instruments of ratification and other diplomatic documents as provided for by law.

Receiving foreign ambassadors and ministers.

Performance of ceremonial functions.

The full text of the constitution can be found on the website of the Japanese prime minister and his cabinet, under the title "The Constitution of Japan." A panel of Columbia University scholars neatly summarized the birth of Japan's postwar constitution this way:

The American Occupation of Japan was premised on the notion that the thorough demilitarization and democratization of the defeated nation would make the world forever safe from the renewed threat of Japanese aggression. The drafting of a new, democratic constitution was considered essential to Japan's recasting as a peaceful member of the community of nations. After a Japanese commission failed to produce a new national constitution sufficiently progressive for the Occupation's liking, a document was drafted (over the span of only a week's time) in-house by American staff and presented to the Japanese government for translation and enactment. The Japanese had no choice but to follow orders and the new constitution, somewhat awkwardly worded as the result of its English-language origins, was promulgated in November 1946 and came into effect on May 3, 1947. Many scholars have noted the irony of the Occupation installing democratic political institutions in Japan through transparently authoritarian means: the Japanese, it has been said, were "forced to be free" by their American occupiers. Nonetheless, the 1947 Constitution was readily embraced by the Japanese people and has endured (with not a single amendment over the past six decades) as a sound basis for Japan's postwar democracy.

For this document, see "Primary Source Document with Questions (DBQs): The Constitution of Japan (1947)," Asia for Educators (website), Columbia University, n.d. And for a discussion of the emperor as prewar divinity, see the following thoughtful piece by the BBC, which argues that Hirohito was mostly seen not as some sort of supernatural being, but "as a vital element of the Japanese patriotic understanding of themselves as a nation rather than a theological reality": "Divinity of the Emperor," BBC (website), last updated September 7, 2009.

2. Herbert P. Bix, *Hirohito and the Making of Modern Japan* (New York: Perennial, 2001), 567.

3. "General of the Army Douglas MacArthur to the Chief of Staff, United States Army (Eisenhower)," January 25, 1946, in *Foreign Relations of the United States, 1946*, vol. 8, *The Far East*, document 308, US Department of State Office of the Historian (website). MacArthur explained in this letter that a trial would trigger a "vendetta for revenge . . . whose cycle may well not be complete for centuries if ever. The whole of Japan," he wrote, "can be expected, in my opinion, to resist the action either by passive or semi-active means," resulting in "a condition of underground chaos and disorder amounting to guerilla warfare."

4. Carol Gluck, "New Hirohito Documents Show Emperor's Thoughts on the War," Nikkei Asia (website), September 13, 2019.

5. Patrick Smith, "Japan: The Real Hirohito Returns," *New York Times*, August 21, 2000.

6. The book was first published in 2000 and won the 2001 Pulitzer Prize for General Nonfiction. The edition cited in this text was published in 2001.

7. Bix, *Hirohito and the Making of Modern Japan*, 18, 15.

8. Herbert P. Bix, "Hirohito: String Puller, Not Puppet," *New York Times*, September 29, 2014. In this opinion piece, Bix reported that a prominent Japanese newspaper had asked him to comment on a newly compiled twelve-thousand-page, sixty-one-volume official biography of Emperor Hirohito. The history was prepared by Japan's Imperial Household Agency, which manages the emperor's affairs. Bix had "politely refused" the request because the paper would not allow him to discuss Hirohito's "role and responsibility" in World War II. Bix wrote: "Japan's Imperial Household Agency, abetted by the Japanese media, has dodged important questions about events before, during and after the war. . . . The new history perpetuates the false but persistent image—endorsed by the Allied military occupation, led by Gen. Douglas MacArthur—of a benign, passive figurehead." The Kyodo News Agency said that the Hirohito volumes portrayed the emperor "as being distressed that he could not stop his country from going to war." See "Japan Compiles 12,000-Page Bio of Emperor Hirohito," Associated Press, September 8, 2014.

9. I interviewed Ruoff by telephone in August 2021. Ruoff, director of the Center for Japanese Studies at Portland State University, is the author of many works about the Japanese monarchy, including *Japan's Imperial House in the Postwar Era, 1945–2019* (Cambridge, MA: Harvard University East Asia Center, 2020).

10. "Hirohito, 124th Emperor of Japan, Is Dead at 87," *New York Times*, January 7, 1989.

11. See Robert Trumbull, "A Leader Who Took Japan to War, to Surrender, and Finally to Peace," *New York Times*, January 7, 1989. In the obituary, Trumbull wrote: "Emperor Hirohito reigned over not one Japan, but three: a Japan consumed

with militarism almost from the time he took over the Chrysanthemum Throne, a Japan that lay in ruins at the end of World War II and seemed destined for years of occupation and dependency, and finally a Japan that, from the shambles of defeat, achieved in peacetime global economic power."

12. Japan's system of naming emperors and labeling their eras has a complicated history. For a concise summary, see Kawashima Shin, "The Historical Background of How Japan Chooses Its Era Names," Nippon.com, May 19, 2017. In brief: when they are alive, Japanese emperors are known in English by their birth names (Emperor Hirohito); in Japanese, personal names are not used, and a living monarch in Japan is simply known as His Majesty the Emperor (Tenno Heika). Posthumously, the dead emperor assumes the name of his era and thereafter is referred to by that era's name (Emperor Showa).

13. Emperors or their advisers once chose imperial-era names (called *gengo* in Japanese), and during the prewar years Hirohito's reign was known as the Showa era. But the Allied occupation officially changed that, at least temporarily. "The two prewar-war decades of Showa were considered a dark and damnable legacy which had fully to be eradicated so that postwar Japan could begin anew," explained Columbia University historian Carol Gluck. So Showa was officially set aside. In 1979, the Era Name Law declared that a *gengo* could only be established by an order of the government's cabinet office, and that a *gengo* name change could only take place when there is an imperial succession. As a result, Showa reemerged as the official label for Hirohito's era only after his death. Imperial eras play a practical role in Japan: they set and reset the calendar. The year 1926, when Hirohito was enthroned, is called Showa 1. He died sixty-four years later, in Showa 64, also known as 1989. That year became year 1 of Akihito's Heisei era, the *gengo* having been decided in advance by the Japanese government. See "Gov't Secretly Drafted Decree on Era Name 'Heisei' before Expert Panel Met: Sources," *Mainichi*, April 1, 2019. Akihito abdicated the throne thirty-one years later, in 2019, or Heisei 31. Akihito's son Naruhito then assumed the throne, and his era was called Reiwa, giving 2019 a new calendar name: Reiwa 1. Reiwa means "beautiful harmony." See Carol Gluck, "The Idea of Showa," *Daedalus* 119, no. 3 (1990): 4; Laney Zhang, "New Era, New Law Number," *In Custodia Legis* (blog), Library of Congress, August 21, 2019; "Heisei in Perspective: Name Proclamation Opened New Era for Japan in 1989," *Japan Times*, December 22, 2018; "Records Bearing Emperor's Seal and Signature and Japan Cabinet Meeting Documents to Be Kept on Paper," *Japan Times*, April 4, 2019.

14. The chrysanthemum is the national flower of Japan and the monarchial symbol. It has been called the "flower of emperors." See Abe Emi, "The Chrysanthemum: Flower of Emperors," Nippon.com, October 22, 2018.

15. "Press Conference on the Occasion of His Majesty's Birthday (2013)," Imperial Household Agency of Japan (website), December 2013.

16. Hashiguchi Kazuhito, "The Road to the First Abdication in 200 Years," NHK World-Japan (website), May 16, 2019.

17. See, e.g., the emperor's address on the occasion of the Memorial Ceremony for the War Dead, in "Addresses by His Majesty the Emperor (2018)," Imperial Household Agency of Japan (website), August 15, 2018. Akihito's remarks generally aligned with government comments on World War II. On one occasion, however, Akihito seemed to break ranks with the prime minister, Shinzo Abe. Speaking at an August 14, 2015, press conference marking the seventieth anniversary of the war's end, Abe noted, "Japan has repeatedly expressed the feelings of deep remorse and heartfelt apology for its actions during the war." He added that future generations should not have to "carry the burden of apology." The next day, at his own event, Akihito again spoke of "deep remorse," and expressed "my deep condolences for those who fell in battle and in the ravages of war." Akihito's comments were interpreted as being more remorseful than those of the prime minister. Kenneth Ruoff wrote that Akihito "seemed to 'up his game'" in 2015 and thereafter, whereas "Abe seemed to find the endless references to the war and claims that Japan bore a special responsibility bothersome to his efforts to make Japan great again." Ruoff, *Japan's Imperial House in the Postwar Era*, 298; see also Justin McCurry, "Japan's Emperor Strikes a More Apologetic Tone Than Abe over Second World War," *Guardian*, August 15. 2015; Anna Fifield with Yuki Oda, "Japan's Emperor Appears to Part Ways with Abe on Pacifism Debate," *Washington Post*, August 15, 2015.

18. Max Hastings, *Retribution: The Battle for Japan, 1944–45* (New York: Vintage Books, 2007), 13.

19. Max Hastings, *Inferno: The World at War, 1939–1945* (New York: Vintage Books, 2012), 415, 646. Historian John Dower's estimates were lower: 10 million Chinese deaths, 30,000 military and 90,000 civilian deaths among Filipinos, and 2.5 million deaths among Japanese; see Dower, *War without Mercy: Race and Power in the Pacific War* (New York: Pantheon, 1986), 296, 299. The US-based National WWII Museum says the number of civilian and military deaths in China is up to 20 million, while its figure for Japan is 2.6–3.1 million; see "Research Starters: Worldwide Deaths in World War II," National WWII Museum (website), n.d.

20. David Sanger, "Japan's Emperor Tells China Only of His 'Sadness' on War," *New York Times*, October 24, 1992; "Emperor Akihito: Japanese 'Must Never Forget' Filipino Lives Lost during WWII," CNN Philippines, January 28, 2016; Nikko Dizon, "Emperor: Japanese People Must Never Forget Loss of Filipino Lives in WWII," *Philippine Daily Inquirer*, January 27, 2016.

21. "Emperor and Empress Visit Okinawa to Commemorate War Victims," *Japan Times*, March 27, 2018.

22. Photos were shot in 2005 at Banzai Cliff on Saipan, where Japanese soldiers and civilians jumped to their deaths to avoid capture by the Americans; in 2015

at the cenotaph for war dead on Peleliu; and in 2018 at the war dead mausoleum on Mabuni Hill, the final Japanese command post on Okinawa, overlooking Pacific waters. For photos, see, respectively, "Symbol of the State: Emperor's Trips to Console Souls of War Dead Symbolize Heisei Era," *Mainichi*, December 18, 2018; "Japan's Akihito Pushed Imperial Boundaries to Reach Out to Asia," *Straits Times*, August 13, 2018; "Japanese Emperor, Empress Visit Okinawa to Honor War Dead on What May Be Last Visit," GMA News Online, March 28, 2018.

23. For these and other examples of imperial poetry, see Kazuhiro Nagata, "'Prayer for Peace' Trips by the Emperor and Empress," Japan Institute of International Affairs (website), March 31, 2020. Nagata described the travels as a "series of journeys to comfort the spirits of the war dead."

24. Richard Lloyd Parry, "Akihito and the Sorrows of Japan," *London Review of Books*, March 19, 2020.

25. Bix, *Hirohito and the Making of Modern Japan*, 687.

26. "Press Conference by Their Majesties the Emperor and Empress of Japan in Commemoration of the 20th Anniversary of His Majesty's Accession to the Throne," Imperial Household Agency of Japan (website), November 6, 2009. In 2006, Akihito was asked at his annual birthday press conference whether he had any "recollections of speaking with Emperor Showa regarding his feelings about the mourning of the war dead or the way to mourn them, or was there anything that Emperor Showa wanted to convey to Your Majesty in this regard?" This might have been an opportunity for Akihito to speak publicly about his father, had he wanted to. Instead, he said: "I had never heard from Emperor Showa regarding the mourning of the dead." See "Press Conference on the Occasion of His Majesty's Birthday (2006)," Imperial Household Agency of Japan (website), December 2006.

27. See "The Annexation of Korea," editorial, *Japan Times*, August 29, 2010; Erin Blakemore, "How Japan Took Control of Korea," History (website), posted February 27, 2018, updated July 28, 2020.

28. F. A. McKenzie, quoted in Doug Kim, "For Future Generations: 100 Years after Samil, Descendants Reap the Legacy of Korea's Independence Movement," *Korean Quarterly*, Winter 2019, n.p.

29. William Underwood, "New Era for Japan-Korea History Issues: Forced Labor Redress Efforts Begin to Bear Fruit," *Asia-Pacific Journal* 6, no. 3 (2008): article 2689 (Korean deaths in the tens of thousands); R. J. Rummel, "Statistics of Japanese Democide Estimates, Calculations, and Sources," Statistics of Democide (website), University of Hawai'i, updated November 23, 2002 (270,000–810,000 Korean deaths in forced labor in 1939–45). See also Choe Sang-Hun and Motoko Rich, "The $89,000 Verdict Tearing Japan and South Korea Apart," *New York Times*, February 13, 2019 (citing South Korean sources, "as many as 7.8 million Koreans were conscripted as forced labor or soldiers during Japan's imperial

expansion before and during World War II"); S. Nathan Park, "Tokyo Keeps Defending World War II Atrocities," *Foreign Policy*, May 29, 2019.

30. Anthropologist Chunghee Sarah Soh has written that the total number of comfort women from all Japanese-occupied territories ranged from seventy thousand to two hundred thousand, "about 80% of whom were Korean." See Soh, "The Korean 'Comfort Women': Movement for Redress," *Asian Survey* 36, no. 12 (1996): 1227; see also Soh, *The Comfort Women: Sexual Violence and Postcolonial Memory in Korea and Japan* (Chicago: University of Chicago Press, 2009); Pyong Gap Min, "Korean 'Comfort Women': The Intersection of Colonial Power, Gender, and Class," *Gender and Society* 17, no. 6 (2003): 939–57; "Military Sexual Slavery, 1931–1945," Columbia Law School Center for Korean Legal Studies (website), n.d.

31. "South Korea and Japan's Feud Explained," BBC News, December 2, 2019.

32. See "Interview with H. E. Koro Bessho, Japanese Ambassador to the Republic of Korea," Asia Society (website), 2015.

33. For a well-written description of imperial press gatherings, see Doug Struck, "Japan's Emperor Meets the Press," *Washington Post*, November 11, 1999.

34. "Press Conference on the Occasion of His Majesty's Birthday (2001), Imperial Household Agency of Japan" (website), December 18, 2001.

35. For more, see Howard French, "Japan Rediscovers Its Korean Past," *New York Times*, March 11, 2002; Jonathan Watts, "The Emperor's New Roots," *Guardian*, December 28, 2001.

36. Parry, "Akihito and the Sorrows of Japan"; Ruoff, *Japan's Imperial House in the Postwar Era*, 301; see also Stephen Murphy-Shigematsu, "Multiethnic Japan and the Monoethnic Myth," *MELUS* 18, no. 4 (1993): 63–80.

37. Ruoff, *Japan's Imperial House in the Postwar Era*, 302. Ruoff said he spoke with palace officials about Akihito's comments, but they "were unwilling to talk on the record about what Akihito was trying to accomplish." Ruoff wrote: "In spite of efforts by palace officials to suggest that Akihito just happened to make the remarks, the emperor's statement, into which considerable preparation surely went, was not to the liking of far-right supporters of the throne," who contend the Japanese race is pure (302).

38. See Kyodo News Agency, "South Korea Visit Left as Unfinished Business for New Emperor," *Japan Times*, May 2, 2019.

39. See Ruoff, *Japan's Imperial House in the Postwar Era*, 8–9.

40. One telling example: Akihito's apologetic remarks in 1990 to the visiting South Korean president, Roh Tae-woo, did not produce an imperial trip to Seoul, even though Roh extended an invitation. Akihito had told Roh: "I think of the sufferings your people underwent during this unfortunate period, which was brought about by my country, and cannot but feel the deepest regret." See Steven Weisman,

"Japanese Express Remorse to Korea," *New York Times*, May 25, 1990. There was debate inside Korea over whether Akihito's apology went far enough; and other nettlesome issues, in particular comfort women, kept the two countries at odds. As a result, the Japanese government shelved plans for an Akihito visit. See "South Korea Wanted More Significant Apology from Japan Emperor in 1990," *Kyodo News*, March 29, 2021.

41. Quote is from Thierry Guthmann, "Nationalist Circles in Japan Today: The Impossibility of Secularization," *Japan Review* 30, special issue (2017): 207. For more on right-wing public opinion and politics in Japan, see Motoko Rich, Makiko Inoue, and Hikari Hida, "A Hard-Line Conservative Hopes to Be Japan's First Female Leader," *New York Times*, October 28, 2021; Kikuko Nagayoshi, "The Political Orientation of Japanese Online Right-Wingers," *Pacific Affairs* 94, no. 1 (2021): 5–31; Yuki Asahina, "Becoming Right-Wing Citizens in Contemporary Japan," *Contemporary Japan* 31, no. 2 (2019): 122–40; Naoto Higuchi, "The Transformation of the Far Right in Japan: From Fascism to Anti-Korean Hate Crimes," *Right Now!* (blog), University of Oslo Center for Research on Extremism, April 26, 2021. For a comprehensive treatment of Yasukuni, see John Breen, *Yasukuni, the War Dead, and the Struggle for Japan's Past* (New York: Columbia University Press, 2008).

42. Parry, "Akihito and the Sorrows of Japan."

43. "Japan's Emperor Thanks Country, Prays for Peace before Abdication," Nikkei Asia (website), April 30, 2019.

44. "Press Conference on the Occasion of His Majesty's Birthday (2018)," Imperial Household Agency of Japan (website), December 2018.

45. At his 2006 birthday press appearance, Akihito said: "I sincerely hope that the facts about the war and the war dead will continue to be correctly conveyed to those of the generations that do not have direct knowledge of the war so that the kind of the ravages of war that we experienced in the past will never be repeated"; see "Press Conference on the Occasion of His Majesty's Birthday (2006)," Imperial Household Agency of Japan (website), December 2006. At his 2015 birthday press conference, Akihito said: "I believe having thorough knowledge about the last war and deepening our thoughts about that war is most important for the future of Japan." "Press Conference on the Occasion of His Majesty's Birthday (2015)," Imperial Household Agency of Japan (website), December 2015.

Part 7

1. "Kobe Marks 27th Anniversary of Deadly Hanshin Quake," *Japan Times*, January 17, 2022 ("about 10,000 severely injured"); James Glanz and Norimitsu Onishi, "Japan's Strict Building Codes Saved Lives," *New York Times*, March 11, 2011 ("injured 26,000").

Chapter 21

1. The speech, with English-language voice-over, can be seen online at "Japanese Emperor Akihito Statement," C-Span (website), March 16, 2011. For the text, see "A Message from His Majesty the Emperor," Imperial Household Agency of Japan (website), March 16, 2011. For Akihito's dress and reception room broadcast venue, see Laura King and Kenji Hall, "Emperor Akihito's Speech Underlines Gravity of Japan's Nuclear Crisis," *Los Angeles Times*, March 14, 2011; Kathryn Tolbert, "Emperor Akihito Gives Message of Comfort in Televised Address," *Washington Post*, March 16, 2011.

2. On Hirohito's radio address and voice, Herbert P. Bix wrote: "The Japanese people gathered around their radio speakers and heard for the first time the high-pitched voice of their emperor"; see Bix, *Hirohito and the Making of Modern Japan* (New York: Perennial, 2001), 526. Teruo Kobayashi, a retired college professor, told the *Washington Post* he was thirteen when he heard Hirohito's address. "I didn't know what he was talking about," Kobayashi said. "He had a strange voice and he was making the speech in very special Japanese dialect just for the emperor. I don't think anyone in the village understood what he was talking about. After he spoke, a broadcaster summed up what the emperor said, and that's when everyone understood." Quoted in Tolbert, "Emperor Akihito Gives Message of Comfort."

3. The plum blossoms were described in "Flowering Bulletin," Shinjuku Gyoen National Garden (website), posted March 11, 2011 (site since discontinued). For weather conditions in Onagawa on March 11, 2011, see "Japan Earthquake, Tsunami," YouTube video, uploaded April 8, 2011, by fuse510112, 1:34 (shows tsunami hitting the town, people watching, wind blowing, and snow and cold rain falling). The low temperature in Onagawa that day was twenty-five degrees Fahrenheit, well below the average temperature range for March in Onagawa, which is thirty-four to forty-nine degrees; see, respectively, "Past Weather in Onagawa Chō, Japan—March 2011" and "Climate & Weather Averages in Onagawa Chō, Japan," TimeandDate.com, n.d.

4. On the height of the waves, see Airi Ryu and Najmedin Meshkati, "Onagawa: The Japanese Nuclear Power Plant That Didn't Melt Down on 3/11," *Bulletin of the Atomic Scientists*, March 10, 2014 (tsunami reached 14.3 meters, or 46.9 feet); Bruno Adriano et al., "Understanding the Extreme Tsunami Inundation in Onagawa Town by the 2011 Tohoku Earthquake, Its Effects in Urban Structures and Coastal Facilities," *Coastal Engineering Journal* 58, no. 4 (2016): article 1640013, p. 15 (tsunami reached up to 14.8 meters, or 48.5 feet).

5. Population and death statistics were provided by Onagawa City Hall in July 2021; additional statistics from Adriano et al., "Understanding the Extreme Tsunami Inundation"; "6 Months On from March 11 Disaster," *Yomiuri Shimbun*, September 11, 2011.

6. Stephen Phelan, "The Fall and Rise of Onagawa," *New Yorker*, March 18, 2016.

7. For summaries of the Fukushima disaster and its consequences, see Hitoshi Ohto et al., "From Devastation to Recovery and Revival in the Aftermath of Fukushima's Nuclear Power Plant Accident," *Asia Pacific Journal of Public Health* 29, no. 2, suppl. (2017): 10S–17S; "Fukushima Disaster: What Happened at the Nuclear Plant?," BBC News, March 10, 2020; Lois Parshley, "Fukushima's Tragic Legacy—Radioactive Soil, Ongoing Leaks, and Unanswered Questions," *National Geographic*, March 10, 2021.

8. The death toll varies, depending on the source: "Police Countermeasures and Damage Situation Associated with 2011 Tohoku District—Off the Pacific Ocean Earthquake," National Police Agency of Japan (website), March 10, 2011 (18,425 dead and missing); "Over 40,000 Still Evacuated 10 Years after Quake, Tsunami and Nuke Disasters in NE Japan," *Mainichi*, March 11, 2021 (22,200 dead or missing); "Tsunami Event Information," NOAA National Centers for Environmental Information (website), n.d. (20,319 deaths).

9. "Japan Quake: Worst Crisis since WWII, Says PM," BBC News, March 14, 2011.

10. Anthony Kuhn, "Japan's Public Broadcaster Responds, Reports Crisis," NPR, *All Things Considered*, April 11, 2011. For a sampling of NHK videos, see "Remembering 3.11: Great East Japan Earthquake Archive," NHK (website), created 2017 (aerial views of the disaster); "3/11—The Tsunami: The First 3 Days," *NHK World Prime*, January 8, 2021; "Raw Video: Tsunami Slams Northeast Japan," YouTube video, uploaded March 11, 2011, by Associated Press, 0:59.

11. See, e.g., "Fukushima Explosion," YouTube video, uploaded March 12, 2011, by squirrelyzaza, 3:29; "Japan Earthquake: YouTube Video of 2nd Hydrogen Explosion at Fukushima Nuclear Plant," Technology blog, *Los Angeles Times*, March 14, 2011. For an annotated timeline of the Fukushima events, see David Biello, "Anatomy of a Nuclear Crisis: A Chronology of Fukushima," *Yale Environment 360*, March 21, 2011.

12. Quoted in Akira Tashiro, "Accounts of A-Bomb Survivors Change in Aftermath of Fukushima Disaster," *Chugoku Shimbun*, Hiroshima Peace Media Center (website), posted October 24, 2011.

13. Quoted in Kohei Okata, "A-Bomb Survivors Hit by the Earthquake and Tsunami Are Reminded of Hiroshima, Anxious about Safety of Other Survivors in the Region," *Chugoku Shimbun*, Hiroshima Peace Media Center (website), posted March 20, 2011.

14. Quoted in Akiko Watanabe, "3/11 Survivor in Kamaishi Recalls U.S. Naval Bombardment," *Japan Times*, April 9, 2015.

15. Quoted in Martin Fackler, "For Elderly, Echoes of World War II Horrors," *New York Times*, March 14, 2011.

16. Fackler.

17. Lucy Birmingham and David McNeill, *Strong in the Rain: Surviving Japan's Earthquake, Tsunami and Fukushima Nuclear Disaster* (New York: Palgrave Macmillan, 2012), 82.

18. "A Message from His Majesty the Emperor," Imperial Household Agency of Japan (website), March 16, 2011.

19. Andrew Higgins, "In Onagawa, Japan's Tsunami Destroys Community," *Washington Post*, March 15, 2011; Chisa Fujioka, "Tsunami Puts Rare Spotlight on Japan Soldiers," Reuters, March 21, 2011; "Jon Snow's Tsunami Diary," YouTube video, uploaded March 20, 2011, by Channel 4 News, 25:50 (see 11:55 for mobilization size).

20. See Makoto Kondo, "Crisis in Japan," *St. Louis Post-Dispatch*, March 16, 2011 (snow and car); Hiromi Tanoue and Vibeke Venema, "Diving into the World of the Dead," BBC News, July 15, 2015 (mangled structure); Koji Sasahara, "AP Journalists Recall Scenes from Japan's 3-Fold Disaster," *Pittsburgh Post-Gazette*, March 8, 2016 (three-story apartment building); "Featured Photojournalist: David Guttenfelder," *Guardian*, March 31, 2011 (fishing boat); "Snow Adds to Japan's Misery," CBS News, March 17, 2011 (melting snow toilets); Facebook Messenger communication to author from Onagawa resident Shigeo Suzuki, September 2021.

21. Skype interview, August 2011, from Nakamura's home in Portland, Oregon.

22. Their stories can be found on the *Oregonian* website, gathered under the topic "Japan Recovery 2011."

23. Melinda Papp, "Molding a Rite of Passage in Urban Japan: Historical and Anthropological Perspectives," *Urbanities* 3, no. 1 (2013): 61–82.

24. See Motoya Nakamura, "To a Photographer Returning to His Native Japan, Tsunami-Ravaged Pictures Speak of Memories Lost," *Oregonian*, May 7, 2011. The essay originally appeared with a photograph of the displaced image of the girl in the kimono; the photograph is no longer posted online.

25. C. Peter Chen, "Bombing of Tokyo and Other Cities," World War II Database (website), n.d.

26. Telephone interview with Tadashi Abe, December 2018. Onagawa City Hall officials curated a website of displaced photos until 2015, when it was taken down.

27. Telephone interview with Masako Abe, September 2020.

28. "Ishinomaki before and after the 2011 Great East Japan Tsunami," UNESCO International Tsunami Information Center (website), n.d.; Mari Saito, "Ten Years On, Grief Never Subsides for Some Survivors of Japan's Tsunami," Reuters, March 10, 2021.

29. Of 15,331 total casualties in Iwate, Miyagi, and Fukushima Prefectures, 7,140 people were seventy years or older. Among the dead, 3,759 were between the ages of seventy and seventy-nine (24.5 percent), and 3,381 were eighty years or

older (22 percent). Cabinet Office, Government of Japan, "Disaster Prevention and Reconstruction from a Gender Equal Society Perspective: Lessons from the Great East Japan Earthquake," June 2012, fig. 1, PreventionWeb.net, UN Office for Disaster Risk Reduction.

Chapter 22

1. Skype interview, May 2011, from Arita's home in Hiroshima.

2. Data available from the Seismic Intensity Database, Japan Meteorological Agency (website), n.d.

3. For "new *hibakusha*," see the awkwardly translated English-language transcript of remarks in Japanese by Kenzaburo Oe, the Nobel laureate, in a 2015 television interview: "It is now, after we are experiencing this nuclear power plant disaster, which was created by us, a self-made, man-made disaster, on such a great scale, this has led to so many new hibakusha, or people surviving this nuclear disaster"; quoted in "Japanese Nobel Laureate Kenzaburo Oe on 70th Anniv. of US Atomic Bombings of Hiroshima and Nagasaki," interview by Amy Goodman, *Democracy Now!*, August 6, 2015. See also Justin Aukema, "A Problem for All Humanity: Nagasaki Writer Hayashi Kyoko Probes the Dangers of Nuclear Energy," *Asia-Pacific Journal* 9, no. 47/3 (2011): article 3670. Aukema notes that after Fukushima, the word *hibakusha* increasingly came to be used for people who had not suffered radiation damage from atomic bombs. For some other examples of "new *hibakusha*," see Ryan Masaaki Yokota, "'No More Hibakusha' Takes on New Meaning after 3/11," *Japan Times*, August 7, 2013; Linda Pentz Gunter, "The Flight from Fukushima— and the Grim Return," *Ecologist*, March 11, 2016; Jesse Barrett-Mills, dir., *The New Hibakusha* (2015), documentary film, 40 min., and the film's IMDb.com page, n.d.

4. Hiroko Tabuchi, "Inquiry Declares Fukushima Crisis a Man-Made Disaster," *New York Times*, July 5, 2012. See also National Diet of Japan, *Fukushima Nuclear Accident Independent Investigation Commission Report*, executive summary, 2012, Nuclear Information and Resource Service (website).

5. Hayashi, known for writing about the A-bomb, won some of the most prestigious literary awards in Japan, including the Akutagawa Prize (1975) and the Tanizaki Prize (1990). See "Obituary / Kyoko Hayashi / Novelist," *Japan News (Yomiuri Shimbun)*, March 2, 2017; "Kyoko Hayashi," Japanese Literature Publishing Project (website), Japanese Agency for Cultural Affairs, n.d.

6. Kyoko Hayashi, "To Rui, Once Again," *Asia-Pacific Journal* 15, no. 7/3 (2017): article 5026.

7. Kenzaburo Oe, "History Repeats," *New Yorker*, March 21, 2011.

8. Hitoshi Ohto et al., "From Devastation to Recovery and Revival in the Aftermath of Fukushima's Nuclear Power Plants Accident," *Asia Pacific Journal of Public Health* 29, no. 2, suppl. (2017): 10S–17S.

9. Severe psychological distress is defined as "stress-related symptoms including depression, anxiety, PTSD, and medically unexplained somatic symptoms": Yasuto Kunii et al., "Severe Psychological Distress of Evacuees in Evacuation Zone Caused by the Fukushima Daiichi Nuclear Power Plant Accident: The Fukushima Health Management Survey," *PLoS ONE* 11, no. 7 (2016): e0158821; see also A. Hasegawa et al., "Emergency Responses and Health Consequences after the Fukushima Accident; Evacuation and Relocation," *Clinical Oncology* 28, no. 4 (2016): 237–44; Shuntaro Ando et al., "Mental Health Problems in a Community after the Great East Japan Earthquake in 2011: A Systematic Review," *Harvard Review of Psychiatry* 25, no. 1 (2017): 15–28.

10. Hasegawa et al., "Emergency Responses and Health Consequences," 237–38.

11. Andrew Buncombe, "The Plight of the Elderly: Japan's Forgotten Victims of the Tsunami," *Independent*, March 20, 2011.

12. Takehari Yasuda, Keishi Takahashi, and Hirofumi Noguchi, "Disaster Hits Elderly with Dementia," *Yomiuri Shimbun*, May 15, 2011.

13. Kunii et al., "Severe Psychological Distress of Evacuees," table 1.

14. Masatsugu Orui et al., "Suicide Rates in Evacuation Areas after the Fukushima Daiichi Nuclear Disaster: A 5-Year Follow-Up Study in Fukushima Prefecture," *Crisis* 39, no. 5 (2018): 353–63.

15. In April 2011, the exclusion zone radius was 12.4 miles; "Transition of Evacuation Designated Zones," Fukushima Prefectural Government (website), last updated March 4, 2019.

16. For a detailed timeline of Fukushima events, see "Fukushima Daiichi Status Updates," International Atomic Energy Agency (website), last updated January 13, 2023. For a brief timeline, see "Fukushima: A Timeline of Significant Events," Fukushima.com, n.d.

17. Arita was referring to handwritten notes found on the walls of a Hiroshima school that was situated about a quarter mile from the A-bomb hypocenter. Part of the school's concrete shell survived, and those remains served as an aid station. Parents and students wrote wall messages there looking for surviving relatives. See Yukina Maeda, "Visitors to Fukuromachi Elementary School Peace Museum reach 500,000," *Chugoku Shimbun*, Hiroshima Peace Media Center (website), posted October 23, 2022. The Fukuromachi Elementary School Peace Museum website has a photo of the wall messages on the "Main Exhibitions" page. For more background and photos, see "Fukuro-Machi Elementary School," Hiroshima Peace Tourism (website), n.d.

18. A 2020 report on the Fukushima meltdown by the UN Scientific Committee on the Effects of Atomic Radiation (UNSCEAR) concluded that "future health effects directly related to radiation exposure are unlikely to be discernible." See "Latest Data Confirms 'Indiscernible' Impact of Fukushima Radiation," World

Nuclear News (website), March 9, 2021; "2020 Report on Radiological Consequences from the Fukushima Accident: 10 Years Later," UNSCEAR (website), launched March 9, 2021.

19. "Hot Spots and Blind Spots," *Economist*, October 8, 2011; Yuka Hayashi, "Murky Science Clouded Japan Nuclear Response," *Wall Street Journal*, August 16, 2011.

20. Telephone interview with Sato, January 2021.

21. For a sample in English translation, see Keiji Nakazawa, "from *Barefoot Gen*," *Mānoa* 13, no. 1 (2001): 124–41.

22. Letter from Akiko Matsumoto to Senta Kato, January 24, 2012.

23. See "Profile: Kenta Sato," *Lives of Fukushima* (website), Greenpeace Japan, 2021; and Seiji Shitakubo, "Accounts of 50 Local Fukushima Residents 10 Years On, Part 3: Challenge for Iitate Village," *Chugoku Shimbun*, Hiroshima Peace Media Center (website), posted March 13, 2021.

24. After 3/11, the Japanese government shut down all of the country's fifty operational nuclear power reactors. They had provided about 30 percent of Japan's electrical power. See, respectively, Martin Fackler, "Last Reactor of 50 in Japan Is Shut Down," *New York Times*, May 5, 2012; "Japan's Nuclear Power Plants in 2021," Nippon.com, March 31, 2021. By December 2022, ten reactors had been restarted after undergoing necessary safety protocols. Prime minister Fumio Kishida had previously announced, citing climate concerns, that a total of seventeen nuclear plants would be back online by the summer of 2023. See Eric Johnston, "Watchdog OKs New Rules to Allow Japan's Nuclear Plants to Operate beyond 60 Years," *Japan Times*, December 21, 2022.

25. According to the Japanese census, Iitate had 1,318 residents in 2020. These were predominantly elderly men and women: 70 percent were sixty or older, and 30 percent of them were over eighty, old enough to have lived through World War II. "Iitate," City Population (website), updated December 16, 2022, data provided by Statistics Bureau of Japan.

26. Masaya Yamauchi, "Alternative Medicine Tried by A-Bomb Survivors Offered to People of Fukushima," *Chugoku Shimbun*, Hiroshima Peace Media Center (website), posted April 4, 2011.

27. Noboru Takamura et al., "Eight Years after Fukushima Nuclear Accident—Community Recovery and Reconstruction from Nuclear and Radiological Disasters—A Case of Kawauchi Village and Tomioka Town in Fukushima," 2019, PreventionWeb.net, UN Office for Disaster Risk Reduction.

28. Seiji Shitakubo and Yo Kono, "Fukushima and Hiroshima: Collected Expertise and Wholehearted Support," *Chugoku Shimbun*, Hiroshima Peace Media Center (website), posted January 12, 2012.

29. Masamoto Nasu, *Children of the Paper Crane: The Story of Sadako Sasaki*

and Her Struggle with the A-Bomb Disease, trans. Elizabeth Baldwin, Steven Leeper, and Kyoko Yoshida (Armonk, NY: M. E. Sharpe, 1991). The book was originally published in Japanese as *Orizuru no Kodomotachi: Genbakusho to tatakatta Sasaki Sadako to kyuyutachi* (Tokyo: PHP Kenkyusho, 1984).

30. "Hiroshima Survivor, Famed Writer Encourages Fukushima Children," *Kyodo News*, July 12, 2011, Hiroshima Peace Media Center (website), posted July 13, 2011.

31. Thomas Wilson and Minami Funakoshi, "Six Years On, Fukushima Child Evacuees Face Menace of School Bullies," Reuters, March 9, 2017; Sayuri Romei, "6 Years after the Fukushima Disaster, Its Victims Are Still Suffering," *Washington Post*, March 10, 2017.

32. Tohoaki Sawano et al., "The Fukushima Daiichi Nuclear Power Plant Accident and School Bullying of Affected Children and Adolescents: The Need for Continuous Radiation Education," *Journal of Radiation Research* 59, no. 3 (2018): 381–84.

33. Martin Fackler, "Japanese Official Resigns over Radiation Joke," *New York Times*, September 10, 2011. Hachiro also called the Fukushima evacuation zone a "town of death," a remark seen by the people who had lived there as insensitive and disheartening.

34. My rendition of Dr. Arita's story is taken verbatim from his May 2011 interview with me, and from a short essay he wrote titled "Kanashimi no Furasshubakku" (Flashback of Sadness), published in the *Hiroshimaken Ishikai Sokuho* [*Hiroshima Prefectural Medical Association Bulletin*], no. 2120 (May 25, 2011): 41.

35. Kenichi Arita, *Watashitachi no kokorozumori: Nanajuuichi nenme no genshi bakudan hibakusha no kokoro* [*Our Mind and Expectations: The Hearts of Hibakusha 71 Years after the Atomic Bombing*] (Hiroshima: Keisuisha, 2018).

36. Email to author, April 2022.

Further Reading

Birmingham, Lucy, and David McNeill. *Strong in the Rain: Surviving Japan's Earthquake, Tsunami, and Fukushima Nuclear Disaster*. New York: Palgrave Macmillan, 2012.

Bix, Herbert P. *Hirohito and the Making of Modern Japan*. New York: HarperCollins, 2000.

Breen, John, ed. *Yasukuni, the War Dead and the Struggle for Japan's Past*. London: Hurst, 2007.

Buruma, Ian. *Inventing Japan, 1853–1964*. New York: Modern Library, 2003.

———. *The Wages of Guilt: Memories of War in Germany and Japan*. New York: Farrar, Straus and Giroux, 1994.

Committee for the Compilation of Materials on Damage Caused by the Atomic Bombs in Hiroshima and Nagasaki. *Hiroshima and Nagasaki: The Physical, Medical, and Social Effects of the Atomic Bombings*. Translated by Eisei Ishikawa and David L. Swain. New York: Basic Books, 1981.

Cook, Haruko Taya, and Theodore F. Cook. *Japan at War: An Oral History*. New York: New Press, 1992.

Dalby, Lisa. *Kimono: Fashioning Culture*. New York: Vintage, 1993.

Dower, John W. *Embracing Defeat: Japan in the Wake of World War II*. New York: Norton, 1999.

———. *War without Mercy: Race & Power in the Pacific War*. New York: Pantheon, 1986.

Endo, Shusaku. *Silence*. Translated by William Johnston. New York: Picador Modern Classics, 1969.

Frank, Anne. *The Diary of a Young Girl*. Definitive ed. London: Puffin, 1997.

Gluck, Carol. "The 'End' of the Postwar: Japan at the Turn of the Millennium." In *States of Memory: Continuities, Conflicts, and Transformations in National*

Retrospection, edited by Jeffrey K. Olick, 289–314. Durham, NC: Duke University Press, 2003.

Gluck, Carol, and Stephen R. Graubard, eds. *Showa: The Japan of Hirohito*. New York: Norton, 1992.

Gordon, Andrew. *A Modern History of Japan: From Tokugawa Times to the Present*. New York: Oxford University Press, 2009.

Hashimoto, Akiko. *The Long Defeat: Cultural Trauma, Memory, and Identity in Japan*. Oxford: Oxford University Press, 2015.

Hastings, Max. *Inferno: The World at War, 1939–1945*. New York: Vintage Books, 2012.

———. *Retribution: The Battle for Japan, 1944–45*. New York: Vintage Books, 2009.

Heftrich, Urs, Robert Jacobs, Bettina Kaibach, and Karoline Thaidigsmann, eds. *Images of Rupture between East and West: The Perception of Auschwitz and Hiroshima in Eastern European Arts and Media*. Heidelberg: Universitätsverlag Winter, 2016.

Hersey, John. *Hiroshima*. New York: Vintage, 1989. Originally published in the *New Yorker*, August 31, 1946.

Horikiri, Tatsuichi. *The Stories Clothes Tell: Voices of Working-Class Japan*. Edited and translated by Rieko Wagoner. Lanham, MD: Rowman and Littlefield, 2016.

Jacobs, Robert A. *The Dragon's Tail: Americans Face the Atomic Age*. Amherst: University of Massachusetts Press, 2010.

———, ed. *Filling the Hole in the Nuclear Future: Art and Popular Culture Respond to the Bomb*. Lanham, MD: Lexington Books, 2010.

Keene, Donald. *Appreciations of Japanese Culture*. Tokyo: Kodansha, 1971.

Landas, Marc. *The Fallen: A True Story of American POWs and Japanese Wartime Atrocities*. Hoboken, NJ: John Wiley and Sons, 2004.

Lifton, Robert Jay. *Death in Life: Survivors of Hiroshima*. New York: Random House, 1967.

Lomax, Eric. *The Railway Man*. London: Vintage, 1996.

McClain, James L. *Japan: A Modern History*. New York: Norton, 2002.

Miyamoto, Yuki. *Beyond the Mushroom Cloud: Commemoration, Religion, and Responsibility after Hiroshima*. New York: Fordham University Press, 2011.

Nagai, Takashi. *The Bells of Nagasaki*. Translated by William Johnston. Tokyo: Kodansha, 1994.

Nagasaki National Peace Memorial Hall for the Atomic Bomb Victims. *The Light of Morning: Memoirs of the Nagasaki Atomic Bomb Survivors*. Translated by Brian Burke-Gaffney. Nagasaki: Nagasaki National Peace Memorial Hall, 2005.

Nie, Jing-Bao, Nanyan Guo, Mark Selden, and Arthur Kleinman, eds. *Japan's Wartime Medical Atrocities: Comparative Inquiries in Science, History, and Ethics.* London: Routledge, 2010.

Nosaka, Akiyuki. *The Cake Tree in the Ruins.* Translated by Ginny Tapley Takemori. London: Pushkin Press, 2018.

———. "A Grave of Fireflies." Translated by James R. Abrams. *Japan Quarterly* 25, no. 4 (1978): 445–63.

Ruoff, Kenneth J. *Japan's Imperial House in the Postwar Era, 1945–2019.* Cambridge, MA: Harvard University Press, 2020.

Schirokauer, Conrad. *A Brief History of Chinese and Japanese Civilizations.* 3rd ed. With Miranda Brown, David Lurie, and Suzanne Gay. Boston: Houghton Mifflin, 2006.

Smith, Robert J. *Ancestor Worship in Contemporary Japan.* Stanford, CA: Stanford University Press, 1974.

Southard, Susan. *Nagasaki: Life after Nuclear War.* New York: Penguin Books, 2015.

Steinberg, Milton. *Basic Judaism.* New York: Harcourt, Brace, 1947.

Tanaka, Yuko. *The Power of the Weave: The Hidden Meanings of Cloth.* Tokyo: International House of Japan, 2013.

Tayor, N. A. J., and Robert Jacobs, eds. *Reimagining Hiroshima and Nagasaki: Nuclear Humanities in the Post–Cold War.* London: Routledge, 2018.

Yamahata, Yosuke, and Rupert Jenkins, eds. *Nagasaki Journey: The Photographs of Yosuke Yamahata, August 10, 1945.* San Francisco: Pomegranate Artbooks, 1995.

Yoneyama, Lisa. *Hiroshima Traces: Time, Space, and the Dialectics of Memory.* Berkeley: University of California Press, 1999.

Yusa, Michiko. *Japanese Religions.* London: Routledge, 2002.

Zwigenberg, Ran. *Hiroshima: The Origins of Global Memory Culture.* Cambridge: Cambridge University Press, 2014.

———. *Japan's Castles: Citadels of Modernity in War and Peace.* Cambridge: Cambridge University Press, 2019.

Index